REHABILITATION AND REMEDIATION OF INTERNATIONALLY ADOPTED CHILDREN

T0372598

This book presents specific methods for the physical rehabilitation, mental health restoration, and academic remediation of post-institutionalized international adoptees. The focus of the book is on the neurological, psychological, and educational consequences of complex childhood trauma in the context of a fundamental change in the social situation of development of former orphanage residents. A discussion of after-adoption traumatic experiences includes a critique of certain "conventional" approaches to the treatment of mental health issues and different disabilities in international adoptees. Using his 30-year background in research and clinical practice, the author expertly describes and analyzes a range of methodologies in order to provide an integrated and practical system of "scaffolding" and "compensation" for the successful rehabilitation and remediation of children with ongoing traumatic experiences. This is essential reading for researchers and practicing clinicians concerned with childhood trauma, remedial education, and issues of international adoption.

BORIS GINDIS is a licensed psychologist and a nationally certified bilingual school psychologist. He was the founder and Chief Psychologist at the Center for Cognitive-Developmental Assessment and Remediation (1989–2021). He served as Full Professor of Psychology and Director of the Bilingual Program at Touro College's Graduate School of Education and Psychology, USA (1996–2006). Dr. Gindis is the author of two books and many research articles and book chapters. He has served as a guest-editor for psychology journals, and has been a keynote speaker at national and international conferences.

REHABILITATION AND REMEDIATION OF INTERNATIONALLY ADOPTED CHILDREN

BORIS GINDIS

Center for Cognitive-Developmental Assessment and Remediation

CAMBRIDGE
UNIVERSITY PRESS

Shaftesbury Road, Cambridge CB2 8EA, United Kingdom

One Liberty Plaza, 20th Floor, New York, NY 10006, USA

477 Williamstown Road, Port Melbourne, VIC 3207, Australia

314–321, 3rd Floor, Plot 3, Splendor Forum, Jasola District Centre, New Delhi – 110025, India

103 Penang Road, #05–06/07, Visioncrest Commercial, Singapore 238467

Cambridge University Press is part of Cambridge University Press & Assessment, a department of the University of Cambridge.

We share the University's mission to contribute to society through the pursuit of education, learning and research at the highest international levels of excellence.

www.cambridge.org
Information on this title: www.cambridge.org/9781009014755

DOI: 10.1017/9781009029629

First published 2021
First paperback edition 2023

A catalogue record for this publication is available from the British Library

Library of Congress Cataloging-in-Publication data
NAMES: Gindis, Boris, author.
TITLE: Rehabilitation and remediation of internationally adopted children /Boris Gindis.
DESCRIPTION: Cambridge, United Kingdom ; New York, NY : Cambridge University Press, 2022. | Includes bibliographical references and index.
IDENTIFIERS: LCCN 2021024692 (print) | LCCN 2021024693 (ebook) | ISBN 9781316516294 (hardback) | ISBN 9781009014755 (paperback) | ISBN 9781009029629 (epub)
SUBJECTS: LCSH: Intercountry adoption–United States–Psychological aspects. | Adopted children–Mental health–United States. | Adopted children–Psychology. | Psychic trauma in children–Treatment. | Problem children–Rehabilitation.
CLASSIFICATION: LCC RJ507.A36 G56 2022 (print) | LCC RJ507.A36 (ebook) | DDC 362.734–dc23
LC record available at https://lccn.loc.gov/2021024692
LC ebook record available at https://lccn.loc.gov/2021024693

ISBN   978-1-316-51629-4   Hardback
ISBN   978-1-009-01475-5   Paperback

Contents

Acknowledgments

This book is an outcome of almost 30 years of my work – in cooperation with specialists in many disciplines – on the assessment and remediation of children adopted by American and Canadian citizens from foreign orphanages. There is no way to mention all my associates, but the staff and consultants at the BGCenter (Center for Cognitive-Developmental Assessment and Remediation) with offices in Nanuet (New York) and Phoenix (Arizona) are to be acknowledged first and foremost: Ida Jeltova, Chun Dong, Carol Napier, Elkhonon Goldberg, Marina Muchnick, and Shylamit Ryshick.

This book was created with the remarkable help and support of my editor Ms. Janka Romero, Commissioning Editor, her wonderful senior editorial assistant Ms. Emily Watton, and Mr. Joshua Penney, Senior Content Manager. Many thanks for your patience, close attention to details, and consideration.

My greatest acknowledgment and gratitude go to my lifelong friends, colleagues, and coauthors Carol Lidz, Alex Kozulin, and Patty Cogan, who influenced me in many ways in writing this book as well as in my day-to-day work. My particular appreciation is for the late Dr. Carl Haywood, a world-renowned scientist and a pioneer in the field of cognitive education and remediation, for his kindness and wisdom, which I will cherish forever.

Many aspects of this book are the result of communication with adoptive parents, particularly from the organizations Families for Russian and Ukrainian Adoption (FRUA), Eastern Europe Adoption Coalition, Families with Children from China, and Latin America Adoptive Parents Association. These communications served as inspiration and a litmus test for my thoughts and actions during my long service as a "first responder" to their problems.

And last, but surely not least, is my dear wife, Tatyana, who helped me in all possible ways in writing this book.

Introduction
Adoption Is Not an Event; It Is a Process

International adoption is a fact of our life. According to the Bureau of Consular Affairs (2020), US Department of State statistics, 278,745 children were adopted from abroad by US citizens from 1999 through 2019. As reported by Johnson (2017), 66,208 children were adopted from abroad by US parents from 1989 to 1999. Therefore, from 1989 through 2019, 344,953 orphans from overseas became parts of American families. As reported by Jones and Placek (2017), international adoption in the United States was peaking between 2004 and 2006 and was gradually declining, particularly after 2011. However, according to a number of recent publications (Mounts & Bradley, 2019; Schrager, 2020), the decline in the number of adopted children from 2006 to 2020 is limited to only young babies. The number of international adoptees between the ages of 5 and 12 has fallen only slightly since 2006, while the number of children under age 1 has fallen 90 percent. Although historically a vast majority (almost 80 percent) of internationally adopted children were infants and toddlers between the ages of 3 months and 3 years, the percentage of older (ages 5–17) adoptees has been growing since 1999, and in the years 2014 through 2019, the majority of international adoptees were children older than 3 at the time of adoption (US Department of State, Bureau of Consular Affairs report dated March 2020). Another definite trend revealed in the last decade is the change in the racial and ethnic composition of adopted children: the proportion of adopted children who were white fell from nearly two-thirds to less than half and the proportion of adopted children who are being raised by parents of a different race from themselves has increased by nearly 40 percent (Zill, 2020; US Department of State (2019), Bureau of Consular Affairs report).

Within the last decade, international adoption has changed its qualitative and quantitative characteristics. As presented in Pinderhughes, Matthews, Deoudes, and Pertman, (2013, p. 12):

> Intercountry adoption has changed comprehensively and is still in the midst of its transformation from a robust but largely unmonitored process through which tens of thousands of infants and toddlers moved into new homes annually, into a smaller but better-regulated system serving primarily children who are older and/or have special needs.

Indeed, we see two distinct trends in the field of international adoption (US Department of State, Annual report on intercountry adoption, 2018) that will likely prevail in the foreseen future:

1. Fewer countries will be on the "donating" side and, due to changing policies in these countries, special needs and older children may constitute the largest percentage of children available for international adoption.
2. Due to improved pre-adoption care (e.g., better conditions in orphanages worldwide) and greater availability of post-adoption services in the United States, adopted children will have better prospects for development than in the past.

"Older" (age 5 and up) internationally adopted (IA) children as a special category of patients in our clinics and students in our schools are the subject of this book, while methods of mental health rehabilitation and academic remediation of international adoptees are its content. I strongly believe that adoption is not an event, but a process that includes restoration of physical health, emotional stability, mental capacity, and learning capability of former orphanage inmates. My 30 years of clinical work with late-adopted (after the age of 5) international adoptees have convinced me that rehabilitation and remediation of this group of children is a highly specialized process. We often hear the saying "it takes a village to raise a child," and nothing could be more relevant to bringing up an international adoptee. Synergetic efforts of the parents, school, professionals, and state-run agencies are the precondition of success. No less important are the methods of rehabilitation and remediation. These are the clinical procedures, teaching mediums, and parents' techniques that are needed to scaffold the victims of prolonged neglect to the level of being self-sufficient and productive members of our society. The description of such methodologies, verified through research and clinical practice, is the substance of this book.

The United States provides the context of clinical practice, mental health rehabilitation, and educational remediation for this book, although a significant part of research data comes from Canada and Western

Europe. The remedial models suggested in the book could be applied in and outside the United States with appropriate modification and adaptation to local circumstances.

Following the major didactic principles, I will start with the definition: who are internationally adopted post-institutionalized children? I suggest the following five distinct attributes that clearly describe IA children and separate them from other groups of our patients and students:

1. IA children are legal orphans, as defined by US Immigration Law: "A child may be considered an orphan because of the death or disappearance of, abandonment or desertion by, or separation or loss from, both parents. The child of an unwed mother or surviving parent may be considered an orphan if that parent is unable to care for the child properly and has, in writing, irrevocably released the child for emigration and adoption" (US Citizenship and Immigration Services Glossary, 2020).
2. IA children were born outside of the countries accepting them, in different racial groups with various languages and diverse social/cultural environments.
3. IA children used to reside in nonfamily settings, such as orphanages, hospitals, or foster care.
4. These children have been legally adopted by citizens of economically advanced countries and brought to these countries to live permanently with their new families. Adoption is the legal process that establishes a parent–child relationship between individuals who are not related biologically (The Free Dictionary by Farlex, 2020).
5. These children are ages 3 months through 17 years at the time of adoption.

The focus in this book is on the so-called "older," or "late-adopted," or "school-age" children. The term "older child" is, of course, a relative one, particularly in the context of adoption. Some adoption literature uses this term to refer to children older than 2 years of age at the time of adoption, while others use it to refer to those from ages 5 to 6 and up to adolescent ages (Robinson, 1998). In this book, the term "older" (and its synonyms "late-adopted" or "school-age at adoption") is used to describe children adopted after their fifth birthday, who on arrival are considered preschoolers, early grade students, or middle school students, or even high school students (ages 14–17). The major point is that these children spent at least 5 years or their early childhood in overseas institutional care and on arrival are to be included in our educational system.

For the sake of parsimony, I use the words "international adoptees" or "internationally adopted (IA) children." Despite their unique physical traits, age, various backgrounds, and distinct language and cultural differences, nearly all international adoptees display certain prominent common features.

First, every one of the "older" international adoptees had to live through painful, trauma-producing experiences in their pre-adoptive life. In addition to a prolonged and severe trauma, international adoptees often have genetic- and epigenetic-based ailments, passed to them by their stressed out and disturbed biological parents. These children often suffer physical and mental imbalances due to environmental toxins and deprivation before adoption. As aptly formulated in the Evan Donaldson Institute report (2010, p. 5):

> Most adopted children, because they suffered early deprivation or maltreatment, come to their new families with elevated risks for developmental, physical, psychological, emotional, or behavioral challenges. Among the factors linked with these higher risks are the following: prenatal malnutrition and low birth weight, prenatal exposure to toxic substances, older age at adoption, early deprivation, abuse or neglect, multiple placements, and emotional conflicts related to loss and identity issues.

Second, the language of the accepting country becomes the adoptees' new native language while their first languages are subjected to rapid attrition. The majority of IA children start learning their new language – whether English, Spanish, Italian, and so on – several years later than their peers, and their process of acquisition of the new language is different from the "typical" ways of mastering the native language in their peers. They go through a process of discarding their native language and learning the new language as a survival skill.

Third, contrary to popular belief, rather than solving all the problems, the child's arrival in the new motherland introduces new challenges. Family life, with its relationships, is uncharted territory for children brought up in orphanages. In the new circumstances, none of their proven behavioral models apply. The loss of culture for an "older" adoptee is just as imminent. Finally, the Western educational system often presents a painful challenge for years to come. Post-adoption traumatization may include a mismatched family, negative school experiences, and rejection by peers.

The majority of older international adoptees are children who experienced complex childhood trauma. Traditionally, the phenomenon of adverse childhood experience is studied in the same cultural and linguistic environment. However, in IA children, a radical change in the social situation of development has taken place: from institutional care to family life, from extreme deprivation and neglect to attentive and protective middle-class style of parenting, from native language and culture to sweeping changes in the cultural/linguistic setting. To the best of my knowledge, only limited research exists regarding the situation when a traumatized person completely changes his/her social/cultural environment as the social situation of development.

The issues presented by the IA children call for creation of a comprehensive system of remediation and rehabilitation specifically for them. Their treatment needs to address physiological, psychological, and social aspects of recovery, be developmentally appropriate for various ages, and aim at maximum recovery possible. A clear understanding that we deal with children whose development has been mediated by complex, prolong, and severe trauma is the basis for their successful healing.

Three professional terms, constantly used in this book, need explanation: rehabilitation, remediation, and compensation.

Rehabilitation is a restoration of a person to a better condition of physical and mental health through training and therapy. The main types of rehabilitation therapy are occupational, physical, speech and language, and mental health, which all aim at the improvement of functioning, reduction of symptoms, and enhancement of the well-being of the patient.

Remediation is a specific process, which uses psychological and educational methods to correct cognitive and academic deficit to the point where it no longer constitutes an obstacle to age-appropriate functioning. Remedial methods and services are therapeutic, corrective, and restorative means, intended for correction or improvement of one's skills in a specific field. To remediate means to correct something deficient, to make up for a lack of something, to get to the root of the problem, and to overcome the issues that prevent successful functioning. In practical terms, remediation involves reteaching of a patient using special remedial methodologies, different from mainstream teaching/learning methods.

Compensation is a process of teaching and learning "work-arounds" for performing a specific task or function. Compensation includes modification and adaptation of the curriculum, usage of the alternative ways to accomplish a goal of the study, application of assistive technologies, accommodations in test taking, and other means of support.

Remediation and compensation should not be considered alternative approaches where either one or the other is selected. The IA children should have both approaches available to them concurrently to enable them to regain as much as possible. The goal with them is to achieve the highest level of their functioning, and finding the right balance between remediation and compensatory approaches is essential.

In a way, international adoption is a "natural experiment" in the study of complex childhood trauma. Scientific research of "older" IA children's development under stress, whether prenatal, postnatal, during the adoption transition, or in post-adoption life, can provide us with discoveries that could be extrapolated to all children who experience severe adversity in their life. We cannot ignore the wealth of data and research opportunities presented by studying internationally adopted children and adoptive families.

In the peak of international adoption in the United States (first decade of the new millennium), Dr. Janet Welsh (2007) and her associates had undertaken a comprehensive literature review to find out about rehabilitation and remedial/therapeutic interventions for IA children and their families. The findings were rather disappointing: very limited treatments and remedial methodologies were in existence specifically for IA children while known methods may not be applied to this very special category of patients/students without significant adaptation. Now, more than a decade later, I have evidence, presented in this book, that there are methodologies – newly invented or substantially modified existing ones – that could be effective for rehabilitation and remediation of international adoptees. This book is fully devoted to the description and critical analysis of what we, as a "village," can do to make victims of systemic neglect and trauma become valuable members of our society.

CHAPTER I

Internationally Adopted Children
Development Mediated by Early Childhood Trauma

What Is a Complex Childhood Trauma?

For the last three decades, a massive, systematic, multidisciplinary, and focused investigation of adverse early childhood experiences has been developing in the United States and many other countries. Researchers and practitioners in the field of mental health came to an understanding that continuous repetitive traumatic experiences during early childhood produce a wide range of distortions in human development. The concept of complex childhood trauma is not uniformed and homogeneous, which is reflected even in the circulating terminology, such as "adverse childhood experience," "prolonged traumatic stress," "repetitive traumatization," "recurring distress," "complex childhood trauma," "relational childhood trauma," "early childhood trauma," "developmental trauma disorder," and so on. What is important to note is that behind all these terms there is an understanding of the affected child's exposure to multiple traumatic events and the wide-ranging, long-term impact of this exposure.

In my view, the most advanced and eloquent conceptualization of this issue is presented in the works of van der Kolk (2003, 2005, 2015) and his associate group of psychologists and psychiatrists. These scientists proposed that multiple and long-term traumatic conditions and events, often against the background of neurological weaknesses and impairments, result in distorted neurodevelopment, designated as developmental trauma disorder (DTD). The concept of DTD was presented to the research and clinical communities as a complex somatic and neuropsychological phenomenon, which is chronic, relational (caused by humans), and significant enough to affect the development of a child (D'Andrea, Ford, Stolbach, Spinazzola, & van der Kolk, 2012). In many cases, DTD is formed before the child has the verbal and reasoning ability to process and store the traumatic experience in memory, resulting in the central nervous system (CNS) accumulating the traumatic incidents as somatic distress and undifferentiated pain/afflicts (van der Kolk, 2015).

In my previously published book (Gindis, 2019), I presented the paradigm that international adoptees bestow the extreme case of development mediated by DTD. In the same book, I suggested the following definition of DTD, which I have assembled from different sources (Gindis, 2019, p. 37):

> Early childhood trauma is a condition caused by repetitive and pervasive, subjectively highly stressful events, mostly within the interpersonal context of the child's life that have an adverse, wide-ranging, and long-term physiological and psychological impact on the development and maturation of high psychological functions, thus compromising neurodevelopmental integration of sensory, emotional and cognitive systems into cohesive whole of a mature socially-adjusted individual.

The subjective nature of the consequences of adverse childhood experiences should be emphasized: what causes the traumatic impact on one child may not produce the same effect on the other. The reaction to the potentially trauma-producing events or conditions is predetermined by the child's genetic equipment, the system of social support available to the child, previous trauma history, and many other factors. When stress is extreme, repetitive, and profound while the social buffering is absent or insufficient, like in the case of abandoned children, it may result in epigenetic modifications and in the formation of behavior patterns that are maladaptive in many contexts and may contribute to the later psychosocial problems with emotional regulation, impulse control, logical thinking, and social behavior (Putnam, 2006).

The stress response, while essential in times of threat, is designed to return to a baseline state when the threat is no longer present: this is a typical pattern of normal human functioning. But we do not see this in many international adoptees: adversity in early life shapes the experience-dependent maturation of stress-regulating pathways underlying emotional functions. Practitioners working with the IA population observed that children who experienced traumatic events in the past continue to experience heightened neurochemical reactions in the present without the existence of a threat (Gunnar & Donzella, 2002; De Bellis, Hooper, Spratt, & Woolley, 2009; Pollak et al., 2010). The release of adrenaline facilitates reinforcement of threat memory, and there is some evidence that failure to regulate the sympathetic nervous system response may lead to a stronger encoding of traumatic memory (Heim & Nemeroff, 2002; Heim & Binder, 2012). The neurological research shows to what extent trauma affects a child on a biological and hormonal level as well as psychologically and behaviorally; it is truly a complex mixture of biological, psychological, and social phenomena (Rothschild, 2000; Ogden, Kekuni, & Pain, 2006). If not addressed, DTD can distort the developmental trajectory for the remainder of the individual's life span, as it is linked to a wide range of problems, including addiction, chronic physical conditions, depression, anxiety, self-harming behaviors, and other psychiatric disorders.

And now, having all that was presented above in mind, let us imagine a child who has been abandoned by birth parents or has lived in an extremely dysfunctional, abusive family as an infant and toddler; was placed in an orphanage to live through the neglect and deprivation of institutional milieu; and then was adopted by strangers into a different sociocultural environment. This child would be at exceptional risk for DTD. This assumption is very true, as revealed by research, clinical practice, and families' experience: the vast majority of IA children does have DTD to some extent – ranging in degree from overwhelming and incurable to mild and recoverable; but no survivor of this abnormal background escapes it without consequences.

There are many factors in a life story of an IA child that cause, sustain, and consistently contribute to the formation of DTD. Among the most significant are the following:

- *Inherited transgenerational trauma* (transmitted from destitute, battered, often homeless, unemployed, and drug- and alcohol-addicted mothers)
- *Organically based encephalopathies* of different etiologies related to prenatal conditions, birth circumstances, and adverse postnatal physical environments. (In some IA children, these impairments are so significant that their entire further development is affected by them, as in the case of Fetal Alcohol Syndrome Disorder)
- *Adverse social circumstances* (dysfunctional and abusive biological family, total abandonment, institutionalization, international adoption, and post-adoption stress)

Contrary to common beliefs, the change from an objectively adverse pre-adoption social situation of development to an objectively favorable post-adoption life does not cut the chain of traumatic impacts in IA children. Adjustment to a new physical, cultural, social, and linguistic environment is a traumatic encounter by itself: the previous experience forms the background, but the new trauma of not fitting in, not connecting with, and not being accepted by the new social milieu creates additional and more subjectively important traumatic events. The long-lasting consequences of earlier traumatization continue to affect the development but are now mediated by the mounting challenges of social adjustment and competition. There are certain factors that mediate the impacts of these conditions, such as the age of the child, the intensity and duration of adverse experience, and resilience forces (a counterbalance to traumatic impacts).

Symptomatic Presentation of DTD in Older IA Children

Symptoms of DTD in older international adoptees could be depicted as mostly physiological and mostly psychological, although in reality both groups of symptoms are closely intertwined. Physiological symptoms of DTD include sensory integration difficulties, musculoskeletal pain, abnormally decreased or increased pain threshold, sleep disturbance, hyper-arousal and hypo-arousal, problems with digestion, oversensitivity to touch or sound, and other physiological indications (Cook, Blaustein, Spinazzola, & van der Kolk, 2003; van der Kolk, 2015). It is a consistent finding that even after years in an adoptive family, IA children may continue to demonstrate an abnormal response to stress on a basic biological level – such as increased cortisol in saliva (Gunnar & Quevedo, 2007), and increased heart rate and blood pressure (van der Kolk, 2003; Fisher, 2014) – and in observable behavior. Physiological symptoms of DTD are most comprehensively presented in a number of monographs, authored by Rothschild (2000), Ogden et al. (2006), Fisher (2014), and van der Kolk (2015), to cite just a few relevant publications. Therefore, I will concentrate on the psychological symptoms of DTD in IA children.

Psychological Symptomatology of DTD

The psychological consequences of DTD reveal themselves in many forms and shapes. Van der Kolk (2003, 2005, 2015) defines psychological symptoms of DTD as an inability to concentrate and pay attention; chronic anger, fear, and anxiety; self-loathing and self-destructive behavior; limitations in self-regulation of feelings and behavior; aggression against others; dissociation; and inability to negotiate satisfactory interpersonal relationships. What is presented below are observable patterns of DTD-caused overt behaviors in IA children, victims of a prolonged complex childhood trauma.

Dysregulated High Psychological Functions

The most prominent feature of psychological symptoms of DTD in older IA children is the impaired regulation of high psychological functions:

poorly modulated emotions, disorganized cognition, disrupted attention, and weakly controlled behavior. Dysregulation of affect and behavior is manifested in both externalized (acting out, tantrums, etc.) and internalized symptoms (depression, anxieties, and phobias). Confirmation of these clinical findings is found in many research publications (Cloitre, 2005; Benjet, Borges, Mendez, Fleiz, & Medina-Mora, 2011; Clarkson-Freeman, 2014; Kumsta et al., 2015). Emotional volatility (inability to modulate emotional responses) is evident in how easily these children can be aroused emotionally and how quickly they move to the extreme of their emotions. Self-regulation of emotions includes the accurate identification of internal emotional states and selection of a socially acceptable way of external expression of emotions. Many traumatized IA children exhibit impairment on both stages. Conversely, some of them may respond with the general numbing of their emotions ("shutting down") and lack responsiveness to the external world, which is known as the state of "disassociation" (Cloitre, 2005; Waters, 2016). In cognitive/motivational domains, dysregulation is seen in impaired "executive functions" (Bick, Zeanah, Fox, & Nelson, 2018; Gindis, 2019). In this respect, many post-institutionalized children are rather similar to much younger children than to their peers. Limitations in executive functions in traumatized IA children in cognitive/academic domains are apparent in their difficulties with sustaining goal-directed behavior, in generation of problem-solving strategies and methods toward achieving goals, in carrying out multistep activities, in following complex instructions, in monitoring and keeping track of performance outcomes, and in their reluctance/unwillingness to perform tasks that are repetitive and uninteresting, require effort, or had not been chosen by the children (Hostinar, Stellern, Schaefer, Carlson, & Gunnar, 2012).

Distorted "Internal Working Model"

The distorted perception of the world and themselves is another significant feature of DTD in IA children. "Internal working model" (IWM) – a term suggested by Bowlby (1980, 1988) – is a cognitive, affective, and motivational framework, encompassing mental representations for understanding the world, the self, and others. It is built on past experiences and helps the individual consider responses and actions; it serves as a mental/emotional "template" or reference criteria for new situations. It determines how individuals perceive themselves, thus impacting their self-confidence and self-esteem. According to Bowlby, in a typical development, IWM is a secure base from which to explore the social and physical world. This "safe base" results from the nurturing interactions with the caregiver. The "internal working model" is constructed through the internalization of emotional and cognitive properties of the young child's relationships with his/her mother. Positive early life experiences allow a child to develop a model of self as generally worthy and competent. In contrast, repetitive experiences of harm or rejection by significant others and the associated failure to develop age-appropriate competencies are likely to lead to the sense of one's self as ineffective, helpless, deficient, and unlovable (Cook et al., 2003). The child's self-perception and worldviews get distorted by rejection, violence, hostility, and fear. Indeed, IA children assemble their internal working model in a manner that depicts the world as a dangerous place to live in and themselves as unwanted and dreadful. Children who perceive themselves as powerless or incompetent and who expect others to reject and despise them have problems eliciting and responding to social support (Cook et al., 2003; Sonuga-Barke, Schlotz, & Kreppner, 2010; Juffer & Ijzendoorn, 2012).

Enduring State of Hyper-arousal and/or Hypo-arousal

These are two opposite states of the central nervous system (CNS) and can be found in the same IA child at different times. Specifically, hyper-arousal presents itself in excessive vigilance, acute flight-or-fight response, agitation, irritability, constant state of rage, and "proactive" aggression, while hypo-arousal is evident in withdrawal, disengagement, and lack of emotional involvement or responsiveness. Each of these response patterns activates a unique combination of neural systems, literally blocking the adequate processing of what is happening in social relations. Chronic trauma exposure may lead to an overreliance on hyper-arousal or dissociation as a coping mechanism that, in turn, can exacerbate difficulties with behavioral management and can affect regulation and self-concept (Hibbard, Barlow, & Macmillan, 2012).

Lack of Developmental Competence ("Mixed Maturity")
as a Direct Consequence of DTD

The essence of this unique phenomenon is that IA children may at one time demonstrate behaviors of a much older person and, at other times, of a much younger one. For example, in terms of self-care, alertness to the environment, and basic survival skills, post-institutional children may be well advanced for their age, but in reaction to stress and frustration, academic learning, and social interaction, they may act like a child several years younger. Their adaptive behavior is often so immature that it puzzles and upsets their adoptive parents and teachers. As a result of "mixed maturity" (the term invented by Dr. Cohen, 2008), it is difficult for IA children to interact with peers, to share interests, to participate in conversation, and to engage in play, sports, or learning activities. "Mixed maturity" is one of the most confusing characteristics of older traumatized IA children for parents, teachers, and therapists (see more in Gindis, 2019).

Difficulties in Forming and Sustaining Social Connectedness: Distorted Attachment as a Direct Consequence of DTD

Traumatized children have difficulty in forming and sustaining reciprocal relationships with others (Cook et al., 2003). The failure to develop a secure attachment in infancy appears to reverberate throughout an individual's life in the form of difficulties with relationships. Indeed, in infancy and early childhood, the quality of attachment is the single most important factor that can predict social connectedness problems later in life (Cozoline, 2014). The security of attachment bonds is the most important alleviating factor against trauma-induced behavior and emotional troubles. International adoption brought a new dimension to the issue of attachment because IA children present an extreme group of attachment deprivation. It was consistently shown in numerous contemporary research publications that a lack of caregiver–child responsive social/emotional interactions is a major contributor to distorted and delayed development, evident in later behavior problems, impaired social skills, and so on. Indeed, the first 36 months of life is a sensitive period for forming the base of social connectedness (Landry, Smith, Swank, & Guttentag, 2008; Bruce, Tarullo, & Gunnar, 2009). Lack of or distorted social connectedness during sensitive periods powerfully interferes with the formation of interpersonal relatedness. Thus, it was found that IA children have difficulty in accurately reading social cues and social demands of the ongoing situation (Bakermans-Kranenburg et al., 2011). Furthermore, they are often out of tune with others, either socially withdrawn or aggressive to other children and family members (Cloitre, 2005). Unable to regulate their emotions, they tend to scare other children away and lack reliable playmates and chums (Merz & McCall, 2010).

Post-orphanage Behavior: "Survival" Behavior Patterns
as Direct Consequences of DTD

The constellation of "survival skills" in IA "older" children includes constant alertness and readiness to react to danger (real or perceived), specific means of coping with a threat (fighting, fleeing, or dissociation), hoarding (mostly food but also some material items), and certain "special" social skills, such as manipulation, triangulation, deception/cheating, and indiscriminate friendliness to strangers. The survival skills of an orphanage resident develop early on and dominate their psychological profile. They forcefully substitute for age-appropriate adaptive skills and patterns of behavior that are not needed for immediate survival, such as academic learning skills, positive socialization skills, and empathy. Traumatic events in IA children's lives are often unpredictable; therefore, a child becomes accustomed to being vigilant in the face of uncertainty, which leads to fear of change in routines. It is to be stressed that survival skills, being repeated numerous times, are deeply embedded into a child's psyche and operate mostly beyond the child's conscious awareness. Once being useful for surviving while the child was in a stressful dysfunctional family or in an institution, survival behavior patterns cause disruptions in the adoptive family's functioning and in their overall post-adoption environment. Survival behavior may impede the ability to meet societal expectations in learning, self-regulating emotions, interpersonal interactions, cognitive functioning, and other age-appropriate competencies.

The rigidity of internalized "survival" skills is astonishing in IA children. To the surprise and frustration of adoptive parents, an international adoptee reacts as if he/she is still in an adverse situation of stress and danger. Early traumatic memories are stored in the more "primitive" areas of the brain, so they are less accessible to language, logic, and reasoning. This may impede adequate responses and lead the child to regression to earlier developmental stages. At the same time, limited language and undifferentiated memories of emotional strain may lower a child's capacity to relieve the pain through verbalization, resulting in tantrums and acting out (Layne, Warren, Watson, & Shalev, 2007).

In the literature related to international adoption, either popular for general public or instructional for adoptive parents and, at times, in research publications as well (Barroso, Barbosa-Ducharne, Coelho, Costa, & Silva, 2017), "survival skills," as described above, are often labeled as post-orphanage behavior (POB) syndrome. Indeed, "survival skills" are the core of POB.

It was convincingly shown in many research publications (Gindis, 2005, 2019; Hawk & McCall, 2011; Marinus & Juffer, 2011) that orphanage as an institution is the breeding ground for specific behavior among children who were deprived of proper positive adult mediation in their early most formative years, were continuously traumatized, and were forced into the survival mode of everyday life. These patterns of behavior and a matching "internal model of the world" become an integral part of a child's psychological profile. The new social situation of development after the adoption contradicts the existing internal representation and patterns of orphanage behavior. However, children are not robots that we can switch from one pattern of behavior to the other: they continue, at least for some time, with the survival mode of conduct that served them well in their pre-adoption life. As a result of the collision of the child's learned, interiorized orphanage behavior and the demands of a new social situation of development, the condition for a trauma-producing state is formed: the IA child may not be accepted by peers, fails in school, and suffers from the ongoing conflicts in the adoptive family. A new layer of trauma forms and consolidates, reinforced by a lack of communicative capacity and appropriate cultural background.

In Chapter 8 of this book, I present a brief description of specific patterns of POB syndrome (for more detailed information, see Gindis, 2019, pp. 74, 140, 143, 144, 148, 164–166) and means of reducing/ eliminating it.

Developmental "Catch-Up" and Long-Lasting Deficiencies in IA Children

In the developmental context, "catching-up" and "long-lasting deficiencies" present one of the most controversial notions in the field of psychology of international adoption. On the one hand, many, if not the majority, of research papers on this subject are excited about the amazing abilities of IA children to improve their functioning to reach the age-appropriate standards (see a comprehensive review in van IJzendoorn & Juffer, 2006). On the other hand, there is a significant number of high-quality research publications proving that the "catch-up" is only relative in regard to the initial status of IA children (Gindis, 1998, 2005, 2019; Hildyard & Wolfe, 2002; van der Vegt, van der Ende, Ferdinand, Verhulst, & Tiemeier, 2009; Sonuga-Barke, Edmund, & Kreppner, 2012; Welsh & Viana, 2012). After years with an adoptive family, a significant number of older IA children score below expectations on general cognitive tests and academic achievement tests, and they exhibit a variety of deficiencies in executive functioning: problems with attention, self-regulation, working memory, and planning. Many of them continue to have attachment, relationship, and social engagement difficulties and a variety of internalized and externalized behavior problems, especially during adolescence. It is particularly applicable to "older" adoptees exposed to traumatic experiences for a longer period of time (Juffer & van IJzendoorn, 2005; Tieman, van der Ende, & Verhulst, 2005; van Londen, Juffer, & van IJzendoorn, 2007; Pollak et al., 2010; Hawk & McCall, 2011; Juffer, Palacios, Lemare, van IJzendoorn, & Verhulst, 2011; Rutter et al., 2015).

While summarizing major findings made within the last 30 years in relation to developmental outcomes in international adoptees, the following transpire:

- The traumatized IA children for years after adoption continue to demonstrate delays and deficiency in many domains of their development.
- The majority (no statistics exists) shows substantial improvement in many domains of functioning following adoption.
- The minority (no statistics exists) demonstrates persistent deficits in one or more developmental domains.
- It is likely that developmental catch-up is domain specific: the existing data suggest that there are certain domains of overall functioning affected more profoundly and persistently than others. Specifically, social/emotional self-regulation recovers more slowly in relation to age expectation (Beckett et al., 2006; Almas, 2012; Stevens, van Rooij, & Jovanovic, 2016).

I am not aware of any specific meta-analysis on what facilitates or inhibits developmental recovery in IA children, but based on about 30 years of following the research literature and my own clinical experience, I may point to two leading factors strongly associated with the negative outcomes:

1. The degree of initial (pre-adoption) impairment in a child, such as cognitive limitations, psychiatric disorders, medical problems, and other special needs. In this respect, the birth ("donor") countries vary considerably in terms of quality of institutional care; thus, the children from low-quality orphanages show greater developmental deficits and slower recovery. According to a number of research reports, children adopted from India, Ethiopia, Russia, and Eastern Europe, particularly from Romania, had more pre-adoptive adversity than children

adopted from South Korea and China. Central American countries have a significant diversity in pre-adoption care as well (Pomerleau et al., 2005; van Londen et al., 2007; Odenstad et al., 2008; Welsh & Viana 2012).

2. The age at adoption and so-called "dose–response" factor: the higher the dose of trauma, the more potentially damaging the effects. This point of view was expressed in many research publications (see Judge, 2003; Bakermans-Kranenburg, van IJzendoorn, & Juffer, 2008; Welsh & Viana 2012; Stevens et al., 2016). However, findings related to the age and duration of institutional experience as a factor in developmental trajectories of children after adoption are inconsistent. I would agree with Welch and Viana (2012) that "[i]t is possible that other factors, such as the quality of care the child received prior to adoption, or biological risks factors, such as premature birth or prenatal substance exposure, are more powerful predictors of outcome than age at placement" (p. 261).

One of the most intriguing and captivating aspects of international adoption is the resilience to the intensely adverse childhood experience IA children lived through in their early childhood. Why do some former orphanage residents carry the deep scars of institutional rearing for life, while the others successfully mix in with the general population? What causes a different outcome after the same traumatic experience? Why do IA children have DTD in different degrees and react differently to the adversity of early childhood and post-adoption stress? It is difficult not to be fascinated by those mysterious sources of resilience in children, whether they are rooted in individual neurological differences, social/emotional support, or learned social skills. Our understanding of the psychological nature of resilience in IA children may bring, potentially, the most significant benefits for therapeutic practice and educational remediation. The variability of outcomes of post-adoption upbringing in children who had similar pre-adoption experience is so remarkable that we need to know what constitutes resilience alongside specific vulnerabilities in IA children.

Resiliency is the ability to cope with life stresses. As a theoretical construct, resilience is defined in various ways, but, essentially, it refers to a dynamic process of forbearance leading to positive adaptation in the face of significant adversity (Luthar, Cicchetti, & Becker, 2000; Bonanno, 2004; Calhoun & Tedeschi, 2006). It implies that the impairment and suffering that follow trauma do not preclude a restorative and successful adjustment, which results in positive development. Based on my clinical experience, the following factors show connections with IA children's resilience to the consequences of DTD:

1. *Social connectedness*. If a child is lucky to have in his/her pre-adoptive and post-adoptive life a person available for productive intimate social/emotional interactions, then the chances of effective resilience increase significantly. Conversely, the greatest threat to resilience is the breakdown of external protective systems.
2. *Individual characteristics* of a child, such as temperament (easy going personality, innate positive disposition, and sociable demeanor) and certain personality traits (adaptability and compatibility, compassion and loyalty along with motivation to learn coping strategies, etc.).
3. *Special talents* (music, sport, art, etc.), creativity, and spirituality.

To conclude, in relation to IA children, the notion of DTD – relational in nature and often on the background of birth-associated neurological weaknesses – is the most productive explanatory paradigm. The acceptance of this concept allows us to determine the underlying causes of many issues in the IA children and better understand their neurophysiological and psychological symptomatic presentations. DTD in IA children differs in many aspects from what we observe in the general population of children affected by adverse childhood experiences. In the IA population, DTD comes as the synergetic effect of weakened neurology, epigenetic-based transgenerational trauma, overwhelming pre-adoption stress, and the stress of culture and language adjustment after the adoption.

Complex trauma has pervasive effects on the biological/physiological, interpersonal, affective, behavioral, and cognitive self-regulatory capacities of a person. Impairments in these domains contribute to childhood psychopathology, which, without adequate intervention, may persist into adulthood. In terms of the factors that facilitate the recovery and developmental catch-up, it should be pointed out the quality and quantity of post-adoption remediation and rehabilitation, the strength of social connectedness with the adoptive family, and the post-adoption social/cultural environment as the decisive forces. The rest of the book is devoted to methods of rehabilitation and remediation of "older" IA children in specific domains of cognition, language, academic, social, and emotional functioning as well as means of therapeutic parenting and preparation of IA students to adulthood.

CHAPTER 2

Developmental, Neuropsychological, Psychoeducational, and "Dynamic" Assessment of Internationally Adopted Children

An accurate assessment of IA children is the first step in the proper understanding and rehabilitation of these survivors of institutional care. Practically all internationally adopted children go through a medical examination upon arrival for possible medical rehabilitation or prevention. Adoptive parents request a thorough medical evaluation on arrival even if a child appears to be healthy: the parents understand the need for medical rehabilitation or prevention. Unfortunately, a psychoeducational or speech and language assessment of a newly arrived school-age child is the exception rather than the rule if the adopted child does not have the evidence of learning or mental health handicapping conditions. Too often, school districts assume a "wait-and-see" position rejecting a request for evaluation in order "to wait until the child learns enough English." Additionally, in many cases, adoptive parents rely on a physician's "clean bill of health" and assume that a physically healthy child should not have any problems in the family or school.

To make things even more complicated, in contrast to the structured and distinctly affirmed medical requirements for initial examination of newly arrived international adoptees (Miller, 2005, Johnson, 2019), there are no clearly stated requirements or procedures regarding psychological screening or full assessment for the same category of children. There is a rather vague understanding of who can provide these evaluations: what are the professionals' qualifications, when does an evaluation have to be done, what kind of evaluation is necessary, and what methods and procedures are to be used? The lack of these guidelines makes it difficult for the adoptive parents to request such an evaluation.

In fact, in many IA children's medical records, court documents, and developmental and educational history, there are "red flags" (see the list of these danger signals in Miller (2005), Eckerle et al. (2014), Tan and Robinson (2018), and Gindis (2019) which make psychological screening and assessment a "must" procedure on arrival. A short list of most popular alarming signs includes a diagnosis or merely a notation of "delay in language and psychological development," the child who did not start school at age 7 or was retained in elementary school, or the child who was a student in a special school, or the child who received remedial services in school in the native country. Some medical diagnoses (e.g., Fetal Alcohol Syndrome Disorder, suspected autistic behaviors, obviously delayed gross and fine motor skills, hearing and vision limitations, etc. require further developmental and psychological evaluations.

One of the most obvious reasons for a psychoeducational evaluation is the issue of school placement and remediation. School districts have a tendency to place newly arrived, school-age, internationally adopted children in a grade according to their chronological age, which is the usual practice for children from immigrant families in the United States and Canada. However, it may be inappropriate for many adopted children.

Pediatricians, who, as a rule, are not familiar with the specifics of school placement, may recommend an "age-appropriate classroom" based on the child's general health. Nevertheless, the chronological age criteria that guide the school district administration and physical soundness that guides pediatricians are only two among many factors to consider. What about trauma-related behavior patterns, language development, social skills, self-regulation and age-appropriate goal-directed social and learning behavior, mastery of age-expected cognitive skills, and ability and willingness to participate in shared and joint classroom activities? An "academic readiness" in relation to an adopted child must be thoroughly examined and properly understood (see more on this topic in Chapter 7). Academic pressure in the "age-based" classroom, along with general adjustment and acculturation, language acquisition, and possible health and neurological problems, may lead to the newly formed traumatic experiences for an IA child and to frustration in the adoptive family.

The legal requirements for a psychoeducational evaluation of non-English speaking children are clearly formulated in IDEA (2009) – the major US educational law. According to IDEA, Sec. 34, CFR300.304, to conduct the evaluation of the English language learners (ELL), the school (public agency) must

(1) *Use a variety of assessment tools and strategies to gather relevant functional, developmental, and academic information about the child, including information provided by the parent,*
(2) *Not use any single measure or assessment as the sole criterion for determining whether a child is a child with a disability and for determining an appropriate educational program for the child; . . .*

(ii) *Are provided and administered in the child's native language or other mode of communication and in the form most likely to yield accurate information on what the child knows and can do academically, developmentally, and functionally.*

(iv) *Are administered by trained and knowledgeable personnel;*

The child is assessed in all areas related to the suspected disability, including, if appropriate, health, vision, hearing, social and emotional status, general intelligence, academic performance, communicative status, and motor abilities.

There is no "one-size-fits-all" recommendation regarding grade placement, specific educational programs, remediation, and support services – the decision should always be highly individualized and based on a thorough consideration of many factors. And this is not possible without a proper screening or full assessment.

The Language of Assessment

The language of the assessment is a unique and a critically important factor in the evaluation of internationally adopted children. One of the most shocking discoveries made with internationally adopted children throughout the years was the swiftness with which they lose their mother tongue (Gindis, 2004a, 2004b, 2019; Glennen, 2014; Genesee, 2016). The evaluation in the native language should be done soon after the arrival before the child's native language is weakened and eventually extinguished. For all children younger than 7, this ought to be done within the first two to five weeks. For those in the 7–10 or older age group who are literate in their native language, the time frame is the first two months at most (see Table on page 22, more information in Gindis, 2019). Please note that these are empirically established data reported by the clinicians who provided testing in Spanish, Russian, and Chinese (both Cantonese and Mandarin) at the BGCenter from 1992 to 2013.

The screening, done within this narrow "window of opportunity" period, is the best investment into the child's future school progress. As time goes by, screening becomes less and less effective, and finally, it becomes impossible; the native language has lost its functionality and cannot be used for an assessment.

If an evaluation in a child's native language is not done by a bilingual professional within the first 3 months, it is difficult to prove this child's eligibility for any remedial services. Too often, school district representatives just say that the learning difficulties, which the parents refer to, are just the normal occurrences in the process of second language learning and

Time frames of language attrition in international adoptees

Age at adoption	Time it takes to lose the functionality of native language
4 to 5 years old	5 to 7 **weeks** after the adoption
Between 6 and 8, emerging literacy in the native language	1 to 2 **months**, but some exceptions are possible
Between 8 and 9, established literacy in the native language	1 to 3 **months** after the adoption
After the age of 9, with well-established literacy in the native language and several years of schooling in the native country	Between 4 and 7 **months** after the adoption (literacy skills are the first casualties in the native language attrition)

the child needs more time within the English language environment to alleviate these difficulties. Without an assessment in the native language, the adoptive parents may not prove the genuine need for remedial help.

An assessment in the English language, on the other hand, should take place only when this language becomes the dominant means not only of communication but also reasoning (cognitive/academic language). The English language dominance and level of proficiency must be established before the psychoeducational assessment is performed.

According to the *Standards for Educational and Psychological Testing* (2014 revision) developed jointly by the American Psychological Association (APA), the American Educational Research Association (AERA), and the National Council on Measurement in Education (NCME), there are certain preliminary procedures that have to be undertaken before administration of psychological and educational tests to a person who is bilingual/bicultural. Specifically, the determination of an examinee's language status (dominant language, proficiency in the cognitive/academic aspect of the dominant language, and cultural determinants of this language application), completed by a competent and properly certified professional, is to be done prior to any psychological testing. The use of verbal tests in English and the first language should be focused according to specific purposes, and the interpretation of the test results is to be done in the context of the known developmental and language history of the examinee.

Following the letter and the spirit of the above *standards,* certain parts of an IA child's assessment could be completed in the native language. In other parts of the examination, the two languages (the native language and English) could be used interchangeably, serving the purpose of objectively estimating the child's actual level of academic functioning and the overall cognitive potential.

Ideally, all standardized tests and behavior rating scales should be administered according to their specific manuals. However, these tests and behavior scales are standardized instruments with limited validity for a foreign-born child with an atypical cultural and developmental background. At times, according to the *standards*, a strictly normative interpretation of the test scores or behavior ratings may not be possible due to deviations from the standard procedures to accommodate bilingual issues. The uniqueness of the child's continually changing language situation should be properly understood in interpreting the numerical findings presented in the psychological report. The best practice regarding all quantitative test results should be considered an approximated estimation of a child's current psychological and educational functioning rather than a measurement; the numerical data should be offered as a baseline for comparison for future assessments, and the performance on all standardized tests should be interpreted as "no less than."

Professional Qualifications of an Assessor

There are certain criteria for selecting professionals to do screening and full assessment of IA children. The ideal choice is a bilingual, in the target language, licensed psychologist with an extensive experience in assessing international adoptees. The professional ought to be capable and willing to analyze the developmental history of the child, often a sizeable amount of paperwork. A lot of useful information could be in these records, and underestimating the child's social and developmental history may lead to misinterpretation of the assessment's findings.

Unfortunately, the chances of finding such a specialist are slim, and compromises are almost unavoidable. One such compromise is to use an interpreter. The issue of selecting an interpreter and working with this specialist is one of the most controversial in the field of bilingual evaluation (Searight & Searight, 2009). But in many areas of the country, adoptive parents simply have no choice and have to accept the least compromised option between the assessment with an interpreter or no assessment at all. It is the psychologist's direct responsibility to ensure that interpreters are competent.

The psychologists must be sensitive to the issues of cultural/language differences and be aware of the specificity of IA children. The evaluator must be familiar with the school environments in order to create an efficient and implementable plan of what to do in school over the next 12–18 months to address the child's developmental and educational needs. Some experts, though being skillful clinicians, may still be unfamiliar with special education procedures and the linkage between assessment and intervention in schools. They may end up with purely medical diagnoses and/or unrealistic, vague, and irrelevant recommendations, which will be rejected by the school as inappropriate. Other clinicians may end up with a "laundry list" of recommendations that are pretty much "one size fits all," and this would take up 24 hours of the child's day if indeed implemented.

A psychologist is a human being. When an adoptive parent brings an IA child to the office of a psychologist, the professional sees a well-groomed and nicely dressed child accompanied by somewhat nervous but otherwise "regular" middle-class, well-educated parent(s). In the perception of a psychologist, this will be a typical family with typical issues (the issues may be serious, but still will be "typical"). Even when the history of the child is known, it is still difficult for a psychologist who never dealt with post-institutionalized children to change the mindset and reexamine the ways of assessing and interpreting the results of his/her testing. This is especially obvious in the evaluation of developmental disabilities and issues related to language processing. It is crucial for the professional working with an IA child to be sensitive to the concerns related to institutionalization, trauma, and adoption in order to be able to interpret the data.

Current Types of Evaluations Available for International Adoptees

As of now, there are four mainstream types of IA children assessments using existing standardized psychological and educational instruments: initial screening, psychoeducational assessment, combined developmental, neuropsychological, and psychoeducational evaluation, and discipline-specific testing (speech/language, occupational and physical therapy, hearing and vision evaluation, etc.). A testing methodology known as "dynamic assessment" is currently outside of a mainstream but has a promising potential in evaluation of IA children. Let us consider each assessment option in more detail.

Initial screening has several distinct goals dictated by the specific timing of the procedure – first several weeks upon arrival to the adoptive family:

1. To determine if the child is developing close to age expectations.
2. To establish if medical conditions have educational/social implications.
3. To detect or rule out issues that should be addressed by a full or specialized assessment.

4. To consult the parents regarding the adjustment period.
5. To determine school readiness and discuss the proper school or preschool placement in the US educational system.

In most cases, at least some of the adoption-related documentations (court decrees, health records, orphanage papers, etc.) are available and have to be carefully reviewed. Depending on a child's age, the screening should take one session of 2–4 hours. Usually, the expected outcomes of a screening are a verbal consultation with the parents and a brief written report that includes interpretation of the findings, immediate in-office discussion of the appropriate actions, and referrals to proper specialists, if needed.

Initial screening by itself is a challenge for a psychologist: a bilingual professional has to evaluate cognitive, language, social/emotional, and current academic skills or pre-academic readiness in a child with "atypical" background. Here is a sample of referral questions, psychoeducational tests, and clinical procedures for an IA child of chronological ages 5–7 (no formal schooling in the country of origin):

Evan is a 6-year-old boy adopted from Peru 16 days ago; he received no formal schooling in his native country.

Referral questions:

- What is Evan's current developmental status in terms of his cognitive, language, and adaptive behavior functioning?
- What are Evan's pre-academic functional strengths and weaknesses and what is his readiness (cognitive, language, and social) for age-appropriate school experience?
- Does Evan need remedial help in the pre-academic, behavioral, and social/emotional domains, and if so, what are the most appropriate plans of actions in the family and in the school setting?

Tests and clinical procedures:

- Clinical observation using NEPSY-ll Observational Tables
- The Bender VMG Test-2 (a standardized test), along with a sample of letter tracing, coloring, and drawings to measure visual perception/processing and graphomotor skills
- The BVAT-NU (2005) – Bilingual Verbal Ability-Normative Update Test (a standardized test for cognitive/academic language in 16 languages)
- The UNIT – 2 (2016), Universal Nonverbal Intelligence Test, Second Edition (a standardized language-free test of general intelligence)

- The Brigance Diagnostic Inventory of Early Development-2 (Brigance, 2004) (a standardized achievement test for preschoolers and early grades)
- An informal evaluation of the verbal communicative fluency/pragmatics in the native language
- A review and interpretation of available medical, court, and educational documentation from the country of origin
- Interview with the adoptive parents using the Developmental Trauma Disorder Questionnaire for Adoptive Parents (DTD-Q-AP) (Gindis, 2019)

A sample of referral questions and psychoeducational instruments assorted for screening of an IA child (chronological age 7–14) with formal schooling in the country of origin:

Katya is an 11-year-old, Ukrainian-dominant bilingual (Russian/Ukrainian) girl, brought from a Ukrainian orphanage 20 days ago. She has repeated the first and second grades twice in her native country. The referral party (the parents and the local school) is interested in knowing the following:

- What are Katya's current academic strengths and weaknesses in the Ukrainian curriculum and what grade level of instruction would be optimal for her in an American school?
- Given that Katya's educational history in Ukraine suggested the presence of significant impediments to learning, does Katya have specific cognitive-based or language-related weaknesses, disabilities, or delays that may prevent her from acquiring academic skills at an age-appropriate level in a local public school?
- How can Katya's learning issues be effectively addressed in school in a way that will positively impact her learning and emotional well-being? Specifically, if Katya needs a modified learning environment, what would be the most appropriate educational accommodations for her?

In order to respond to the above-presented referral questions, the following set of tests and clinical procedures was used in this screening:

1. Review of the original adoption-related legal, medical, and educational documentation
2. Intake conference with the adoptive parents using the DTD-Q-AP (Developmental Trauma Disorder Questionnaire for Adoptive Parents, Gindis, 2019)
3. Clinical observations and rating of behavior and social interaction during testing using Direct Observational Assessment during Test Sessions and Child Clinical Interviews (McConaughey, 2005)

4. The Universal Nonverbal Intelligence Test – Second Edition (UNIT-2) – a standardized test to determine intellectual potential without direct language involvement
5. The Bender Visual-Motor Gestalt Test, Second Edition, and samples of handwriting and drawings
6. The BVAT-NU (2005) – Bilingual Verbal Ability-Normative Update Test (a standardized test for cognitive/academic language in English and Ukrainian)
7. The Luria Language Processing Test (LLPT, 1996 revision) – a nonstandardized test for evaluation of communicative fluency/pragmatics and reasoning/comprehension in the Ukrainian language
8. Woodcock-Johnson lll, Tests of Achievement, *Normative Update* – math subtests translated into Ukrainian
9. An estimation of academic skills according to the Ukrainian official curriculum for the first through fourth grades (Olma Press instructional material – Kiev, 2003 and 2009 editions) in reading, writing, mathematics, and general fund of information

An initial screening as a procedure has certain limitations, which the parents and teachers of internationally adopted children should know about in order to make appropriate choices. Initial screening can detect the presence of a problem but will not necessarily show the nature and scope of it. Thus, it may be sufficient for the children that do not have any "red flags" in their medical documentation or educational history. But if any "red flags" are present, the full evaluation may be in order and more beneficial for the child. Initial screening will not be able to positively detect long-term emotional/behavioral issues, and in most cases, the initial screening summary document is not sufficient for obtaining the remedial and special education services at school; only a full assessment report will qualify for this.

Combined Developmental, Neuropsychological, and Educational Assessment

In my professional judgment, supported by 30 years of clinical practice evaluating internationally adopted children ages 5–17, the most effective and remedial-oriented approach is the combined developmental, neuropsychological, and educational assessment (combined DNE). This approach is definitely trauma-focused and includes considerations of the neurological causes of behavioral, emotional, and cognitive impairments and strengths of a patient. This model of assessment is customized for the unique nature and needs of IA children. This approach would be the preferable mode of assessment when a child has certain confirmed medical conditions, such as Fetal Alcohol Syndrome Disorder, or exposure to environmental toxins such as led, heavy metals, radiation, and so on (Gabowitz, Zucker, & Cook, 2008, Gindis, 2009, 2019) because it connects the clinical presentation with a particular etiology, thus guiding the child's treatment plan that may include family, school, and community. In combined DNE, in response to referral questions, some aspects of a child's functioning are measured more in depth. A particular strong point of combined DNE is the in-depth developmental history (based on adoption-relevant documentation) and data from the child's parents, therapists, teachers, and other related individuals. Below is a sample of referral questions and a list of instruments used in a combined developmental, neuropsychological, and educational assessment.

Gabriela is a 15-year-old eighth-grade student adopted from Guatemala 7 years ago. English is her dominant language, while Spanish is not functional even for simple social communication. She was referred for significant learning and behavior issues.

Referral questions:

• What is the nature of Gabriela's behavioral/emotional difficulties? Specifically, does Gabriela have organically based neurological impairment(s), developmental delay(s), or a psychological disorder(s) underlying her current behavioral and emotional issues? In this context, what is (are) her differential diagnosis or diagnoses?
• To what extent does Gabriela's developmental history contribute to her current adaptive functioning, academic performance, and social interaction and how can this factor be addressed educationally and therapeutically?
• What would be the most appropriate academic placement, remedial methodologies, supportive services, instructional accommodations, and test modifications for Gabriela in the next 4 years of her education in the local public school?

In order to respond to these referral questions, the following tests and clinical procedures are to be used in this assessment:

Domain: Developmental History

1. Review of the adoption-related medical and legal documentation
2. Review of school records including the most current individual educational plan and the progress reports/narratives from Gabriella's teachers

3. An initial interview with the parents using Developmental Trauma Disorder Questionnaire for Adoptive Parents (DTD-Q-AP) – adverse childhood experience survey related to international adoption

Domain: Adaptive Behavior/Skills and Social/Emotional Functioning

4. Clinical observations of behavior and social interaction during testing using the guideline for NEPSY-II (a developmental neuropsychological assessment) and Behavior Observations Table
5. Interview with the parents and school personnel using
   • Devereux Behavior Rating Scale (Parent and Teacher Forms) – psychopathology of behavior
   • DSM-5-based Generic Checklist of Child Depression Disorder Symptoms
   • DSM-5-based ADHD Symptoms Checklist, Parent and Teacher Form
   • Adaptive Behavior Assessment System – 3 (Parent and Teacher Forms) – general adaptive behavior
   • Social Responsiveness Scale, Second Edition (Parent and Teacher Form) – a standardized measure of reciprocal social behavior
   • Behavior Rating Inventory for Executive Function, Second Edition (BRIEF-2), Parent and Teacher Forms – a measure of self-regulation and goal-directed behavior
   • Randolph Attachment Disorder Parent's Questionnaire, Long Form
6. Clinical interview with Gabriella using
   • Beck Depression Inventory, Second Edition – self-report of depression symptoms
   • Incomplete Sentences Inventory Blank, High School Form
   • Revised Children's Manifest Anxiety Scale, Second Edition – self-report of anxiety symptoms
   • Projective Questionnaire

Domain: Neuropsychological Assessment of Specific Psychological Functions

7. Quick Neurological Screening Test-3, Revised (QNST-3R) – a screening test for "soft" neurological signs in observable behavior
8. Neurocognitive Assessment Battery – CNS Vital Signs (NECOG), a computerized measure of attention, visual and verbal working memory, processing speed, and executive functioning
9. NEPSY-II (developmental neuropsychological assessment) – selected tests for different psychological functions

Domain: General Intellectual Functioning and Specific Cognitive Processes/Skills

10. Woodcock-Johnson IV, Tests of Cognitive Abilities (WJ-IV-C) – selected tests for processing speed, attention, and high-order reasoning
11. NEPSY-II – selected tests of specific cognitive capacities and skills
12. Wechsler Intelligence Scale for Children, Fifth Edition (WISC-V) – a standardized test of general cognitive abilities and processes

Domain: Language – Cognitive/Academic and Social Aspects

13. Woodcock-Johnson IV, Tests of Oral Language – a measure of cognitive/academic language
14. Social Language Development – Adolescent – a semi-standardized social/communicative language test

Domain: Academic Knowledge and Skills

15. Woodcock-Johnson IV, Tests of Achievement, Extended Battery – a standardized assessment of academic curriculum for the appropriate age and grade in reading, writing, and math
16. Curriculum-Based Dynamic Assessment for reading, writing, and math (according to specific methodology for each subject matter)

This comprehensive assessment should result in differential diagnosis (or diagnoses) and practical and convincingly presented recommendations for the school and family (see samples below).

Specialized Evaluations

Specialized evaluation is a domain-specific examination, concentrating on a specified function, such as speech and language, fine-motor skills, hearing or vision, auditory processing, and so on. It is normally requested after screening or full assessment in order to clarify a particular issue. There is a significant volume of literature related to these specialized assessments, and I prefer to refer the reader to these sources of special knowledge.

Dynamic Assessment

The issue of the adequate means of psychological evaluation of IA children emerged concurrently with the first wave of massive international adoption in early 1990. Very soon, the professionals working with IA population realized that norm-referenced tests and standardized behavior scales may not be proper instruments for the evaluation of children with a grossly "atypical" background. It would be morally unfair and methodologically inappropriate to compare newly arrived former foreign orphanage residents with their peers in this country. It was obvious that due to their neglectful and traumatic background, IA children were delayed in many developmental competencies. It was quickly found that their academic knowledge base is weaker and different from the one acquired by their peers in American or Canadian schools. In order to help these children, we should have assessed not only their current level of functioning but their cognitive modifiability, their responses to instruction and guidance, their motivation to learn, and other learning-related capacities. The answers to these questions were the ultimate goal of our assessment that could provide the direct passage to effective remediation. It is my deepest conviction that the best practice in this respect is the psychological methodology known as dynamic assessment – DA (Haywood & Lidz, 2007).

DA is a "family" of different procedures that share a set of common principles (Kozulin, 1998, p. 70) that:

1) Cognitive processes are modifiable, and an important task of assessment is to ascertain their degree of modifiability, rather than remain limited to estimation of the child's manifest level of functioning.
2) Interactive assessment that includes a learning phase provides better insight into the child's learning capacities than unaided performance.
3) The primary goal of assessment is to suggest psychoeducational interventions aimed at the enhancement and realization of the child's latent abilities to learn.

As summarized by Lidz (2000), "The essential characteristics of DA are that they are interactive, open ended, and generate information about the responsiveness of the learner to intervention" (p. 7). Moreover, DA addresses the issue of closing the gap between assessment and intervention with specific, teachable strategies (Lidz, 2007).

In the context of an IA child assessment, DA is a testing procedure that follows a test–teach–retest format focusing on the cognitive processes and social-behavioral aspects of the child's learning. Therefore, the DA provides information, not readily available through standardized testing, crucial for effective remediation – the ultimate goal of this assessment.

The description and analysis of the use of DA with the IA children were presented by this writer and his collaborators in a number of publications (Gindis & Karpov, 2000; Lidz & Gindis, 2003; Gindis, 2019). There is no room in this chapter to discuss the ideas, principles, and practices of DA in detail. I refer those interested to the most comprehensive, in-depth, and remarkably practical book, published by the Cambridge University Press in 2007, titled *Dynamic Assessment in Practice: Clinical and Educational Application*, authored by two leading experts in this matter: Dr. Carl Haywood and Dr. Carol Lidz.

Before presenting the application of DA to the assessment of IA children, I need to make these remarks:

First, along with the other clinicians using DA, I believe that it should not be a dilemma of standardized testing vs. DA. These are two approaches to an assessment of children, each with its specific possibilities and limitations. These methodologies should both be included in a combined developmental neuropsychological and educational assessment as presented above (Gabriela's case).

Second, DA is a diverse paradigm that includes many approaches, methods, tests, and so on. In our work with the IA children, we used a specific DA instrument known as the Application of Cognitive Function Scale (authors: Carol Lidz and Ruthanne Jepsen; please see full description in Haywood & Lidz, 2007, Chapter 6). A few words about the ACFS in order to appreciate its usefulness for the IA children's assessment. The scale was originally designed for children functioning between the ages of 3 and 5, but in our practice in the last 20 years, it has been successfully used for IA children ages 5 through 9. ACFS taps basic cognitive processes and learning strategies associated with typical learning activities. There are six subscales in the ACFS. Please see a brief description of each subtest included in the clinical case that appears below.

Each ACFS activity is presented in the typical DA format of pretest (independent performance) scripted intervention by the examiner and post-test (independent performance). Each subtest provides an indication of the degree of mastery of a task, thus reflecting the underlying cognitive skills and, at the same time, the child's responsiveness to intervention. The interventions consist of standard instructions, as formulated by the authors (in Haywood & Lidz, 2007, pp. 162–175), and emphasize the strategies that are involved in successful completion of the activity. Although the ACFS can be scored, in our assessment of the IA children, the standardized procedure was not strictly followed: the procedure was used to help in differential diagnosis and for qualitative exploration of the child's functioning in the areas tapped by the activities.

The ACFS also contains a Behavior Rating Scale – the same for all subtests – which describes the qualitative aspects of the child's interaction with the materials and the examiner and includes self-regulation (child maintains attention and refrains from impulsive interaction with materials), persistence (child completes the task without seeking to terminate), frustration tolerance (when the child shows upset from frustration, he/she is readily calmed and redirected), motivation (child shows enthusiastic reaction to the materials and task), flexibility (child does not repeat unsuccessful task solutions and develops alternative approaches to the task), responsivity (child is willing to learn and open to input from the mediator), and interactivity (child engages in turn-taking conversational exchanges with the examiner).

Clinical Case: Nicole

Nicole is a 6-year-9-month-old second grader in a local public school. She was adopted from China at the age of almost 4 years, being considered "delayed" in her native country. English is her only language at the time of this assessment. She was referred because of consistent difficulties in learning and social interaction during preschool and her first year of elementary school. In school, she has received speech and language services, some academic support within the classroom, and counseling on an "as-needed" basis. She was described as a "smart" but "nervous" girl by her parents. Psychoeducational testing using the standardized tests was attempted but not completed due to the lack of cooperation. Academically, Nicole performed below expectations for her grade placement. Both her parents and her teachers agreed that she has at least average cognitive capacity, but they are confused about her inconsistency in cognitive functioning, her sudden regressions in behavior, her debilitating anxiety, and some "autistic-like" patterns of behavior.

Following the school referral, Nicole was administered a comprehensive combined developmental, neuropsychological, and educational evaluation that included DA using the Application of Cognitive Function Scale (ACFS). The description of that part of Nicole's assessment appears below. Please note that the subscales were not scored in order to stress the qualitative nature of the DA. The brief description of every scale (taken from Lidz, 2000 and Haywood & Lidz, 2007) precedes the qualitative description.

Classification: Nicole was asked to sort blocks into groups (based on color, shape, or size). The intervention focused on what to notice about the blocks that served as a basis for grouping. The examiner's observations concentrated on her ability to respond to directions and to make groups based on an abstracted distinctive feature and on evidence of flexible thinking.

During the pretest, Nicole immediately recognized the concept of "grouping": she piled four flat red rectangles together and said: "This is a group." She was not able to explain, however, why she made this particular group. She could not make other groups (e.g., based on shape or size). When I explained that ". . . a group is when things belong together. . ." she exclaimed: "Like people! We have groups in school!" During the intervention phase, she seemed to understand the principle of grouping and nodded affirmatively when I made groups using paper-made geometrical forms different in colors, shape, and size. However, when she was asked to make a group based on a characteristic other than color, she looked confused and failed to do this. I returned to the paper representations and repeated the explanation with modeling one more time. She was offered a set of blocks again, and she routinely made four "color groups" looking expectedly at me. Suddenly, just before I was ready to terminate this activity, she smiled as if she got an "insight" and quickly made three groups based on shape, and later, after encouragement to continue, she made another group based on size. In order to test the limits, the initial set of blocks was offered, and Nicole again showed her ability to cross the category from color to shape or size.

Perspective Taking: Nicole was asked to take on the role of teacher and teach the examiner how to draw a picture. The teaching phase provides a model for the child of how to communicate to influence the performance of another person emphasizing the ability to read behavioral cues of others, ability to comprehend and distinguish among verbal communications of others (such as statements vs. questions vs. commands), and ability to provide verbal and behavioral communications to allow another person to engage in reciprocal interchanges. This activity provides a good sample of language pragmatics.

During the pretest, Nicole was very reluctant to take on the role of a teacher. In fact, she was scared by the very proposal of being a teacher (to be in control). She looked away from me, started trembling, and wanted to see her mom right away. Being assured and encouraged by her mother, she finally gave her directions for drawing a picture of a boy. All her instructions were nonverbal: she just pointed where to draw. During the intervention phase – when the examiner assumed and modeled the role of teacher – Nicole seemed to be more at ease, although she claimed that she "cannot draw." She visibly warmed up and drew according to my instructions: her drawing was completed in accord with the sequential order of my directions. During the posttest, Nicole was, again, reluctant to be in control of my actions. Most of her directions were by gestures, but she did use several words, like "... circle here (pointed), eyes (pointed) ... now ears ...." This activity revealed a great deal about Nicole's most vulnerable area: pragmatics (her use of language to interact with others).

Short-Term Auditory Memory: Nicole was asked to retell a short story read by her mother. (Nicole's mother was asked to participate to overcome Nicole's debilitating anxiety that resulted in "avoidance" behavior.) During the intervention phase, Nicole was taught to build a chain of tangible symbols for the story and to use visual imagery to facilitate story recall. Interpretation of the results of this activity focused on the ability to communicate in the sequential narrative form and the ability to visualize the contents and activities of stories read, as well as attention span, requiring Nicole to sit and listen to an entire story sequence.

During the pretest, Nicole conveyed not a single word and clearly expressed her dislike of this activity. She was not interested in the material presented (a magnet board) and refused to make symbols on her own. Her mother indicated that Nicole might not understand the whole idea of this activity; therefore, I modified the instructions and started making symbols for the recall myself, modeling for Nicole, and later invited Nicole to do this together with me. She cautiously agreed and later even engaged in turn-taking conversational exchanges regarding the construction of the represented symbols. During the third reading, she was expected to touch every appropriate symbol while listening to the story. However, she obviously missed the very point of the purpose of this action. I explained more than once why we needed these symbols, but she appeared unable to grasp the idea as if she had completely blocked it out. During her posttest recall, she produced only one name and one action related to the story. She was stubborn in her unwillingness to work anymore on this activity and appeared upset. Her anxiety caused by the "unknown" and her unwilling-ness to try something new were the stumbling blocks in this activity.

Short-Term Visual Memory: Nicole was asked to remember eight toys placed in front of her and then removed. The intervention focused on memory strategies of rehearsal, "chunking," and visual imagery. The outcome included evidence of awareness of the need for application of a memory strategy, as well as the number of items recalled.

During the pretest, Nicole named both sets of eight toys correctly (which is in sharp contrast to her poor performance on the Picture Vocabulary subtest from the W-J Test tried previously by the school psychologist). However, she recalled only two items (out of eight) during the pretest trial. During the intervention phase, Nicole appeared interested and attentive. I presented three mnemonic techniques (repeating names, making groups, and knowing functions). During the posttest, when I said, "Show me how you will help yourself remember things," Nicole demonstrated no signs of the taught mnemonic devices. She named the same two items as during the pretest. No evidence of any "spontaneous" mnemonic strategy was demonstrated. Moreover, when the toys were taken away, she demonstrated a kind of "separation anxiety" asking when the toys would be returned and if they would ever be shown to her again. It was impossible for her to do any mental operations with the toys out of her immediate view: to name them, to recall their function, to group them, and so on. However, as soon as the objects were presented to her, she was able to make different mental manipulations with them, such as separating them into groups without touching them, just naming them.

Verbal Planning: Nicole was asked to tell the plan for making cookies. The intervention focuses on telling the steps of a sequential plan and using planning words. The outcome emphasized her awareness of multiple and sequential steps toward an identified goal, ability to retrieve and keep in working memory an activity sequence, ability to detect when something is out of order, ability to anticipate what comes next, comprehension of planning words such as first, next, last, and use of planning words to communicate a sequence.

During the pretest, Nicole enthusiastically acknowledged that she knows how to make cookies. However, she could only say "you take flour . . ." and then "tuned out" for good. In spite of her mother's help and prodding, Nicole appeared tired, started yawning, asking for "a break," and practically refused to participate in this activity. During the intervention phase (presented with the sequencing cards), Nicole demonstrated her "avoidance" behavior brazenly: she refused to sort cards out together with the examiner and turned her back. It was the only episode during the whole evaluation when she demonstrated her active opposition to a joint activity. Overcoming her resistance, I tried to introduce the concepts "first, next, after this, and last" using both the visual presentation (with the sequential cards) and auditory-visual, "modeling" how to make a peanut butter sandwich. During the posttest, however, Nicole again was not able to go beyond the "flour" stage. Soon she refused to cooperate in this task at all and was ready to cry.

Sequential Pattern Completion: After a lunch break, Nicole was asked to complete a repetitive sequential pattern started by the examiner, using tangrams. The intervention focused on helping her to sense the rhythm of a pattern and to learn to use the cues provided by the examiner to determine what comes next. The outcome included knowledge base for objects (vocabulary and experience), awareness of distinctive features of sequenced pattern pieces, detection of repetitive features (rhythm) of pattern, comprehension of the concept of "next," and her justification of the basis for each response.

During the pretest, Nicole just played with the pieces making no patterns and not responding to my request: "Try to figure out what comes next." During the intervention phase, Nicole was receptive and interactive. She maintained good attention, and her reaction was consistently enthusiastic. Interestingly enough, perseveration, which seemed to be a stable characteristic of her mental performance in previous activities, did not interfere with this particular activity. As with the first subtest (grouping), Nicole surprised me with her quick grasp of the concept of "pattern" in all modalities (auditory, visual, or kinesthetic). She not only understood my explanation but also gave her own example by drawing two samples of patterns: one based on color and another on shape. During the posttest, she correctly completed the first three sets of tangrams and gave a proper explanation for the first set (size) and the second set (color). She failed, however, with three other sets that required more than one discriminator for the determination of the pattern.

Summing up, the DA indicated that Nicole possessed many of the cognitive skills needed to perform academic tasks required for first graders in elementary school. At the same time, the DA showed that Nicole had elevated anxiety, a lack of persistence in her mental efforts, and immature self-regulation in mental activities. Her tolerance for frustration and her flexibility in mental activities were low: she could not handle even a minor frustration in an age-appropriate manner. Her responsiveness (an ability to be socially engaged) was very inconsistent, and her interaction with adults in a teaching role was "defensive" and manipulative. Her responsiveness to the interventions was inconsistent, and she tended to resort to her initial immature behaviors, having difficulty in generalizing and transferring her new learning experience. Her resistance to learning in a socially collaborative context was due not to cognitive weaknesses per se (as may be suggested by the standardized tests) but rather to her "noncognitive" emotional, motivational, and behavioral characteristics. It was her level of anxiety and her fragile sense of security that blocked her amenability to an age-expected level of cognitive functioning. Nicole's desire to be always on the known and manageable "turf" was rooted in her early childhood experiences of deprivation and insecurity.

This pattern of behavior is typical for children with a background of prolonged and severe adverse childhood experience. It was the trauma-produced behavioral pattern that blocked her ability to benefit from a scaffolding cognitive activity provided by adults. This was definitely an obstacle to her learning: to be a good learner means to take risks, to step into unknown territory, to be sure of one's own ability to cope, and to be ready to accept help from an adult (or more competent peer). In fact, DA documented the depth of the challenge in addressing her learning needs. DA showed that "role playing," "modeling," and "imitating" are not easy for Nicole; unfortunately, these are major learning/teaching "mechanisms" for her age. In order for learning to occur and be transferable, Nicole would require a more structured learning environment and considerably longer duration and intensity of collaborative learning experience than expected for her peers.

The following specific features related to the processes of teaching/learning were observed during the dynamic format of Nicole's testing:

- Nicole's super-sensitivity to the texture of learning material might interfere with her cognitive functioning: it was evident in her total absorption by the tactile or perceptual qualities of the objects offered to her as the bases for cognitive activities. Thus, during the story-telling activity (Short-Term Auditory Memory), I explained more than once what was the purpose of using the material symbols (beads), but Nicole appeared completely distracted by the material property of these symbols and just played with them (even licking them) instead of using the objects for higher mental process.

- Perseveration (that is, making the same cognitive operations over and over again without being able to switch to a new point of view that is more appropriate to solving the problem) seemed to be a stable characteristic of her mental performance. It was observed that when Nicole was presented with problems that she failed to comprehend or did not know how to solve, she would get caught in perseveration first and then become quite confused and disorganized, losing track of what she was doing.

- Another characteristic that transpired via the interactive assessment was that while Nicole demonstrated a mild-to-moderate receptive and expressive language deficit, her pragmatic language abilities to initiate, maintain, and terminate joint interactions were significantly impaired. It was difficult for Nicole to engage in goal-directed dialogue. Her limited pragmatics contributed substantially to the weakness of her social skills as well as her cognitive functioning.

- The degree of structure of a cognitive activity seemed to be the key element in Nicole successful performance: a lack of structure or a completely unknown activity at the beginning of tests escalated her anxiety to the extent that she was not able to perform at all. On the other hand, her performance tended to improve due to an introduction of even a minimal structure or a pattern.

The dynamic assessment revealed that Nicole was not an easily modifiable child. Overcoming the consequences of early childhood trauma is the major challenge in addressing Nicole's learning and social/emotional needs.

Curriculum-Based Dynamic Assessment (CBDA)

One of the surprising and upsetting findings during the initial screening or full psychoeducational testing of school-age (7–16) international adoptees on arrival is that there is a wide range of discrepancy between the formal grade assignment in their native country and actual academic knowledge and skills in a student. In my experience, this discrepancy may reach from 2 to 4 (sic!) years: an 11-year-old boy from Ukraine may formally graduate from the fourth grade in an orphanage-based "corrective" (special education) school and be a nonreader. A 12-year-old girl from Guatemala may read in Spanish on the first grade level and do math no higher than the second grade in an American school. In most of these cases, no standard educational testing either in native language or with a translated American educational testing is possible. The only option is a CBDA according to the procedures described in Chapter 7 of "Dynamic Assessment in Practice" (Haywood & Lidz, 2007).

Still another common situation of using CBDA is the educational part of the combined developmental, neuropsychological, and educational assessment of the school-age IA children after several years (no less than two full school years) in adoptive families and the American educational system. Here the CBDA is a valuable addition to a standardized educational assessment (in our practice, it is mostly Woodcock-Johnson IV Tests of Achievement, Extended Battery) that gives vital information about the "responsiveness to intervention" – what are the students' limitations and possibilities to benefit from mainstream instruction vs. specialized/individualized remediation. There is a wide range of CBDA procedures for school subjects and different disciplines, like speech and language (Lidz & Elliott, 2000). Using WJ-IV Achievement tests in combination with CBDA procedures is a "win–win" situation in an assessment of IA children: the first allows determining the current baseline of the mastery of a subject matter (e.g., comprehension in reading) and the second, the responsiveness to the mainstream or remedial instructions as well as "testing the limits" in the student's collaborative learning. With this information, it was possible to observe differential contributions of cognitive vs. social–emotional factors to learner's performance, as well as elaborating the qualitative aspects of their functioning on a variety of tasks. Indeed, the unique information about responsiveness to intervention and transfer of learning following intervention becomes available with dynamic assessment.

Trauma Assessment in IA Children

The need for the assessment of consequences of trauma constitutes the most significant difference between a psychological evaluation of IA children, freshly arrived children from immigrant families, and their peers in the population at large. In fact, one of the major goals of the psychological assessment of international adoptees is the determination of the degree of DTD and the recommendation of appropriate means of addressing it in the family, school, and community.

The interpretation of neuropsychological test results within the trauma framework is critical in designing effective intervention strategies. Without this context, any IA child is likely to be diagnosed based on specific behavioral manifestations (e.g., oppositional defiant disorder, mood disorder, attention deficit hyperactivity disorder, and the like), and the treatment would be targeting correspondent symptoms. The application of a trauma-informed approach to evaluation, on the other hand, leads to understanding underlining these behavior problems. For example, in a particular IA child, early trauma may result in extremely immature executive functioning and broad dissociative psychopathology, but due to his overt behavior, a child may appear as a "typical" ADHD patient for a clinician not familiar with the consequences of early trauma. The developmental aspect of trauma assessment is crucial, as children younger than 5 rarely demonstrate clear-cut trauma symptomatology; with them, the focus is on the determination of the objectively existed stressful events.

Young children who have been traumatized multiple times often experience developmental delays across a broad spectrum, including cognitive, language, motor, and socialization skills; they tend to display multiple disturbances with various presentations, thus meeting numerous clinical diagnoses. And yet, as observed by van der Kolk and his associates, each of these diagnoses captures only a limited aspect of the traumatized child, while a more comprehensive view of the impact of complex trauma provides a focused developmental approach (Cook, Blaustein, Spinazzola, & van der Kolk 2003).

Trauma verification during the initial screening aims at determining whether a newly arrived IA child has experienced continuous trauma and indeed displays symptoms of DTD. If so, the recommendation is to alert the parents about the possibility of DTD and the need to make a referral for a comprehensive trauma-informed mental health assessment. Please note that at this point, we are talking only about the likelihood of a complex childhood trauma condition: not all children who experienced negative events present trauma-specific symptoms as a result. The available instruments for detecting a possibility of trauma are different questionnaires, which are used to detect the objective conditions and events that may potentially produce psychological trauma (Bernstein & Fink, 1998; Dennis, Chan & Funk, 2006). All these surveys are designed for the population at large and are heavily loaded culturally. To the best of my knowledge, the only questionnaire composed specifically for internationally adopted older children is the DTD-Q-AP (Gindis, 2019, presented in the Appendix of this book).

There are no specific tests for DTD; currently, the diagnosis is an outcome of the analysis of four major sources of information:

- Developmental history based on medical, legal, adoption, and school documentation
- Interview with adoptive parents using the Developmental Trauma Disorder Questionnaire for Adoptive Parents (DTD-Q-AP) and other relevant questionnaires
- Direct observation of behavior and the surveys of parents/teachers (and other individuals, if needed) using specialized forms, for example, to determine the presence and degree of post-orphanage behavior syndrome (Gindis, 2019)
- Psychological testing (using standardized procedures in order to compare IA children with existing norms of functioning in different domains) and dynamic assessment (to verify cognitive modifiability, responses to instruction and guidance, and other learning-related capacities) in order to determine psychological functions affected by traumatic past experiences

The review of existing models of trauma-focused psychological assessments (see a comprehensive study of Dr. A. Wevodau, 2016; also, International Society for Traumatic Stress Studies, 2020) leads to the unfortunate conclusion that a vast majority of existing methodologies are concentrated on PTSD, but not on the complex childhood trauma that results in DTD. Thus, the International Society for Traumatic Stress Studies (2020) promotes the instruments exclusively devoted to PTSD conditions. As of now, there are only two mental health assessment strategies, designed for children and adolescents, that go above and beyond the PTSD realm, such as

- A *Trauma Assessment Pathway Model*, developed by the Chadwick Center for Children and Families, with a concentration on the understanding of a child's developmental level, traumatic experience, child's family, community, and cultural systems (Conradi, Taylor-Kletzka, & Oliver, 2010).
- The *Child and Adolescent Needs and Strengths (CANS) – Trauma Comprehensive Version.* The "CANS-Trauma" is a multipurpose tool concentrating on the needs of a particular child-serving system (Kisiel, Fehrenbach, Small, & Lyons, 2009), such as trauma experiences, traumatic stress symptoms, emotional and behavioral needs, and risk behaviors.

Still, there are no methods developed specifically for the study of DTD in internationally adopted children that would include the specifics of this category of trauma survivors. As of now, DTD-Q-AP (Gindis, 2019) is the only one survey designed specifically for international adoptees.

Trauma assessment, in IA children especially, is a rather sophisticated and challenging task for any mental health professional due to the subjective nature of adverse childhood experience. Exposure to clearly traumatic events or conditions does not automatically lead to the formation of DTD. On the other hand, the absence of documented traumatic events or conditions does not preclude the presence of physiological and psychological symptoms of DTD. In my 30 years of clinical practice, I encountered a significant number of cases when children came from the same orphanage with a similar developmental history and a common list of objectively traumatic events. Moreover, these children were of similar age, and sometimes even siblings were adopted to one family. But the outcome, the developmental path for each, was very different: what causes a traumatic impact on one child may not produce the same effect on the other. As the joke goes, one person's irritation is another person's pain. Alas, it is true! Here is an example.

Clinical Case: Twin Brother and Sister

Two children, the twin brother and sister, were adopted from a Polish orphanage before their fourth birthdays. Both were abandoned at the age of 5 months and lived in the church-run orphanage until adoption. The adoptive parents, originally from Poland themselves, were successful professionals in the United States (an engineer and a nurse). The family lived in a middle-class neighborhood, and the children attended a good public school. The parents maintained the Polish language at home. Both children, although far from being exemplary students, graduated from high school. The brother began working in a small landscaping company, soon became a manager there, married the daughter of the owner of the business, then sold the company, and moved on to become a large company's employee (building maintenance manager). His wife worked as a salesperson in a retail store. They have two children, kept steadily their employment, and own a house; they were an established, successful middle-class family. The brother – a handsome, jovial man, very social, with many friends, an active participant in his community life – is loved and welcomed in his former school, where he volunteers to be a teacher's assistant in the automotive class.

The twin sister is another story that includes two unsuccessful marriages, several felonies and 3 months in jail, in-and-out of drug rehabilitation centers, many therapies paid for by her parents, and an unsuccessful attempt to return to live in Poland. She depleted most of the money left to her by her parents on cars and jewels, alcohol, and drugs. Finally, she had a court order to be supervised by her brother, who now manages her finances. At the age of 40, she is single, works as a cleaning lady at a local "Home Depot," rents a room, and, as far as I know, is sober and stays clean from drugs.

Both siblings did not remember their pre-adoption life, and the parents never told them that they were adopted (an old European tradition – BG). Finally, at the age of 9, they confronted their parents, asking for their baby photos needed for a school project. The family sat at the dinner table, and the parents, after careful preparation and consultation with a social worker, told the children that they were adopted. The boy accepted this news very calmly and said that he was so lucky to have his adoptive parents. The girl was devastated. She started screaming at her mother: "That's why I do not look like you or him (the father)." "Who were my real parents?" The brother told me that nothing had changed in his life after this revelation, and he loved and respected his adoptive parents immensely and was very sad when they passed away in their late 60s. His twin sister seemed to be unhappy, depressed, and angry throughout her late high school year and her young adulthood. She tried to find her biological mother, traveled to Poland, and found out that her late biological mother was an unemployed, homeless, alcohol-addicted women with many "husbands," and on return, the sister declared that she herself was the "trash" who does not deserve love, acceptance, and respect. Her recovery from that trauma took about 20 years, and who knows if the relapse is still ahead.

As you see, adverse childhood experience (ACE) is associated with the actual trauma-produced disturbances, but those objective troubles may not necessarily produce a subjective psychological trauma. Why two individuals with similar genetic equipment and similar traumatic childhood experiences, such as abandonment and institutionalization, resulted in different life outcomes as adults? We know from history that many famous people, high achievers in their field, suffered from adverse childhood experience (ACE) during their childhood and still thrived as adults. Under extreme or chronic adversity, many individuals are forced to grow: "What does not kill us makes us stronger," as Friedrich Nietzsche said. Among those who have high ACE scores, we see that some are unaffected, leading successful lives, some are affected but still function well, while others are devastated.

Still another aspect of trauma is the concealed nature of traumatic events and situations. In most cases, DTD had formed before the child has the verbal and reasoning ability to process and store a traumatic experience in memory. In this case, the central nervous system (CNS) accumulates the traumatic reminiscences as somatic distress and pain. A child, many years after the traumatic events, may experience undifferentiated diffused pain, tension, and discomfort and unbearable urge to relive this tension through some actions, but the cause may remain unknown (see more on this subject in van der Kolk, 2015). Here is another clinical case to illustrate this situation.

Clinical Case: A Girl Refuses to Take a Bath

An 8-year-old girl was brought for a psychoeducational assessment. She was adopted from Russia before her third birthday. As reported by her adoptive parents, the biological mother was deprived of her parental rights and incarcerated for a long term for an "unknown crime." Adoptive parents handed me a thick folder with adoption documentation mostly in the Russian language not translated to them. They listed the problems their daughter had in school and at home. Among other things, they mentioned one "bizarre issue": the girl was afraid of hot or even warm water. The bathing has been a problem since her arrival, and even when she sees the steam coming from the teapot, she may be scared and may go to the other room or even cry without any apparent reason. The parents asked me about this behavior, and I said that for me, it looks like a PTSD reaction but, basically, I have no idea where it came from. In the evening of the first day of that assessment, I started reviewing the adoption documentation, mostly in Russian. I found that the biological mother of the girl was in jail for an attempt to kill her 3-month-old daughter by throwing her into the tub with boiling water. (This information was not translated and was unknown to the adoptive parents.) The relatives rescued the girl and rushed her to the hospital. The girl survived, though a significant part of her body had some unexplainable little marks. The girl, who was 3 months at the time, did not remember the pain and suffering, but her body remembered, which resulted in a seemingly bizarre behavior related to hot water.

It is important to realize that the consequences of DTD have shared overt behavioral symptoms with a number of different mental health disorders. Therefore, those professionals who have no experience with post-institutionalized children may be easily confused and find a host of disorders from ADHD to attachment disorder, to autism spectrum disorder and affective disorders in children, who in fact demonstrate symptoms of DTD. On the other hand, DTD may be, in addition, reinforced by neurologically based genuine disorders, such as bipolar disorder or ADHD. In discussing DTD, by no means I discount the possibility that some of IA children along with DTD symptomatology may have childhood depression, post-traumatic stress disorder, or ADHD. Hopefully, a skillful clinician is able to recognize the roots of the issue before putting these children on medication or in specialized rehabilitation programs.

In conclusion, the appropriate assessments, starting from initial screening in the native language on arrival to a follow-up with comprehensive combined bilingual developmental, neuropsychological, and educational assessment along with special disciplines evaluations of IA children, are the needed steps in proper understanding and rehabilitation of these survivors of institutional care. Dynamic assessment plays a special role in the psychological assessment of IA students. The bilingual aspect of all kinds of assessments of IA children, particularly during the initial screening, is crucial. It imposes certain requirements for professional qualifications of the assessors. The evaluation of trauma consequences in international adoptees is the core of proper assessments of their needs, weaknesses, and resilience capacities. Additionally, experience with this specific population is needed for the detection of psychological symptomatology of DTD and making differential diagnoses in post-orphanage children. Each and every psychological assessment of IA children must present a workable, focused, highly individualized plan for their rehabilitation and remediation.

CHAPTER 3

Differential Diagnoses and the Structure of School-Based Recommendations for Internationally Adopted Children

The issue of differential diagnosis and comorbidity of different medical conditions in IA children has an utmost significance as the consequences of misdiagnosing children with complex childhood trauma are grave and long-lasting. One of the promises within the Hippocratic Oath "first, do no harm" is fully applicable here: misdiagnosis means ineffective or even harmful treatment. Thus, adopted children who, due to DTD, are constantly aroused and hypervigilant to real or imagined adverse events or conditions may be easily diagnosed with ADHD. Youngsters who are unresponsive, avoidant, and withdrawn as a consequence of DTD may be diagnosed as depressed. Those who are conditioned by DTD to acting out or presenting "proactive" (not provoked) aggressive behaviors may be mistakenly recognized as having oppositional defiant disorder. However, for children who have been experiencing prolonged traumatization in early childhood, "acting out" behaviors, a lack of empathy, and self-centeredness can be deeply embedded survival skills as the consequences of DTD. As a result, many IA children are given a range of diagnoses that are missing the underlying general cause of their conditions, thus subjecting these children to maltreatment.

Developmental Trauma Disorder (DTD) vs. Post-traumatic Syndrome Disorder (PTSD)

Interconnectedness between DTD and PTSD makes a differential diagnosis a real challenge due to a number of common presentations in overt behavior. It is necessary to realize that a child afflicted with DTD may also have symptoms of and even the full-blown condition of PTSD. Still, there is a distinct difference between these two conditions (Cloitre, 2005; De Bellis, Hooper, Spratt, & Woolley, 2009). PTSD is typically originated in a discrete, traumatic incident rather than an ongoing pattern of repetitive traumatization. PTSD has a set of well-defined manifestations, but none include developmental characteristics. PTSD implies the existence of so-called "triggers," which are the reminders of some traumatic incident. In clinical practice, when PTSD can't account for all the symptoms present, other diagnoses are often used to explain additional symptoms (Friedman, Keane, & Resnick, 2014). On the other hand, DTD occurs as a result of a continuous process, possibly comprising multiple discrete incidents. For this reason, such events do not warrant a diagnosis of PTSD because the events were not "imminently life threatening," a criterion for PTSD in the DSM-5 (2013). From the developmental perspective, neglect and exposure to multiple adverse occurrences have a much more pervasive effect than a single traumatic incident. As observed by van der Kolk (2003, p. 293), PTSD cannot capture the multiplicity of exposures over critical developmental periods: ". . . isolated traumatic incidents tend to produce discrete conditioned behavioral and biologic responses to reminders of the trauma, whereas chronic maltreatment or unavoidable recurring traumatization . . . has pervasive effects on neurobiological development." Finally, DTD has roots in pre-birth conditions, while PTSD can happen only after birth.

PTSD is diagnosed in many internationally adopted post-institutionalized children. Moreover, there is an opinion that all international adoptees have PTSD to some degree (Hoksbergen & Dijkum, 2001). This view is somewhat speculative because it is based not on clinical or research data, but rather on the assumption that if institutionalization and previous life in a neglectful and abusive family are so traumatic, it must result in PTSD. However, even hypothetically, this is not accurate because we know that PTSD is the product of the interplay between the nature of a specific traumatic experience and the psychological makeup of the person experiencing it. In other words, the same experience may lead to PTSD in some individuals but not in others. Vulnerability to PTSD depends on many factors, such as age, previous experiences, general sensitivity, preexisting medical and psychological conditions, and so on.

From educational and mental health perspectives, it is not productive to accept the notion that all former orphanage-raised children have PTSD as part of their psychological makeup. Although it is true that they as a group are more at risk for PTSD than their peers at large (Loitre, 2005), this diagnosis must be made on an individual basis because the triggers of PTSD reactions in international adoptees are so diverse and so different from our cultural background that it takes a specialist in psychological issues of international adoption to figure it out. Thus, some of the triggers could be as common as a threat of physical punishment: it was reported by many adoptive parents that any action that had even a remote resemblance to corporal punishment could trigger a reaction that can only be explained by previous traumatic experiences. At the same time, some triggers could be rather "exotic," such as the sight of falling snow or the sound of the child's native language (Gindis, 2019).

Therapies that have been proven effective to treat PTSD in adults may not be useful with children, particularly internationally adopted children: any sensible treatment of PTSD via "talking" therapy is based on the person's language ability. This ability is in itself an issue for international adoptees: their limited English (or quickly disappearing native language capacity) may result in their inability to express feelings and verbalize memories, thus blocking PTSD rehabilitation.

As with other behavior issues in IA children, it's important to determine which PTSD symptoms are mild, manageable, and probably transitional in nature and which are threatening symptoms of a long-lasting trouble. For example, if the symptoms are observed during the first several weeks at home, they may still be due to the initial adjustment period, produced by the situation of unsettledness, anxiety, native language loss, and new language development. In such a case, time is needed to get over the culture shock and test the new environment; time is needed to switch from old orphanage behavior to a new family-acceptable behavior.

DTD vs. ADHD

A constant state of hyper-arousal, a direct product of DTD, is typical for many "older" IA children. As a result, a child with DTD may present patterns of behavior often associated with ADHD, such as difficulty with sustaining attention, restlessness, and impulsivity. There is evidence of high rates of ADHD diagnoses in the IA population, reported by parents, teachers, and mental health professionals (see reviews in Miller, 2005; Gunnar & van Dulmen, 2007; Sonuga-Barke, Schlotz, & Kreppner, 2010). In fact, according to several research publications, IA children are diagnosed with this disorder 3–4 times more often than their peers in the population at large (Lindblad, Ringback Weitoft, & Hjern, 2010; Abrines et al., 2012).

The first researcher who attracted attention to this issue was M. Rutter and his group of associates (Rutter, Kreppner, O'Connor, 2001). They indicated that there was a very high rate of what they called a "hyperactive-inattentive syndrome" in their sample of IA children, but they made a point of not calling it ADHD because the clinical picture did not fit ADHD typical presentation. One study (Loman, 2012) compared the clinical and symptomatic profiles of the 11- to 15-year-old IA children with the nonadopted children diagnosed with ADHD. (Note that the majority of IA children in that sample were adopted from Eastern European countries following longer periods of institutionalization.) It was found that IA children with symptoms of ADHD revealed an elevated disinhibited social behavior and, among males, more distinct impulsivity. In addition to typical ADHD features, the IA group had a few unique features usually not found in the typical ADHD population, such as PTSD symptomatology and a high rate of aggressive behavior. The author stopped short of naming trauma but listed several trauma-related characteristics among causes of ADHD-like behaviors.

There is a growing understanding (Abrines et al., 2012) that many IA children have been misdiagnosed with ADHD when the difficulties (hyperactivity, inattention, behavioral issues) are actually related to trauma. One thing that most orphanage survivors have in common is poor emotional and behavioral self-regulation. Hyperactive, disorganized, and dis-regulated behaviors that are typical for children with ADHD may reflect in internationally adopted children the impact of early childhood trauma facilitated by abnormal environment of orphanage life. Their hyper-arousal is the result of a sensitized neural response stemming from a specific pattern of repetitive neural activation due to recurring traumatizing experiences. Sensitization occurs when this pattern of activation results in an altered, more sensitive neural system. Once sensitized, the same neural activity can be elicited by less intense external stimuli (Perry, 2006). In other words, the traumatic events in early childhood have the capacity to "redefine" the baseline level of the central nervous systems involved in the stress response. Research suggests that when a child with a history of adverse childhood experience perceives a threat (real or imagined), it reinforces the sensitized neuronal pathways with resulted heightened fear/stress response. Being constantly tense and easily aroused, IA children produce intensely restless behaviors similar to those observed in children with ADHD (Roskam et al., 2013).

I may add two factors that may explain the ADHD-like behavior in IA children in supplement to trauma. One is the lack of modeling, mediating, and assisting, usually provided by caregivers in the family-based upbringing. This is the effect of missing prior adequate social/cultural influences. The second factor is the abrupt loss of the first language and slowly emerging new language. It is well known that the language is a powerful force in the development of self-regulation. The lack of this psychological "tool" does not allow IA children to gain enhanced control over manifestations of their feelings and to inhibit impulsive responses. The clinical picture becomes even more complex when ADHD-like behavior in international adoptees coexists with anxiety. In the clinical and research community, there is an ongoing debate regarding the diagnostic overlap between ADHD and generalized anxiety disorder (Berlin, Bohlin, & Rydell, 2003; Nemeroff, 2004). In an IA child, the ADHD-like condition includes a significant emotional component that mediates behavior.

DTD vs. Autistic Spectrum Disorder

The prevalence of autism and other developmental disabilities in internationally adopted children is unknown, though there is a widespread belief that orphanage residents are more prone to developmental disabilities than their peers at large (Miller, 2005; Welsh, Andres, Viana, Petrill, & Mathias, 2007). It is understood that in addition to general risk factors such as heredity and the neurological makeup, there are secondary factors, social in nature, such as a lack of postnatal care and negative conditions of development in institutions, which facilitate the formation of developmental delays and disabilities in this population.

Certain displays of post-orphanage behavior (POB) may look like autism spectrum disorder (ASD) patterns of behavior. Because POB was a new phenomenon in Western psychology (to be exact, a well-forgotten phenomenon) and ASD was at its peak of popularity in the early 1990s, no wonder that the term *institutional autism* has emerged with the influx of children born overseas, raised in orphanages, and adopted by the Western countries' families. Actually, several similar terms have been used interchangeably: *institutionally induced autism* (Federici, 1998), *quasi-autism* (Rutter, 1999, 2001), *acquired institutional autism* (Miller, 2005), and *post-institutional autistic syndrome* (Hoksbergen, Laak, Rijk, Dijkum, & Stoutjesdijk, 2005). The base for all these modifiers of the term "autism" was that children may acquire either autistic condition or just autistic symptoms due to their early life in orphanages, hospitals, and other similar nonfamily institutions. Those interested in the history, development, short-lived popularity, and eventual vanishing of the notion of "institutional autism" are referred to my book (Gindis, 2019) and other publications (Gindis, 2008). The misconception of "institutional autism" has such a dramatic practical significance for remediation of IA children that I need to repeat, in brief, the essence of this issue.

According to the existing research literature, the first significant group of international adoptees in the Western countries adopted from Romanian orphanages presented, in many children, the following patterns of overt behavior:

- Self-stimulating behaviors, such as rocking, head banging, shaking of hands, face shielding, and making weird and animal-like sounds
- Self-soothing: withdrawal with finger sucking or clothes sucking, hair twisting, full-body spinning and rocking, head spinning and banging, and covering ears to block out even ordinary sounds
- Self-mutilating behaviors and picking at the body
- Unusual responses to sensory stimulation of taste, smell, and touch
- Temper tantrums in response to change in routine and seemingly unmotivated, uncontrollable outbursts of rage and aggression

These patterns of behavior were mostly evident in children younger than 5 years on arrival and diminished in intensity or disappeared over time in the families. However, a small minority of children continued to exhibit these behavior patterns for many years and were eventually diagnosed with autism according to diagnostic categories presented in DSM-5 and ICD-10-C. In my clinical experience, if these behaviors were found in children older than 5 years, these patterns were typically more persistent and, in many cases, turned out to be symptoms of genuine autism.

Eventually, in Rutter's (1999, 2001, 2007, 2015) publications, it was found that among Romanian adoptees, there were two categories of children: those who had genuine autism and those who demonstrated a rather heterogeneous cluster of behaviors, with some patterns similar to those observed in truly autistic children. Both the nature and the psychological mechanism of these autistic-like behaviors that varied in intensity and being mostly transitory remained unexplained. In many ways, such abnormal behaviors may be a typical human reaction to a new and unmanageable situation. A careful review of the developmental history after adoption is crucial because such features of institutional behavior as repetitive self-stimulating, self-soothing, and a lack of the appropriate spontaneous social interactions show dramatic improvement with time, in contrast to symptoms associated with the genuine autistic spectrum disorders.

What was really lacking in all these research studies about "institutional autism" or "autism-like behavior" is the issue of an abrupt native language loss as one of the major causes in behavior regression to more primitive, "autism-like" patterns. The rapid native language attrition significantly limits verbal communication during the first several weeks and months of the child's life in the family, when institutional behavior is at its peak.

A lack of or severe limitation in verbal communication typically leads to significant regression in the child's behavior and the emergence of the autistic-like self-stimulating and self-soothing conduct. The verbal communication deficiency during the initial adjustment period, followed by abrupt first language attrition, provokes patterns of behavior that fit a description of genuine autism very well. Unfortunately, no research has been done on the links between the transient autistic symptoms and the language transition experienced by international adoptees within the first several months in an adoptive family.

Making a differential diagnosis between autism, post-institutional behavior, and temporary patterns of behavior related to the adjustment period and abrupt language attrition is one of the most daunting tasks in the field of mental health and rehabilitation of IA children. A major distinguisher between organic-based autism and temporary autistic-like institutional behavior is the presence of positive dynamics in the child's development in the family. While most behaviors originating in organic-based autism persist, showing only small and slow, if any, changes, the same identifiable behaviors associated with institutional behavior and loss of language should diminish progressively until they completely disappear, although they may resurface in response to stress and environmental challenges. The timetable depends on a child's age and a host of individual differences, but if autistic-like behavior patterns do not diminish in intensity after about 6 months in the family, it is likely that we are dealing with organic-based autism or another variation of developmental disability.

Another distinguishing feature is the severity of the problem within a constellation of symptoms. In organic-based autism, the symptoms are usually more clearly defined and presented in well-known clusters described in the professional literature (Freitag, 2007). Institutional behavior reflects only separate patterns of autistic behavior that are not consistent and combined with the features that just cannot be found in "classical" autism and can often be explained by environmental circumstances. No wonder, in contrast to organic-based genuine autism, post-institutional behavior is the product of specific social conditions. It is to be recognized as a learned maladaptive behavior and should be addressed with behavior modification methodologies commonly used for nonautistic children. One time-tested recommendation is that children with institutional behavior should not be placed in the same programs as children with organic-based autism (which is happened, unfortunately, too often) to prevent their mimicking and reinforcing inappropriate behaviors. Parental consultation and counseling, modification of parenting techniques, change of parental expectations and attitudes using short-term behavior programs, and addressing specific behavior have proven to be effective in addressing issues of institutional behavior.

DTD vs. Attachment Difficulties

For adoptive parents, there is no more emotionally charged issue than attachment. No wonder, attachment is the core of adoption and failed attachment ruins the very nature of adoption. Attachment difficulties and their extreme presentation, known as attachment disorder, mean the inability to form and maintain age-appropriate intimate relationships within the family. Little is known about the biological causes of this condition, and a mainstream understanding is that attachment disorder is due to pathological care, that is, a disregard for the child's basic emotional needs for security, comfort, stimulation, and affection in early, most formative years.

The American Psychiatric Association in its Diagnostic and Statistical Manual, fifth edition (DSM-5, 2013) defines reactive attachment disorder (DSM-5 code 313.89) with three criteria (pp. 265–266):

A. *A consistent pattern of inhibited, emotionally withdrawn behavior towards adult caregivers.*

B. *A persistent social and emotional disturbance characterized . . . by minimal social and emotional responsiveness, limited positive effect, episode of unexplained irritability, sadness, or fearfulness.*

C. *The child has experienced a pattern of extremes of insufficient care as evidenced by . . . social neglect or deprivation . . . including . . . rearing in unusual settings that severely limit opportunities to form selective attachments, e.g., institutions with high child-to-caregiver rations.*

As seen from the definition above, attachment disorder (AD) stems from unusual early experiences of systematic neglect and deprivation of the child's basic physical and emotional needs. It can happen because of an abrupt separation from caregivers or a lack of caregiver's responsiveness to the child, or frequent change of caregivers. All the above are typical for children in overseas orphanages and make them "at-risk" for developing attachment difficulties. No wonder that there is a widespread opinion that attachment issues are to be found in all international adoptees, and we can talk only about the degree of this disorder (Bakermans-Kranenburg et al., 2011). At first glance, it makes sense: practically all internationally adopted post-orphanage children come to adoptive homes after experiencing what is defined above as "pathogenic care." Real life, however, is more complex than the theory: pathogenic care must meet with certain personality qualities to result in damaged attachment.

Like many other psychological conditions, attachment disorder ranges from severe to mild, from incurable to a transient and minor state. Only a few children are damaged beyond their ability to form a connection. Only a few children bond almost instantly and forever. But for the vast majority of older IA children, the individual capacity to form an attachment to the newly acquired parents and siblings is somewhere in between two extremes.

Attachment is a behaviorally defined phenomenon: no litmus paper or laboratory test can detect it. Based on the observed patterns of behavior and relationships, a competent professional can determine whether attachment difficulties are present in the patient, as well as the degree of this disturbance. Initially, adoptive parents and their children meet as strangers, and it would be a miracle if any internationally adopted child was completely attached to the adoptive parents on arrival or even within the first several months. Attachment is a two-way street: attachment of the parents to the child and attachment of the child to his/her adoptive parents. It is unfair morally and unproductive clinically to place the burden on a child and focus on forcing him/her to develop the bond. Unfortunately, rather than moving toward one another, some parents, clinicians, and therapists expect the adopted children to make the adjustment.

A particularly frustrating situation is with the children in the autistic spectrum disorder who were diagnosed with attachment disorder. The two conditions are incompatible (Mercer, 2006; Murin, Willis, Minnis, Mandy, & Skuse 2011), but on a number of occasions, I met children in my practice who spent years in attachment therapy having autism spectrum disorder. In my clinical experience, two other occurrences – learned "orphanage survival skills" and behavior during an acute adjustment period – are the major producers of behavioral patterns that may be mistakenly interpreted as symptoms of attachment disorder.

In practice, it may take a long time of slow progression until the final realization that the attachment is not going to form. The reasons for it may become apparent only years later, and again, it is mutual/reciprocal action/obligation: inappropriate parental techniques, deep-seated developmental trauma disorder, depression in a parent, strong disagreement in the family, and many other causes, often combined and thus facilitating each other.

Differential diagnosis or diagnoses in the context of developmental trauma disorder are the core for creating a focused, practical, and effective rehabilitative and remedial plan for the treatment of IA children. This cure is to be spread through the family, school, and community.

The school setting is one of the major factors in the remediation of IA children. Based on three decades of working with "older" international adoptees, the following empirically validated structure of psychoeducational remedial recommendations for IA children could be suggested in the school environment.

Major Components of Remedial Recommendations for the School Settings

1. Diagnosis or diagnoses based on ICD-10-C or DSM-5 nomenclature with a brief explanation of the practical meaning of these medical conditions
2. Creation of an Individual Educational Program (IEP) with the following components:
   • Educational classification based on the Individuals with Disabilities Education Act (IDEA-2004)
   • Educational and therapeutic placement (primary educational and therapeutic environment)
   • School-based related services (e.g., speech and language therapy) – needed to sustain a student in special education class
   • School-based supplemental services (e.g., social skills training) – needed to support a student in general education class
   • School-based crisis intervention procedures
   • Specific remedial methodologies for reading, writing, and math
   • Specific methodologies for social/emotional rehabilitation and behavior improvement in school
   • Classroom accommodation
   • Test-taking modification
   • Extended school year – ESY option
   • Suggested specific goals for a student's IEP
   • Trauma-informed safety plan (if needed).
   • Recommendations for Individual Transition Plan (ITP) for IA children age 14 and older who have educational classification

Below are samples of the components of recommendations listed above. These samples are written for a 10-year-old girl named Marina, adopted soon after her seventh birthday from Kazakhstan. Marina was referred due to significant learning, social/emotional difficulties, and aggressive behavior in a regular education classroom.

Sample #1: Diagnoses

- Mixed anxiety and depressive disorder (F41.8; ICD-10-CM code)
- Childhood disorder of social functioning, unspecified (F94.9; ICD-10-CM code)
- Other developmental disorders of scholastic skills (reading and math) (F81.89; ICD-10-CM code)

Mixed anxiety and depressive disorder (MADD) is a diagnostic category, defining patients who have both anxiety and depressive symptoms of roughly equal intensity accompanied by at least some autonomic symptoms. Marina has a number of autonomic features, usually caused by an overactive nervous system, such as involuntary physical indications, "soft" neurological signs, intestinal distress, and others. Marina consistently, and for a long time, shows excessive worry and sad/irritable feelings that interfere with her daily functioning. Disturbance in mood regulation and emotional behavior inappropriate for her age or circumstances were reported in school and at home alike. This state of mind is very common among children with developmental trauma disorder, mostly as a secondary disability developed in reaction to their traumatic experiences. Immature self-regulation of emotions and behavior contributes to a socially inappropriate response to routine school and family events. As presented in clinical data in this and other psychological reports, Marina consistently demonstrates many major disorder-specific symptoms of this medical condition.

Childhood disorder of social functioning, unspecified is a disorder resulting in abnormalities in social functioning that begins during the developmental period. In many instances, serious environmental distortions or privations play a crucial role in etiology. It leads to impairments in the ability to effectively communicate, participate socially, maintain social relationships, or otherwise perform academically or socially. Symptoms must be present in early childhood even if they are not recognized until later. Please note that in the past (before the publication of DSM-5), many individuals with such symptoms may have been grouped under the Not Otherwise Specified category of Pervasive Development Disorder (PDD-NOS). In Marina, the combination of organically based developmental delays in many domains of life (language, social, cognitive) and post-institutional background (a social condition of extreme deprivation of basic physical and emotional needs) creates a complicated psychoeducational profile: the synergistic effect is greater than the sum of each condition and leads to a greater educational challenge.

Specific developmental disorders of scholastic skills are measured by individually administered standardized tests of math, writing, and reading being substantially below that expected given the person's chronological age, measured intelligence, and age-appropriate education. This disability may have roots in some neuropsychological traits (e.g., slow processing speed) described in this report.

Sample #2: Educational Classification

In the school context, there is a specific system of educational classifications, stipulated by the Individuals with Disabilities Education Act (IDEA), as opposed to medical diagnoses as presented in the DSM-5 system or ICD-10-CM nomenclature. Educational classification means the presence of educational handicapping conditions that substantially interfere with the student's ability to learn and behave in school. The educational classifications are not medical diagnoses; rather, these are descriptions of educational needs. The school's obligation to provide remediation to a student with classification is at least 3 years of a guaranteed service, with a mandatory annual review of the progress. All school obligations are spelled out in the legal document called Individual Educational Program (IEP).

It is recommended that Marina's educational classification be "emotional disturbance." IDEA defines emotional disturbance as follows (Code of Federal Regulations, Title 34, §300.8(c)(4)(i)):

> . . . a condition exhibiting one or more of the following characteristics over a long period of time and to a marked degree that adversely affects a child's educational performance:
>
> (A) An inability to learn that cannot be explained by intellectual, sensory, or health factors.
> (B) An inability to build or maintain satisfactory interpersonal relationships with peers and teachers.
> (C) Inappropriate types of behavior or feelings under normal circumstances.
> (D) A general pervasive mood of unhappiness or depression.
> (E) A tendency to develop physical symptoms or fears associated with personal or school problems.

At least four conditions (B, C, D, and E) can be recognized in Marina. This educational classification reflects on the "core" of her educational needs and substantiates her eligibility for certain special education programs and supportive services. Typically, educational programs for students with this educational classification ought to include emotional and behavioral support in order to develop social skills and increase self-awareness, self-control, and self-esteem.

Sample #3: Educational and Therapeutic Placement

The most appropriate and least restrictive educational environment to meet Marina's current educational and mental health needs is a specialized educational and therapeutic school, public or private. This therapeutic/educational setting is to be a program specializing in the treatment of adolescents with anxieties, complex childhood traumas, and specific learning disabilities. Any successful school program for Marina should be based on her active engagement at least 30 hours per week, 12 months per year, in systematically planned, developmentally appropriate therapeutic and educational activities designed to address identified educational and therapeutic objectives.

The specificity of Marina's educational needs requires an educational environment that emphasizes structure and behavioral support, language and academic remediation using appropriate teaching methodologies, has an individualized curriculum and is able to provide the appropriate intensity and organization of remedial efforts. In order to maintain a satisfactory level of functioning and secure her further progress, Marina must have a comprehensive and structured scaffolding system properly spelled out in her Individual Educational Program (IEP). In such a program, teachers are to be partners to the therapeutic staff utilizing a strategic, comprehensive approach for attaining educational goals. The level of instruction is to be individualized for each academic subject and to be adjusted according to Marina's "zone of proximal development": the level of work at which she can succeed with the help of her teacher. Marina's education is to encompass not only academic learning but also socialization, communication, amelioration of interfering behaviors, and generalization of abilities across multiple environments.

Sample #4: School-Based Related Services

Based on the IDEA legislation, in our educational system, there is a range of school-based remedial treatments (called "related services"), such as speech and language therapy, occupational and physical therapy, rehabilitation counseling, special transportation, and so on, available for eligible students. Any recommendation for such a service or services is to be based on the findings obtained during an assessment. For example, "Language remediation is the key to Marina's overall academic and social progress. The frequency, group size, and duration of therapy sessions should be adequate for Marina's needs in this area. Having English as her native language makes Marina eligible for language remediation because her current functioning in her native language constitutes a weakened educational base and negatively affects her ability to advance her reading and writing skills. Proper methodology is the crucial factor in Marina's language remediation."

Sample #5: School-Based Supportive Services

School-based counseling is recommended on an as-needed basis: to consult about conflicts, to promote socially acceptable means of self-advocacy, to request mediation, or to protect Marina from bullies. Due to Marina's emotional condition, she may occasionally violate school rules and regulations and therefore face disciplinary actions according to existing school policies. We must not punish Marina for her disability but rehabilitate her by developing age-appropriate means of self-regulation. Whenever and if Marina violates school rules, the IEP team, which includes her parents, should consider strategies to address these specific behaviors that impede Marina's learning or that of others. IEP members or a designated staff member should conduct a manifestation determination review whenever Marina demonstrates inappropriate behavior, using the guidelines recommended by the National Association of School Psychologists and legal experts (see WrightsLaw at https://www.wrightslaw.com/info/discipl.mdr.strategy.htm).

Sample #6: Specific Remedial Methodologies for Reading and Math

Based on the findings presented in the current assessment, the most appropriate remedial methodology for Marina in reading and writing is Orton–Gillingham-based approaches, such as the Wilson Reading System (www.wilsonlanguage.com) or a similar "multisensory" program. It is this examiner's professional opinion that Marina needs multisensory (based on visual, auditory, and kinesthetic learning styles) language-based instruction with a focus on structured phonics, reading fluency, vocabulary, and comprehension.

It is necessary to rebuild Marina's foundation (or build a new one) for math comprehension, reasoning, and handling math operations. For this, we have to go to the most basic math skills. One of the most proven methods is Stern structural arithmetic, available at http://sternmath.com/about-the-program.html. Please note that the Stern method is based on the "scaffolding" concept, which should be particularly helpful for Marina.

Sample #7: Specific Methodologies for Social/Emotional Rehabilitation and Behavior Improvement

In practical terms, this is a system of classroom and schoolwide accommodations, including special crisis prevention and de-escalation techniques, called the "trauma-informed safety plan" – TISP. (See more information on TISP in Chapter 4.) This is the most therapeutically effective and educationally appropriate plan for Marina because it includes crisis de-escalation and crisis-prevention techniques along with the teaching of alternative positive behavior, such as a means of calming down. According to TISP methodology, in instances where Marina's emotional self-regulation fails and her words or actions require intervention, there are steps and actions that can make the likelihood of a positive outcome higher (see more information on specifics of "trauma-informed safety plan" in Chapter 4).

Sample #8: School/Classroom Accommodations to Reduce Anxiety in Marina

1. Accommodation in the classroom environment (such as extended time, manner of presentation of material, certain teaching techniques, etc.) is a nonmedical means of anxiety reduction for Marina.
2. Overlearning certain academic skills and knowledge is necessary to reduce her anxiety: a base of automated (overlearned) skills is needed in order to perform with expected speed and accuracy and thus to reduce the anxiety of underperforming in comparison with the classmates.
3. Preprocessing (also called pre-teaching) as a means of anxiety reduction is helpful, particularly around topics, new situations, or anything that is stressing Marina or triggers her anxiety. For a new situation, it's important to let Marina know what to expect and to answer any questions she may have (but keep her focused on the topic).
4. If something is triggering her anxiety, help Marina to identify what strategies she can put in place to support her self-regulation.

Sample #9: Test-Taking Modification

A test modification clause is to be included in Marina's IEP. Based on her educational classification and addressing her self-regulation weaknesses, the following test-taking modifications are to be included in Marina's IEP:

- Extended (doubled, if needed) time.
- Separate location/small group setting for test-taking.

- Questions to be read aloud for Marina (math testing only).
- Instructions to be read and reread for her (both math and ELA).
- "Proctor rule": during statewide testing, the proctor will not accept Marina's work if Marina makes an attempt to submit it before the time allocated for the test is over. Marina will be advised to return to her work and use the rest of the time for a thorough review of her responses.

Sample #10: Extended School Year (ESY Option)

It is crucially important to provide Marina with summer school classes in order to prevent regression after a prolonged school vacation. The existing research in cognitive psychology and remediation, as well as the best practice in special education, indicates "incessant input" and "regular reviewing" as two basic conditions for the remediation of learners with Marina's learning characteristics. It is known from research and clinical experience that students with Marina's psychoeducational profile and background tend to regress during the summer vacation much faster and deeper than their typically developing peers. Based on the presented analysis of the specific characteristics of Marina's educational needs, it is this examiner's professional judgment that a summer break from academics would cause Marina to regress significantly, with a recoupment period that would significantly exceed the usual recoupment time for children without disabilities. Summer school, summer tutoring, and privately run summer remedial programs present a range of possibilities to prevent such regression.

Sample #11: Suggested Specific Goals for Marina's IEP

At this developmental stage, Marina's self-regulation (executive functions) is her most urgent educational need, the one which mediates her academic and social performance. As Marina continues to advance through school, increasingly more independent work will be required of Marina and organizational and time-management skills will gain in importance. It is necessary to include specific goals related to Marina's self-regulation of behavior and emotions in her IEP. Because her limitation in executive function affects all aspects of school performance, IEP goals should link directly to all key academic content areas (reading, writing, math, science, etc.) and communication and social-emotional performance. Based on Marina's psychological "profile," presented in her combined developmental, neuro-psychological, and educational report, specific goals in the domain of self-regulation (executive functions) are to be introduced into Marina's IEP:

1. Goal setting: Marina will cooperate with teachers in setting instructional goals (e.g., "I want to be able to complete this assignment"); given explicit instruction, visual reminders, and diminishing teacher's support, Marina will successfully distinguish target goals (e.g., completing school assignment) from interfering goals.
2. Planning: Given a routine (e.g., complete sheet of math problems), Marina will indicate what steps or items are needed and the order of the events. Given a selection of three activities for an instructional session, Marina will indicate their order, create a plan on paper, and stick to the plan. Given a task, Marina will create a plan for accomplishing the task.
3. Organizing: Given visual cues and diminishing teacher's support, Marina will select and use a system to organize her assignments, including the materials needed, the steps to accomplish the task, and a time frame. Using learned strategies and given diminishing teacher's support, Marina will prepare an organized outline before proceeding with multistep school projects.
4. Self-monitoring and self-evaluating: Given diminishing teacher's support, Marina will accurately predict how effectively she will accomplish a task. For example, she will accurately predict whether or not she will be able to complete a task, predict how many (of something) she can finish, predict how many problems she will be able to complete in a specific time period, and so on.
5. Self-awareness and self-advocacy: Marina will accurately identify tasks that are easy/difficult for her and will explain why some tasks are easy/difficult for her; Marina will request help when tasks are difficult.

In conclusion, proper differential diagnosis has the utmost significance for rehabilitation and remediation of IA children who may present symptoms of many childhood mental health ailments while the core of their conditions is developmental trauma disorder. DTD may result in overt behavior that has similar patterns with post-traumatic stress disorder, attention deficit/hyperactivity disorder, autistic spectrum disorder, attachment disorder, generalized anxiety disorder, conduct disorder, childhood depression, and other mental health disturbances. Too often, IA children are given a range of diagnoses that are missing the underlying general cause of their conditions, thus subjecting these children to maltreatment. Recommendations for the rehabilitation and remediation of a patient are the primary outcomes of a psychological assessment. There is no "one-fits-all" set of recommendations; each and every piece of advice and direction contained in recommendations is to be as individual as the child's issues. In the school domain, there is a set of laws and procedures known as Individuals with Disabilities Education Act (IDEA-2004) that determines the ways and means of remediation in this institution. The major instrument of school-based remediation is the Individual Educational Program (IEP) that includes many specific components and could be an effective instrument in rehabilitation and remediation of IA children.

CHAPTER 4

Developmental Trauma Disorder Rehabilitation in Internationally Adopted Children

Although international adoption on a large scale has been in existence for about 30 years in the United States and Canada, no rehabilitative and remedial programs designed specifically for IA children exist. On the other hand, there is a wide range of different clinical treatments, mental health interventions, academic remedial methods, and specialized services for children affected by adverse childhood experiences. Some of these methodologies could be useful – with a different degree of effectiveness – for the IA children; others are ineffective and even counterproductive for them, despite remaining relevant for other groups of children with adverse childhood experience.

IA Child as a Subject for Rehabilitation, Remediation, and Compensation

Before analyzing the existing and emerging remedial and therapeutic methodologies, I need to present a collective portrait of the subjects – the IA children as therapy patients and service recipients. In my own clinical practice and my numerous encounters and discussions with therapists and service providers in the "trenches," those who work with IA children and their families on a daily basis for years, I have formed a stable impression that IA children are, in most cases, rather "unusual" and "challenging" patients. There are subjective and objective social factors at play in making them "tough" and "difficult." The first factor is the children themselves: it's their "survival" mode of thinking and interacting. A typical older IA post-institutional child tends not to trust anyone and uses primitive but still effective means of manipulation and avoidance in his/her interactions with the service provider or assessing the psychologist/ educator. Indiscriminate superficial friendliness with a stranger – a frequent behavior pattern of an IA older child – may completely disorient an inexperienced mental health professional. Their systematic and stubborn answers "I do not know" or obstinate silence, their lack of cooperation, restlessness and impulsivity, sudden shifts in mood, extreme emotional reactions, refusal to cooperate (e.g., maintain appointments), and so on can be very frustrating for a therapist. Survival perception and primitive self-protective behaviors are deeply ingrained in the psyche of post-institutionalized children, preventing them from an age-appropriate behavior, proper socializing, and academic learning. As noted by van der Kolk (2003, p. 310) in relation to victims of complex childhood trauma,

> ... only after acquiring an internal sense of personal competence and gaining a feeling of predictability are children likely to gain sufficient physiologic control over their arousal to start learning from new experiences and learn to respond flexibly to new challenges. Traumatized children must be helped actively to overcome their habitual fight/flight/freeze reactions by engaging their attention in actions that (1) are not related to trauma triggers and (2) provide them with a sense of mastery and pleasure.

Traditional therapies rely on either "meaning-making" verbal communication or, with very young children, establishing a connection via play. With the IA children, one of the major stumbling blocks for any "talking" therapy is the language issue per se. For the majority of them, their adverse childhood experiences took place in the very young age, and at the time of therapy, the patients experience just undifferentiated pain and discomfort, which they are unable to verbalize or even present through nonverbal means such as drawing, play, and so on. They simply have no "story" to share. Further, the therapy that is "talking" in nature may be useless if started at the time when the new language in the IA child has not reached the level of functionality needed for sensible therapeutic exchange. The child may not understand what was said, not being familiar with the second meaning of an expression, or be confused with a presumably funny phrase or idiom. For the older IA children, adopted at the preadolescent and adolescent age, a therapy is a culturally unknown territory.

The other set of difficulties may stem from attitudes of the therapists themselves when they lack experience with the IA children and may consider these patients as "typical" middle-class children (even when they are different from the parents racially or ethnically). Big mistake! Behind this appearance of a typical childhood, there lies the most atypical child's development mediated by trauma.

Trauma-Focused Therapies and IA Children

A significant volume of published scientific and internet-based information exists regarding the treatment of childhood trauma (see National

Child Traumatic Stress Network, 2020). I would like to single out a comprehensive review of neuroscience research related to trauma and applied clinical practice with trauma survivors presented by Evans and Coccoma (2014) and "Comparative Effectiveness Review No. 89," prepared by the Agency for Healthcare Research and Quality (Goldman, Lloyd, & Murphy, 2013). Unfortunately, in these detailed and wide-ranging reviews, the adoption population was not even mentioned! No doubt, some of the trauma-focused therapies are more attuned to the issues of international adoptees than others in addressing specific issues such as attachment, conduct problems, and family dynamics (Zamostny, O'Leary, O'Brien, Lee, & Baden, 2003), but none has in focus international adoptees (over 345,000 subjects in the United States alone and growing).

In my selection of the existing therapeutic approaches to DTD-related problems of the IA children, I relied on the following criteria I have developed in my many years of clinical practice along with recommendations of colleagues in the field and a review of current research literature:

- *Theoretical foundation*: the methodology needs to be consistent with a well-defined body of information on the nature of complex developmental trauma.
- *Appropriateness to the age and developmental level*: the notions of "mixed maturity," developmental delays in cognitive functioning, and emotional self-regulation at different ages have to be integrated into the treatment methodology. This often means the engagement in treatment activities that might be more characteristic of younger children.
- *Focus on "what can be changed"*: the primary targets of a therapeutic approach have to be the major personality characteristics of complex childhood trauma.
- *Attention on transfer and generalization of learned social skills, attitudes, and patterns of behavior*.
- *Multidimensionality*: the rehabilitation/remediation process should include psychological, physiological, educational, and social/cultural components and ought to involve not only the patients but engage their parents, therapists, service providers, and educators.
- *Evidence of effectiveness*: it is important to have empirical evidence of program/method efficiency.

Based on the above criteria, I reviewed and observed in actions many treatment programs within a number of years. I consider two internally rather diverse clusters of therapeutic methodologies that can be called conditionally as mostly neurophysiological therapies and mostly psychosocial therapies. Both groups of therapies have to be engaged in treatment at certain periods of the child's life, mostly in a sequential manner but in some cases simultaneously. For example, eye movement desensitization and reprocessing has to be applied first and trauma-based relational therapy later. It's possible that the therapies will need to be used concurrently; for example, sensory integration therapy is used simultaneously with trauma-focused cognitive behavioral therapy. The synergetic effect of both groups of therapies is the best possible approach in the treatment of IA children with complex childhood trauma.

Below I present only a brief synopsis of selected therapies. There is a significant volume of literature on each listed therapy, partially presented in the references (Cohen, 2005; Evans & Coccoma, 2014; Hartinger-Saunders, Semanchin-Jones, & Rittner, 2016). The subjective nature of my choices is evident and the only – but valid – excuse is that I have in mind the best interests of my patients – internationally adopted post-institutionalized children.

Neurophysiological Therapies

Sensory Integration Therapy: Children with histories of trauma and institutionalization often have sensory processing difficulties that can negatively impact behavior, social skills, motor proficiency, and academic performance. (For a comprehensive account, please see Cermak, 2009.) Sensory processing deficits can be addressed with the appropriate interventions. Thus, the application of daily systematic, focused sensory stimulation showed significant improvements in children with sensory issues. Sensory activities, sensory diets, and sensory rooms (Warner, Koomar, & Lary, 2013) have all shown to be helpful in organizing children's and adolescents' mental and emotional states (Purvis & Cross, 2007; Dorman et al., 2009).

The idea behind sensory integration (SI) therapy is that the repeated specially organized stimulation of the child's nervous system will allow it to respond to sensations and movement in a more ordered way. SI therapy is often used alone or as a part of a broader program of occupational therapy. The goal of SI therapy is not just to teach specific skills or behaviors but to remediate deficits in sensory processing per se, allowing the child to interact with the environment in a more organized fashion. Sensory activities may be helpful with calming down the child, or reinforcing a desired behavior, or helping with transitions between activities. The parents may consult with the child's occupational therapist regarding follow-up at home with some SI techniques such as brushing, breath exercises, and so on.

Neurofeedback Therapy: Neurofeedback is a therapeutic intervention that provides a response from a computer-based program that assesses a patient's brainwave activity. The program then uses sound or visual signals to reorganize or retrain emotional states that produce these signals. By responding to this process, patients learn to regulate their emotional responses and to alleviate symptoms of various mental health disorders. The mainstream medical community considers neurofeedback therapy mostly as a method of managing different psychological functions, such as attention, emotional arousal, relaxation, and so on (Marzbani, Marateb, & Mansourian, 2016). However, Fisher (2014) provides evidence that neurofeedback can treat symptoms of developmental trauma, fostering more effective self-regulation through persistent training. In his foreword to Fisher's book, van der Kolk, one of the "founding fathers" of the concept of DTD, calls neurofeedback therapy a new frontier, one of the most promising methods in the treatment of complex childhood trauma (p. XVll).

I know a number of clinical cases when neurofeedback was effective in helping IA children; however, from parents' surveys and sketchy description of individual cases (see http://www.attach-china.org/whatneurohasdone .html), it appears that a "typical" range of 15–40 sessions may not be adequate for the IA children: their treatment may require several months and over 100 sessions (Fisher, 2014, p. 349). Neurofeedback therapy session usually takes up to an hour and a half and requires a patient to cooperate and sit still, which is an issue for many IA children.

Overall, neurofeedback is a research-supported treatment with many studies published in major peer-reviewed scientific publications. These studies have demonstrated a highly significant improvement in executive functioning – the capacity to focus, attend, inhibit impulses, and so on, which is a major indicator for being able to function in school and in community.

Eye Movement Desensitization and Reprocessing (EMDR): EMDR therapy targets the unprocessed memory as well as the emotions, beliefs, and bodily sensations associated with it. According to the World Health Organization practice guide (2013, p. 83), "EMDR is based on the idea that negative thoughts, feelings and behaviors are the result of unprocessed memories. The treatment involves standardized procedures that include focusing simultaneously on (a) spontaneous associations of traumatic images, thoughts, emotions and bodily sensations and (b) bilateral stimulation that is most commonly in the form of repeated eye movements."

Bilateral stimulation – usually the eye movements, tapping, or tones – activates the brain's information processing system, allowing the old memories to be reprocessed and stored in an adaptive way. Over a series of sessions, symptoms are reduced, and beliefs associated with the memories or experiences are shifted to a more positive and adaptive state (Luber, 2009; Shapiro & Laliotis, 2015).

In the book *Neurobiology and Treatment of Traumatic Dissociation: Toward an Embodied Self*, the authors (Lanius, Paulsen, & Corrigan, 2014) reported success with EMDR, applied for healing of developmental trauma. They described the sequences in therapy as follows (p. 13): "After gathering history and establishing rapport, the therapist and person in therapy work together to establish target memories and present triggers that are causing suffering and/or interfering with daily life. The targets are the starting points of the session and a point of reference to trace the memory back in time."

For many adoptees, their trauma had happened before they developed the language to explain the events, so the memory is primarily somatic in nature and stored in the nervous system. As it was found working with IA children, the EMDR treatment method may not be suitable for the younger children or those who are severely oppositional because it does require cooperation on the part of the patient.

Please note that all three above-described treatments are not fully recognized by the mainstream medical, psychological, and educational communities. Some insurance companies do not reimburse for these therapies, and in a number of states these treatments will not be recognized as "approved" in mental health and educational settings. Nevertheless, I know from my clinical practice, from my colleagues' feedback, and from the adoptive parents' reports that in many cases these methodologies work effectively with the IA children.

Psychosocial Therapies

Three interventions, discussed below, have been developed specifically for patients suffering from childhood complex trauma and were designed to address a range of developmental concerns and competencies. The age range is rather wide: from preschool children through young adulthood. The therapies I consider the most effective for IA children are: Attachment, Regulation, and Competence (ARC), NeuroAffective Relational Model (NARM), and Trust-Based Relational Intervention (TBRI).

Like all psychological theories and techniques, these treatment models have their admired adherents and strong critics. What is common for all three approaches, despite using different labels for practically the same psychological attributes and functions, is multidimensionality I described earlier: attention to the neuropsychological aspect of trauma, teaching parents and service providers about trauma, affect regulation training, concentration on the social aspect of rehabilitation, and understanding of the role of competency in the formation of healthy self. In my view, the most appealing element in all three approaches is the social context of the treatment: family, school, and community are considered the crucial factors in the healing of the treated child. Based on the clinical work, I would like to point out that these methodologies have been and continue to be used effectively with the group of children I care about: internationally adopted post-institutionalized children ages 5–16.

Attachment, Regulation, and Competency (ARC) Model: The ARC model is a comprehensive intervention framework for working with traumatized children using a variety of psychoeducational, somatic, cognitive/behavioral, and social/relational methods to build attachments, enhance child's self-regulation, and increase competencies in different domains. At the end of treatment, the focus is on transferring a variety of skills, which the child and caregiver have learned, into a broader social context (Blaustein & Kinniburgh, 2010; Arvidson et al., 2011). The model focuses on (a) creating a structured and predictable environment by establishing rituals and routines; (b) increasing caregiver capacity to manage intense affect; (c) improving caregiver–child attunement; and (d) increasing the use of praise and reinforcement (Kinniburgh, Blaustein, Spinazzola, & van der Kolk, 2005).

According to Hodgdon, Kinniburgh, Gabowitz, Blaustein and Spinazzola (2013), ARC addresses three core domains impacted by exposure to chronic interpersonal trauma: attachment, self-regulation, and developmental competencies. The attachment methodologies are directed at providing children with a sense of security and safety, necessary for mastering a variety of capabilities including the ability to self-regulate, develop positive relationships, and acquire cognitive skills relevant to learning. The crucial element here is to develop the ability of the caregiver to recognize and regulate the child's emotional experiences via attunement, consistent responses, and routines. ARC specifically teaches caregivers and children to identify and label their affect and then modulate and express their feelings in a positive and effective manner. The competency domain presents techniques to help children increase their executive functioning skills in order to effectively engage in problem solving, anticipation, and planning. The goal is to develop a positive sense of self.

There is a number of empirical studies confirming the effectiveness of ARC in reducing trauma symptomatology in adopted children and minimizing caregivers' stress (Hodgdon et al, 2015). I had a number of patients who benefited from the application of the ARC model, and I continue to follow the development of this promising paradigm for IA children. More detailed information about the ARC model is available in Blaustein (2012).

The NeuroAffective Relational Model (NARM). Although I have limited personal familiarity with this approach in comparison with ARC and TBRT, I found it potentially very promising for the IA children. NARM is particularly attractive as a somatically based psychotherapy, using developmentally informed clinical interventions together with somatic mindfulness. NARM methodology effectively links somatic and psychological capacities to form and strengthen self-regulatory capacities.

From the point of view of my clinical experience, the great advantage of NARM is that, while not ignoring the child's past, it emphasizes work on the present moment, addressing the ongoing traumatic experience. It helps in bringing into awareness the disorganized and dysfunctional elements of consciousness without making them the primary theme of the therapy. NARM emphasizes the person's strengths, capacities, resources, and resiliency and is a powerful tool for working with both nervous system regulation and distortions of identity, such as low self-esteem, shame, and chronic self-judgment. NARM works simultaneously with the physiology and the psychology of individuals who have experienced developmental trauma (Heller & LaPierre, 2012). Although the authors of NARM never mention the IA children, they describe patterns of behavior which very much fit the patterns found in post-institutional children. Thus, the authors wrote that the survival behavior can be adaptive for certain situations and at a certain time. This survival behavior becomes ingrained in the child's CNS. The survival skills, which were appropriate for the past, distort the present experience and create a strong disconnect. Survival styles, once having outlived their usefulness, become the source of pathological symptoms. This is the amazingly accurate descriptions of what happened to IA children.

Trust-Based Relational Intervention (TBRI): To the best of my current knowledge, TBRI is the only trauma-based therapy that explicitly has international adoptees as a focused group, calling them "children from hard places." As formulated by the authors of this intervention (Purvis & Cross, 2007; Purvis, Cross, & Sunshine, 2007), TBRI is an attachment-based and trauma-informed "caregiving model." Indeed, this treatment approach offers practical tools for the parents, caregivers, teachers, and trained psychotherapists that can be used in homes, residential treatment facilities, group homes, schools, camps, and even overseas orphanages. In brief, TBRI has three guiding principles: empowerment, connection, and correction (Purvis, Cross, & Pennings, 2009; Purvis, Cross, Dansereau, & Parris, 2013). The empowerment principle focuses on the physiological, largely internal, needs of the child and the environmentally related needs. The connection principle focuses on self-awareness, attachment, and relational needs. The correction principle focuses on the regulation of behavioral needs of the child, including teaching self-regulation skills and maintenance of healthy boundaries.

As described by Dr. Purvis (2009), for each principle there are corresponding activities, which the parent or a professional working with a child will find easy to implement. The activities consist of verbal reminders, behavioral rehearsals, and role-playing with others or with puppets. Modeling is a substantial part of this therapy, like demonstrating rule-following or socially appropriate behaviors. For example, role-playing involves practicing a "script" between the caregiver and the child to allow the child to practice appropriate responses to frustrations he/she may encounter. The goal is to sustain connectedness while guiding the children to appropriate behaviors and responses and for the children to know that a protective adult will help them regulate until they are able to master self-regulation. Negotiation is a critical component of all TBRI strategies, in both proactive and responding modes, because many traumatized children have learned to use violence, manipulation, control, or triangulation to keep themselves safe and to get their needs met. In terms of practical social skills, TBRI methodology includes teaching/learning of showing respect, making eye contact, using words to replace negative behaviors, being gentle and kind, accepting consequences, accepting "no" for an answer, asking permission, and others. When proactive strategies are practiced regularly, problem behaviors become less frequent as children internalize appropriate behaviors for getting their needs met. It is important to remember that it takes sustained, consistent repetitions over time in order for the youngster to be able to self-regulate with the support of an attentive adult.

In our private conversations, Dr. Karyn Purvis conveyed that aiming their methodology on changing the internal working model of the world in international adoptees requires, in most cases, literally months of intensive work to develop new beliefs and new behaviors.

The BGCenter Approach: Four-Level Model of Treatment of Developmental Trauma Disorder in IA Children

A remedial model of psychophysiological (mind/body) regulatory rehabilitation, academic remediation, and peer socialization for the older IA post-institutionalized children with complex childhood trauma has been proposed at the BGCenter (http://www.bgcenter.com/) for children adopted after their fifth birthday. Our approach integrates services at home, at school, and in the community. The theoretical underpinnings of the approach are the concept of developmental trauma disorder (van der Kolk, 2003, 2015) and Vygotsky's theory of social connectedness and mediated learning (Vygotsky, 1987–1998). Our methodology offers guidelines for the treatment of IA children starting with the initial psychoeducational and developmental assessment (see Chapter 2) and through the sequential stages of development from preschool to young adulthood, including specific methods in remediation in cognitive, language, and academic domains (Chapters 5, 6, and 7) along with peer socialization and acculturation (Chapter 8). According to our approach, the major principles of and requirements for the successful rehabilitation/remediation of IA children are as follows:

1. *Totally safe environment*: This is a major and absolutely necessary condition for the emotional stability and reduction of survival post-orphanage behavior in IA children. The concept of safe environment implies that there are no trauma-producing or trauma-associated factors in daily living and therefore there is no need to activate fight/flight/freeze responses for a child. Trauma-related reactions such as fear, proactive aggressiveness, escape or avoidance, learned helpless-ness, tantrums, and so on are deeply embedded emotional states and patterns of behavior, which stay potentially active during many months and even years of the IA child's post-adoption life. The notion of safety has objective and subjective (based on the individual's perception) aspects. Perceived safety is achieved when a child is involved in activities that are successful, when there is a certain degree of predictability, when there is an adult or more competent peer who is here and now to help, protect, and scaffold the child, and when a child masters the socially acceptable means of self-regulation in deal-ing with academic and social challengers. Subconsciously, the sense of safety occurs concurrently with the sense of trust in an adult caregiver, available protection, and helping.

2. *Social connectedness through acculturation, socialization, attachment, and acceptance*: The connectedness is built in the process of transfor-mation of the overt post-orphanage survival behavior to the one based on socially and culturally acceptable norms, customs, values, and roles of the society in which IA children now live. This process reflects the

fundamental change in the "internal working model" of the social milieu from insecure and hostile to trustworthy and helpful. The transformation takes place if the child is involved in the purposeful and socially meaningful activities together with the leading adults and peers; in the process of these joint activities moderated by adults, the appropriate peer relations in the group are modeled, formed, and practiced. The result is to be the formation of self-assertiveness, cooperation/reciprocity, social empathy, and the capacity for physical and emotional intimacy.

3. *Cognitive, language, and academic remediation*: Remediation is expected to bring the feeling of mastery and physical, academic, and social proficiency that facilitates the engagement in the focused efforts to accomplish the goals. Social and academic competencies are the best remedy for trauma-produced anxiety, helplessness, and misery.

The idea behind our remedial paradigm is that the child's treatment should take place concurrently in two directions: "bottom-up" – with mostly neurophysiological rehabilitation – and "top-down" – with the predominantly psychosocial remediation. There are four chronological levels in this model, which have a certain intentional overlapping. At every stage of an IA child's life, the main level is shifting sequentially and chronologically with the child's maturation and socialization while the previous level(s) is (are) present in the forms of interiorized skills and emotional states. The notion of coinciding/interrelating in goals and methods of achieving them in each level with the previous level is vitally important.

Level One (Chronological Ages 5 through 12): The Basic Physiological Regulatory Restoration

The goal is to establish, refine, and facilitate age-appropriate self-regulation of major neurophysiological functions: "Traumatized children must learn to tolerate trauma-related bodily sensations and emotional states" (van der Kolk, 2003, p. 310). IA children clearly demonstrate that trauma affects not only the psychological but, first of all, the physiological state of the central nervous system: hyper-arousal and hypo-arousal are the state of the whole human organism. Early institutional rearing that typically involves both sensory and social deprivation is associated with problems in sensory modulation capacities (Cermak, 2009).

This goal could be achieved through specialized age-appropriate sensorimotor "experiential" individual therapies (e.g., sensory integration therapy, neurofeedback therapy, eye movement desensitization and reprocessing therapy), proper nutrition, and intense physical exercise (sports). Safety and predictability provided by parental methodology known as therapeutic parenting (see Chapter 9) are to be established to promote the formation of physiological self-regulation. These are the preconditions to relinquish their habitual fight/flight/freeze reactions and develop the capacity to interact positively with peers and adults, to engage properly in classroom activities, and to deal age-appropriately with inevitable frustration, which is a part of life. A special methodology called "Trauma-Informed Safety Plan" (TISP) could be first introduced at this level and be modified and properly customized through Levels Two and Three (see the clinical case below).

Level Two (Chronological Ages 6 through 18): Academic Remediation

School learning and peer socialization are the major, most significant activities in the preadolescent and adolescent ages. These activities must not be blocked, impaired, or distorted. The main goal at this stage is to maintain progress in the academic achievement of the child along with the productive peer interaction.

This is achieved through intense and focused academic remediation, using specific methodologies combined with concerted efforts of the family (therapeutic parenting model, presented in Chapter 9), school (Individual Education Program and Individual Transitional Planning, presented in Chapters 7 and 10), and community (public or private remedial agencies discussed above). Level One and Level Two are closely connected and intertwined: cognition regulates affect, and sensorimotor experiences support compensatory cognitive processing and adaptive behavior. Participation in the shared and socially meaningful activities under the leadership of a competent and dedicated adult to facilitate socialization of the child is a must on all levels, but it becomes especially important on Level Two. The detailed programs of cognitive, language, academic, and social remediation are presented in Chapters 5, 6, 7, and 8, respectively.

Level Three (Chronological Ages 5 through 18): Peer Socialization and Social Connectedness

It is commonplace in practically all developmental theories and a practical knowledge of all parents that peer interactions, connections, and communication are the major factors during adolescent times and young adulthood. Any impairments of these activities have long-lasting negative consequences. Unfortunately, difficulties with socialization and peer inter-actions are very common among children adopted internationally as pre-schoolers through adolescent time. There are two groups of reasons for this: subjective (certain personal qualities of many older international adoptees described in Chapter 1, such as "mixed maturity" in self-regulation, chronic hyper-arousal or dissociation, etc.) and such objective factors as a lack of language skills and age-specific cultural and social adjustment, as well as the differences in cultural background and values. A comprehensive system of socialization of an IA child within positive peer-group relationships in school and outside of school does not come into existence on its own: the teachers, parents, and mental health pro-fessionals must work together to develop and maintain it. Therefore, particular attention is paid to the creation of a needed "controlled envi-ronment" by selecting those activities that facilitate proper peer interac-tion. The time frame of Level Three is basically the same as on Level Two: these two levels are closely interconnected and intertwined. The remedial methodologies in this domain are presented in Chapters 8 and 9.

Level Four (Chronological Ages 14 through 21): Transitioning to Adulthood

The goals of Level Four are the identification of the areas of personal strength, reinforcement of skills and special giftedness applicable to future job training, adjusting to an independent living, and reinforcement of emotional self-regulation and self-confidence. The major tool of the Level Four is the Individual Transition Plan (ITP), for which any child who has an Individual Educational Program (IEP) is entitled at the age of 16 (according to the IDEA, certain transitional services or even the whole ITP may start at the age of 14). Specific methodologies are presented in Chapter 10, which discusses the specificity of the ITP for international adoptees in comparison with the population at large; the structure, con-tent, and goals for international adoptees' ITP; specifics of occupational evaluation and development of vocational and postsecondary education goals for the IA person; and the special role of social/emotional behavior goals in ITP for the international adoptees.

As one can see, all levels are closely connected and entangled: partici-pation in shared and socially meaningful activities for gaining age-appropriate academic and social competence facilitates socialization and integration into society. This Four-Level model is proactive in nature, addresses the specificity of the IA population and the nature of its neurological and social traumatization, and uses properly modified research-based and clinically proven methodologies.

Below please find a sample of clinical case based on the four-level model with the school-based recommendations for an IA child afflicted with DTD:

Clinical Case

Max, a 10-year-9-month-old boy, was adopted from the Philippines at the age of 6 years and 4 months. He lived with his homeless and drug-addicted mother until the age of 10 months, stayed in a local hospital for 4 months, lived through two foster care placements, spent 2 years in a church-run orphanage.

Through the combined developmental neuropsychological and educational assessment, it was determined that Max has a dysregulated autonomic nervous system (ANS), which is the primary mechanism in control of the fight-or-flight and freeze-and-dissociate responses. The ANS dysfunction impacts his somatosensory awareness of surroundings through sight, sound, touch, smell, taste, and so on, as well as motor movements. Max experiences the underlying sensory processing deficits, which contribute to his challenges with self-regulation and thus reducing his ability to participate in everyday activities as well as his ability to respond with appropriate emotional control and behavior to challenges or frustration.

Max was recognized by his local school district as a student with educational handicapping conditions. His educational classification (the designation of educational handicapping condition) is Other Health Impaired (OHI). According to his Individual Educational Program (IEP), Max's remediation ought to encompass not only academic learning but also socialization, adaptive skills, communication, amelioration of interfering behaviors, and generalization of abilities across multiple environments. The IEP contains specific academic goals and means of attaining these goals, school-based related services, and a behavior support system for addressing his emotional needs.

Related services designed for Max include occupational therapy (OT), school-based counseling, and Trauma-Informed Safety Plan (TISP).

School-based occupational therapy (OT) is beneficial for Max in reducing tension/anxiety and practicing goal-directed behavior and self-regulation. The goal of the application of OT is to initiate a positive change in Max's ability to effectively regulate sensory modulation – the degree to which one is influenced by various sensory inputs. Particular attention is to be paid to the issue of sensory discrimination – the ability to correctly process sensory information and sensory-based motor coordination. The following sensory modulation techniques are to be used by OT professionals: orienting/ alerting and relaxation/calming activities, self-soothing actions, stretching exercise, creation of a personalized sensory kit, use of weighted vest, brushing techniques, and beanbag tapping. The OT professional will monitor the use of a "sensory diet" – a daily schedule which is integrating specific prevention strategies and crisis intervention techniques.

School-based counseling. For Max, a program that teaches how to recognize his own emotional state and, through this recognition, to regulate himself at school will be particularly beneficial. Therefore, the methodology known as "zones of regulation" is to be used by a school counselor. This program classifies states of arousal into four easily identified color-coded zones: red (means stop), yellow (a warning to slow down and be cautious), green (good to go), and blue (a rest area). Within the course of five to eight sessions, Max will learn ways to identify his different states of arousal and his capacity for emotional control. He will learn about different tools for moving from one zone to another, including tools for staying in the green zone, a zone he needs to be in to function well in class. The "zones of regulation" program focuses on teaching the self-regulation skills necessary for making and keeping friends. The parents can learn more about zones of regulation by logging on to the website www.zonesofregulation.com and/or reading Leah Kuypers' book (2011), which contains a CD-ROM with reproducible visuals and handouts related to the lessons.

Trauma-Informed Safety Plan (TISP): Given the nature of Max's social/ emotional problems, a Trauma-Informed Safety Plan (TISP) needs to be the central part of Max's individualized educational program. As of now, the behavior modification plan (BMP) offered by the school is not successful. Max is a child with complex childhood trauma and a grossly dysregulated autonomic nervous system: his reaction to everyday events in school could be different from what is expected from a student of his age. In children like Max, consequences, whether rewards, privileges, or penalty, are often ineffective when the behavior is outside of his/her ability to control. The use of behavior modification programming with a child with emotional trauma puts this child in a perpetually defensive state, or in a state of anxiety that leaves him/her feeling unsafe and thus unable to learn and socialize in an age-appropriate manner. On the other hand, a carefully crafted plan aimed at creating an environment that is proactive in preventing Max's escalating emotional distress and is based on social connectedness rather than on rewards and punishment is likely to be helpful and productive. It is important to note that in relation to Max the focus should be on "connection," not "control." TISP includes special crisis prevention and de-escalation techniques teaching positive alternative behaviors, such as ways of calming down. The core of the TISP is the school-wide and classroom accommodations aimed at reducing and controlling Max's ongoing frustration and teaching him to practice calming techniques and develop age-appropriate social skills.

In a situation of crisis (e.g., disobedience in following school rules and regulations), the following actions are more likely to help Max regulate his emotions:

- The most important thing for a teacher or a teacher's aide involved in the crisis is to ensure his/her own state is calm, and his/her actions, posture, position, and tone communicate that calmness. First and foremost, an adult must be in control of his/her own emotions and thoughts if he/she hopes to engender feelings of safety and calm in Max.
- It is critical to communicate with Max at the level at which his nervous system is currently functioning. Empathy beats logic every time; logic doesn't register with a child whose brain is functioning in survival mode. Max's chronological age is irrelevant in such a situation. Communication, both verbal and nonverbal, must assure Max that he is safe both physically and emotionally. When Max feels safe (when he believes the other individual sees, knows, and understands him), he will be more able to regulate his own emotions. Such empathy often begets conversation and confidences from the traumatized child. This is not the time for talking about consequences. Let Max talk. Talking is preferable to acting out. Give him time to fully vent his feelings of stress and listen while he talks.
- Finally, when the situation has calmed, Max should be allowed to collaborate with those in authority to determine the appropriate course of action, including disciplinary consequences. If Max can articulate what went wrong and identify his own part in it, there is no need for a lecture: it is more effective when the answer comes from within.

It is only when Max is calm, cooperating, and in a good mood, try to teach him alternative and adaptive behavior that will be used in the situation of crisis:

- Teach strategies to calm down, such as breathing, counting, and walking/stretching. Those techniques are to be interiorized by Max to the degree of automaticity in order to be implemented in the time of crisis.

- Max will be trained in self-regulatory scripts such as "big deal/little deal," "choice/no choice," and "plan A/plan B."
- Using a "frustration card": Max will be taught to show a card that he can use to signal feelings of frustration. When he shows this card, he will be removed from the frustrating situation.
- Max will have a "finish later" folder or box to be used when he is not yet done with an assignment.

A routine structure introduced into his day and predictability can help Max with transitions. It is not possible to control for all of the changes that happen during a typical school day, but concentrating on a transition routine that can cut across activities may help. A visual schedule that depicts the major activities of the day can be created and shared with Max. Upon arriving at school, Max might sit down for a few minutes with a teacher's aide (TA) assigned to him, explore how he feels, practice a calming routine, for example, take two deep breaths, count to 10, and go over the morning schedule of activities. After each activity, the TA can give him positive feedback, ask how he feels, check his schedule for the next activity, practice his calming routine again if needed, remind him to use his calming routine when he needs it, answer any questions he may have, and help him move to the next activity. The goal of this type of routine is to teach Max to internalize the steps so that he can follow the routine on his own as he gets older. He might have a list of steps he can refer to when needed.

Consider providing Max with positive feedback and incentives for doing his work. Max needs a large amount of positive feedback: positive comments should far outnumber negative comments across his day. For activities that Max finds particularly difficult (e.g., writing assignments), extra incentives should be considered, such as being allowed to engage in a favorite activity following the difficult activity.

In conclusion, as presented in this chapter, therapeutic systems and treatment methodologies have proved their effectiveness in addressing developmental trauma disorder in international adoptees. The bottom line is that the physiological, psychological, and social aspects of DTD and their synergetic effect on development have to be addressed in a cohesive, integrated manner. Trauma-specific treatment of international adoptees should facilitate recovery by creating a safe environment, develop emotional self-regulation and academic competence, and enhance integration into a social network. Relationships and social support are identified as decisive factors in trauma recovery for children and adult survivors of childhood trauma: relationships either hinder or contribute to resilience, coping, and recovery.

CHAPTER 5

Cognitive Remediation of Internationally Adopted Children in School and Family

My son (adopted at 5, now 9-year-old) keeps struggling with school learning . . . and I keep telling his teachers that it is as if he has no "hooks" to clip information on to in his brain . . . that he needs to learn how to learn. How can I help my son? (From an adoptive parent's letter)

Deficits in General Cognitive Abilities and Specific Cognitive Skills in IA Children

Cognition refers to thinking processes and skills: it is an intellectual competence that allows a human being to acquire, understand, and respond to information. Cognition, as a major psychological function, includes the abilities to regulate attention, remember, process, and organize information with a certain speed, communicate, and act upon this information. It has an individualized nature; people are different in their cognitive capacities. Cognitive skills develop and change over time; they can be measured and improved, or they may deteriorate under certain circumstances. All these abilities work in a close, interdependent fashion with emotions and motivation to allow the persons to function in their environment.

In humans, cognition is a developmental psychological function, and cognitive development is a synergetic result of the interplay between biological and environmental (social in nature) factors. In the case of IA children, we know very little about the first factor; as for the second factor, we are aware of the environmental characteristics of neglect, deprivation, and an overload of traumatic experiences. The presence of adverse conditions during gestation and after birth may have long-lasting negative effects on the developing brain. Still, there are many individual differences at play.

The review of literature on cognitive capacities of IA children (Gindis, 2019) revealed that general cognitive capacity and specific cognitive skills and processes in many IA children were below age expectations in comparison with their peers in the general population. It was found that cognitive impairments persist even after placement in a socially enriched environment, but a favorable social situation of development facilitates positive gains in the overall cognitive capacity of IA children (van IJzendoorn, Juffer, & Klein, 2005). Still, a considerable number, if not the majority, of IA children continued to experience an enduring deficiency in general and specific domains of cognitive functioning. The most common and leading specific neurocognitive deficits found in IA children as a group were (a) executive dysfunction, (b) cognitive/academic language issues, (c) problems with working memory, and (d) low processing speed (Connor & Rutter, 1999; Behen, Helder, Rothermel, Solomon, & Chugani, 2008; Camelia et al., 2012; Gindis, 2019).

Cumulative Cognitive Deficit as a Specific Feature of the Cognitive Profile of IA Children

An important fact, confirmed by many research findings (Welsh, Andres, Viana, Petrill, & Mathias, 2007; Dalen, 2010; Zill, 2016, 2017), clinical practice (Gindis, 2005, 2019), and teachers' and parents' experiences (Price, 2000; Clauss & Baxter, 1997) is that after an initial phase of seemingly fast new language acquisition and adjustment to their new homes and schools, many international adoptees have significant difficulty in their academic work, which leads to behavioral and emotional problems. Their learning difficulties may persist and worsen long past the time when their academic problems could be attributed to new language learning and adjustment issues. Moreover, as international adoptees progress through the developmental stages and school grades, many of them seem to fall farther and farther behind age norms in their performance on academic tasks and intelligence tests (Zill & Bradford, 2018). In many international adoptees, the overall pace of academic performance is too slow and inconsistent, thus failing to match comprehensive and relentless efforts of their adoptive parents and professionals in different fields.

One of the compelling explanations of this phenomenon is that these children experience what is known as "cumulative cognitive deficit" (CCD), a term coined by psychologist Martin Deutsch in the 1960s (Jachuck & Mohanty, 1974; Cox, 1983). Although the issue of CCD in international adoptees has been described in a number of my publications (Gindis, 2005, 2019), in order to present recommendations for cognitive remediation of IA children, I need to describe the basic concept of this phenomenon here.

CCD is a psychological construct referring to a downward trend in the measured cognitive and scholastic achievement of culturally or socially disadvantaged children relative to age-appropriate societal norms and expectations. The evidence of CCD existence comes from a variety of sources (Jensen, 1974, 1977; Kamin, 1978; Saco-Pollitt, Pollitt, & Greenfield, 1985, Haywood, 1987, Mackner, Starr, & Black, 1997). The theory behind cumulative cognitive deficit is that ". . . children who are deprived of enriching cognitive experiences during their early years are less able to profit from environmental situations because of a mismatch between their cognitive schemata and the requirements of the new advanced learning situation" (Sattler, 1992, pp. 575–576).

Etiology, Structure, Contributing Factors, and Specifics of CCD in IA Children

It is common knowledge that young children learn in two major ways: directly through observing, experimenting, experiencing, and imitating and indirectly through adults, who mediate knowledge for children by selecting and modifying input from the outside world and directing children's responses. Through direct and mediated learning, major cognitive skills and processes are formed and put into action. Deprived of such experiences, children are indeed disadvantaged and may have problems moving to more advanced levels of cognitive functioning and school learning. When a child misses certain stages of normal cognitive development and fails to learn certain generic concepts that are necessary for successful schooling, the educational matter this child is taught simply does not have any structural cognitive support, upon which to be understood, remembered, and used. No wonder, all high order cognitive abilities such as abstract thinking, concept formation, analysis/synthesis, perceptual organization, sequential/simultaneous processing, and handling symbolic signs are developmentally hierarchical: the appearance of more complex cognitive structures resting upon the prior emergence of simpler cognitive components. For example, the ability to compare appears prior to classifying, classifying prior to seriating, and so on (Bruner, 1966). The psychological roots of CCD are developed in the absence of a viable foundation for the productive development of more complex cognitive skills and processes. For example, elementary cognitive skills such as patterning or sequencing are normally formed between the ages of 3 and 5 in a typically developing child through direct experience and mediated learning (Rittle-Johnson, Fyfe, McLean, & McEldoon, 2013). As clinical experience has revealed, the same patterning and sequencing skills are often absent in a 7- or 8-year-old former orphanage resident (Gindis & Karpov, 2000, Gindis, 2019); however, more complex math and reading skills rest on these basic cognitive notions, and without rebuilding the base, no successful remediation is possible. Severe educational and cultural deprivation (a lack of direct and mediated learning in early childhood) combined with a host of trauma-producing factors constitutes the core of CCD in IA children.

The analysis of empirical research publications on CCD in the population at large (see more on this subject in Gindis, 2019, pp. 118–130) revealed the following major characteristics of the cognitive profile of children with CCD:

- Lack of age-appropriate cognitive skills and limited or nonexistent metacognitive skills, such as monitoring one's own thinking or learning, which leads to progressive cognitive incompetence.
- Poor organization of knowledge bases, resulting in ineffective learning, constant forgetting of learned material, and inability to transfer knowledge and skills from one situation to another.
- Cognitive/academic language, a major mediator of cognitive processes, is deficient but often exists concurrently with the fully functional social "everyday" language.
- Chronic mismatch between a student's learning aptitude and his/her learning environment, level of instructions, and the manner of the teacher's presentation and instruction.
- Immature self-regulation of behavior that results in poor concentration and limited attention span.
- Diminished intrinsic motivation for learning or achieving in learning activities, which grows with age and becomes one of the major characteristics of CCD.

Resembling the population at large in its nature and dynamic of development, CCD in the IA children has its specificity that must be recognized and addressed in our remedial efforts.

First and foremost, CCD in IA children exists against a background of developmental trauma disorder (DTD), which is the major contributing factor in their deficiency of cognitive functioning. Observable immature self-regulation of goal-directed learning activities, inability to concentrate and be attentive, fatigue and nervous tension during mental efforts, decreased memory capacity, and other symptoms of learning difficulties are all attributes of DTD.

In international adoptees with CCD, there is a high likelihood of neurological weakness, mostly related to premature birth, birth-related traumas, malnutrition, and many subtle neurological impairments, not easily detectable at a later age. The correlation between these medical conditions and a substandard school performance is a well-established fact. It means that, even when a child had been adopted within the first 24 months of life, the risk of CCD may still be present. Neurological weaknesses of IA children constitute the biological background of their cognitive limitations.

Abrupt first language attrition in adoptees and failure to transfer cognitive skills from a first to a second language is another unique feature of CCD in IA children adopted as preschoolers and at school ages. Language is a medium through which cognitive skills and knowledge are formed, present, and further developed. Most international adoptees ages 5 and up learn their new language according to the so-called "subtractive" model, with English quickly replacing the first language. The subtractive nature of new language acquisition definitely contributes to CCD, which is reinforced when the first language is lost for all practical purposes and the second one is barely functional communicatively and nonexistent cognitively. The overall length of this period depends on the child's age and individual differences, but practically all international adoptees, who join their adoptive family after their fifth birthday, appear to undergo this period, and for some of them, it is the time when their cognitive weaknesses are consolidated into CCD.

Learning always includes the emotional and motivational components that mediate cognitive functioning. As noted by Haywood (1987, p. 198), ". . . constant failure in cognitive/academic activities . . . feeds upon itself in a negative spiraling fashion which results in low self-esteem and/or lack of interest in and constant frustration associated with cognitive efforts." It is likely that emotional, behavioral, and cognitive difficulties are closely intertwined and constitute a very important characteristic of CCD in post-institutionalized adoptees.

The IA children, arriving to their adoptive families at school age between 5 and 17 years of age, have cultural differences that may contribute to CCD being a part of their adaptive behavior patterns. Valuing of cognitive activity, intrinsic motivation in cognitive operations, learning behavior in general, and attitude toward teaching authority may be influenced by cultural differences (Haywood, 2005). The relationship between the cultural differences (in both internationally adopted children and the adoptive families) and CCD should be further explored and explained.

CCD in the population at large is attributed to cultural/educational deprivation experienced in the early formative years and is traditionally associated with children from poor and uneducated families. Most international adoptees are now a part of middle-class families with well-educated parents. Probably for the first time in the history of CCD, their families are not ongoing contributing factors in CCD; on the contrary, they may be considered powerful remedial factors. Now symptoms of CCD are more often subjected to professional attention due to adoptive parents' sensitivity to the issue and their awareness of possible learning problems in children combined with higher parental expectations in this respect.

To summarize, in contrast to a single cause (e.g., the "culture of poverty"), the determinants of CCD in international adoptees may be associated with a combination of factors, such as developmental trauma disorder, neurological weakness, educational/cultural neglect and deprivation in early childhood, abrupt first language attrition, and a lack of proper remedial education after adoption. Consequently, the remedial efforts should be multifaceted as well. To complicate the picture further, due to its "summative" nature, CCD can go undetected in the early stages of the child's educational journey. It takes time for the cognitive deficit to consolidate and become "cumulative." Full-blown CCD is normally observed in third- to fifth-grade students (ages 8–12). An appropriate academic placement and remedial education are the most effective ways to address CCD in IA children in order to prevent further deterioration in learning capacity and motivation to learn.

What is the prevalence of CCD in international adoptees? It is unknown at the moment, and this question needs further research. Although we do not have any reliable statistical data so far, some clinical empirical findings do exist. Based on the research completed in Western Europe (van IJzendoorn & Juffer, 2006; Beckett et al., 2006; Beckett, Castle, Rutter, & Sonuga-Barke, 2010; Dalen et al., 2010), about two-thirds of international adoptees have academic difficulties in school. Welsh et al. with associates (2007) did a meta-analysis of 30 published research articles in the United States and Canada and came to a similar conclusion: over 75 percent of international adoptees of school age were in need of special education placement or services. Four major parent surveys completed between 1996 and 2002 by the Eastern European Adoption Coalition (http://www.eeac.org) and the Families for Russian and Ukrainian Adoption (http://www.frua.org/) provided approximately the same numbers: from 60 to 80 percent of parents reported that their children either have been receiving or are in the process of obtaining special education services. Not all international adoptees who receive or eligible to receive special education services or placements in our school do have CCD; they may have different educational handicaps. Still, a significant number of IA students in need of special education may be an indirect indication of the urgent need for cognitive remediation.

Remediation of CCD in the School and Family Environments

The question of great practical significance for many adoptive families is whether, and to what degree, CCD can be remedied and what are the most effective prevention and treatment(s) of such an impediment. Although our current experience with international adoptees with CCD is limited, there are some research data, as well as practical "know-how" related to CCD in the population at large, which are applicable, with appropriate modifications, to IA students.

The biggest problem with the school-based remediation is that the schools often do not know how to address the specificity of international adoptees in their remedial efforts – "how to fit these round pegs into the square holes of special education programs," as one adoptive parent defined this situation. We know by now that traditional remediation with more intensive work individually or in a small group using basically the same teaching methodology as in regular classrooms is not effective with overcoming CCD (Conway & Hopton, 2000). In other words, simply doing more intensely what has not worked in the past is not a good solution. The problem is that traditional remediation assumes the presence of an appropriate base in cognition upon which it tries to build the compensatory structures; however, the lack of the proper cognitive foundation itself constitutes a major source of difficulty in reversing the negative trend in CCD. Special remedial methods should be applied toward developing basic cognitive processes such as sequencing, patterning, elementary classification/discrimination, associations, and the like. Thus, cognitive education is one of the most effective methods of remediation of CCD in international adoptees.

Criteria for Selecting and Evaluating Cognitive Education Programs

There are many cognitive education approaches created for different age groups (see a comprehensive review in Hessels & Hessels, 2013; Haywood, 2010). All these systems of cognitive remediation are based on the idea that cognitive processes are acquired mental operations that can be mastered and improved through appropriate learning. In order to compensate for the detrimental effect of CCD in international adoptees, cognitive intervention should be applied within four closely connected educational domains, suggested by Haywood (1987): (a) enriching cognitive language, (b) teaching specific cognitive processes that increase cognitive competence, (c) facilitating task-intrinsic motivation, and (d) providing optimal learning settings.

Commercially available programs of cognitive education fluctuate in their applicability from preschool to secondary and postsecondary levels. Programs vary in terms of their theoretical background regarding cognitive development and teacher–learner interaction. Only a few current programs contain plans, methods, or materials that are useful for both classroom and home-based remedial education, but those that do contain these elements (Haywood, Brooks, & Burns, 1992; Greenberg, 2000, 2005, Lidz & Gindis, 2000; Bodrova & Leong, 2007) have demonstrated greater success when parent participation is implemented.

Haywood suggested the following criteria for selecting a cognitive education/remediation program (2010, pp. 23–24):

- Classroom activities and teaching methods should be derived from and consistent with a well-defined body of theory regarding the nature of cognitive remediation.
- Both the content of classroom exercises and the specific cognitive processes to be acquired and elaborated should fit developmental levels of cognitive functioning of the learners.
- Cognitive education programs should complement rather than replace those curricula, with emphasis on both cognitive development and content acquisition goals.
- The program must take deliberate, planned, and frequent efforts to achieve generalization.
- A major goal is to help children become independent learners who find reward within tasks themselves; cognitive education programs should promote metacognitive activity when children need to think about their own thinking and to devise their own strategies for thinking, learning, and behaving more effectively.

Based on the above criteria, I selected and reviewed five major cognitive education systems developed in the United States, Canada, and Israel: my major concern was the compatibility of a specific program and characteristics of IA children.

1. Instrumental enrichment (Feuerstein, Feuerstein, Falik, & Rand, 2006)
2. COGNET (cognitive enhancement training) (Das, 2004; Das, Hayward, Samantaray, & Panda, 2006)
3. Transactional metacognitive approach (Haywood, 2010)
4. Cognitive enrichment advantage (Greenberg, 2005)
5. Tools of the mind (Bodrova & Leong, 2007)

In my professional opinion, among the listed, one specific program – namely transactional metacognitive approach, developed by C. Haywood and his associates – would be most suitable for the IA students. Based on this theoretical platform, a practical methodology titled "Bright Start. Cognitive Curriculum for Young Children" was developed and perfected (Haywood et al., 1992; Brooks & Haywood, 2003). Please note that this program was originally created for preschoolers. However, in our practical remedial work with international adoptees, we successfully applied it (with some adaptations) to children ages 4 through 9. A brief synopsis of this program is presented below.

Bright Start

"Bright Start" was developed for children who were at risk of failure in school due to being socioeconomically underprivileged, migrant, language-different, victims of early childhood deprivation and neglect, and children with various learning disabilities (Brooks & Haywood, 2003). Clinical experience in application of this program (Gindis, 2006, 2019) attests to its suitability for internationally adopted children. The program consists of eight curriculum units that may be taught in one-on-one situations or in small groups of children interacting with an adult (a parent, a tutor, or a teacher in school) for a period of about 20 to 40 minutes each day. It is recommended that these units be taught in the following sequence:

Unit 1. Self-regulation: children learn to bring their bodies under the control first of external stimuli and then of internal stimuli (self-control). Children then learn to use their self-control in a social context.

Unit 2. Number concepts: introduces basic number concepts – quantity, numbers, ordinal relations, conservation. Starting with one-on-one correspondence, children learn concepts that help them respond to events in a quantitative, organized way.

Unit 3. Comparison: introduces the concept that we can identify similarities and differences in a systematic way. Children learn to define and make comparisons based on such characteristics as size, shape, and color.

Unit 4. Role-taking: develops the ability to see different perspectives, first on the physical level and then on the social level. Children learn to consider other people's feelings and viewpoints. This unit, like self-regulation, is primarily social in nature.

Unit 5. Classification: develops the function of classifying across three dimensions – color, size, shape – and evolves into representational classification (classifying without pictures).

Unit 6. Sequence and pattern: children learn to identify items within classes according to their serial position. The lessons focus on number and pattern progression and finding patterns in groups of stimuli.

Unit 7. Letter-shape concepts: children learn to identify and classify objects and events according to certain prominent characteristics, which will be crucial to the learning of the letters of the alphabet.

Unit 8. Transformation: children learn to induce rules related to change and to deduce the application of the change rules in new situations, to create changes that follow rules, and to track what changes and what stays the same. This unit is the most cognitively advanced and can be used with primary-grade children.

Each unit is composed of a number of lessons – over 190 lessons all in all. The program is appropriate for the IA children from age 4 through 9 and is, indeed, well equipped to help them, among other things, to learn cognitive academic English, needed for cognitive operations that are pre-requisites for learning in the primary grades.

There are many features in this program beneficial for IA students. One of them is the possibility of collaboration of teachers and parents. There is an optional "follow-up" component in the program that is based on the special parent manual with parent–child activities that are performed by the parents and any children who are at home. An adoptive parent can ask an ESL and/or regular teacher to include elements of the program in their curriculum and do a follow-up at home. Also, the program is closely connected with the activities of daily living and takes advantage of ordinary daily experiences.

In the context of educating the IA children, the most distinctive characteristic of the "Bright Start" is the "mediational teaching style" and a "cognitive-mediational behavior management system," which the IA children were deprived of in their pre-adoption life. The Bright Start program contains detailed directions on mediation techniques and guidelines for fostering task-intrinsic motivation. The mediational teaching style explains the methods of forming basic thinking skills in the children, generalizing meanings of their own experiences, and managing their meta-cognitive processes. Thus, during the structured activities, teachers, parents, and therapists try to elicit evidence of systematic thinking ("give me a reason why we should look carefully at this picture before describing it"), use process-oriented questioning ("why do you think it's better to count this way?"), and accept children's responses while challenging their answers and requiring justification ("that's a correct answer, but can you tell me why it is correct?"). By using the mediational teaching style, the teachers facilitate children's understanding of the generalized meaning of their experiences, efficient strategies of gathering information and its elaboration, systematic thinking processes, and accurate communication strategies.

During each lesson, the teacher encourages discussion about the activities in the lessons. For example, in the self-regulation unit, the teacher presents activities dealing with cues that help in monitoring fast and slow body movements. The teacher might present a picture (or a rhythm on a small drum) and ask the child to walk slow or fast as a response to the picture (or the rhythm). Later, the teacher presents symbols and abstract cues that tell the child how to self-regulate the behavior. After each activity, the teacher tries to elicit meaningful examples of the cognitive principle learned, based on the child's experiences at home, in the kindergarten, or the playground (Haywood et al., 1992).

The effectiveness of Bright Start as a remedial program has been tested repeatedly in different countries (Tzuriel, Isman, Klung, & Haywood, 2017; Haywood, 2020). It is important to note that children with backgrounds similar to those of international adoptees were included in practically all experimental groups during those evaluation studies. The overall outcome of these studies has been positively reflected in cognitive development, intelligence test scores, language skills, intrinsic motivation, and classroom behavior (Brooks & Haywood, 2003; Haywood, 2020).

Home-Based Cognitive and Language Remediation Program

Although the role of a parent as a remedial teacher is not free from controversy (Mottan & Shanmugam, 2018), particularly in the context of attachment issues, many parents of international adoptees are involved in remedial work with their children at home. There is a number of remedial methodologies developed specifically for home use, such as Barton Reading and Spelling System (https://bartonreading.com/tutors/#), Stern Structured Arithmetic (https://sternmath.com/), Parent Wilson

Language Program (https://www.wilsonlanguage.com/parents/), and many others. None of these methodologies, however, are good match with the needs and specificity of international adoptees. The challenges of creating an effective home-based remedial system for IA children are very specific, as seen from the following listing. The methodology should not require of the adoptive parents special skills and prolonged training; rather, it should strengthen the parents' role rather than that of teachers; it should promote attachment and bonding inside the family, being a family affair rather than a school-like activity. (Parents should not be the second-shift teachers in their own home.) At the same time, the home-based program should maintain a link between home- and school-based learning and complement the school-based remediation. Finally, such a program should address the emotional and social issues of IA children along with cognitive and language problems. As of now, the only specialized home-based cognitive remedial program is the SmartStart, available at www .bgcenter.com/smartstart.htm.

The SmartStart Program: **Helping Your Internationally Adopted Child Develop a Foundation for Learning**

The SmartStart program (Lidz & Gindis, 2000) was created for international adoptees ages 4 through 8 with all the foregoing requirements in mind. The program offers specific activities that focus on the processes that have been found to positively influence the cognitive development of young children. This curriculum can be applied at any time within the first 2 years in an adoptive family, but it is especially beneficial if implemented in the very early stages of the child's adjustment to a new life and continued over months of cognitive remediation. The SmartStart program is designed to address the missing links in a child's cognitive and language development by introducing basic abstract concepts and verbal notions that should be mastered at earlier developmental ages. The program consciously provides metacognitive skill formation along with academic language development in children ages 4 to 8. The program consists of seven units:

1. Noticing our world. The unit focuses on learning to use the senses to experience the environment. The unit addresses learning what and how to notice, and how to talk about what is noticed, how to help a child to pay attention to patterns and sequences, and how to make groups based on perceived features.
2. Let's make a plan. The unit focuses on connecting the present with the future by learning to think strategically, to set goals, to make a

plan, to evaluate the results, and to make changes in response to this evaluation. The concepts of this unit form the essential basis for cooperation with others in achieving a goal.

3. That's fantastic! The unit focuses on developing imagination, as well as divergent and hypothetical thinking. Children are encouraged to make "what if?" speculations and to entertain strange combinations and alternative approaches.

4. The nimble symbol. The unit directly addresses the use of symbols in our environment and focuses on laying a foundation for emerging literacy and numeracy.

5. What's the big idea? The unit focuses on making rules, getting the main idea, and learning from general principles. This unit instructs children how to form the concepts derived from their empirical experiences.

6. Who is in charge? The unit focuses on the development of self-regulation. Children need to learn to control themselves and to reduce their dependence upon control by others. Self-regulation is a primary domain in which international adoptees are lagging behind their peers.

7. Making connections: understanding the past – facilitating the future. The unit emphasizes the ability to reflect on the past and to connect the past with present events. It emphasizes recalling and understanding the linkages between the past, as parent and child build it, and the present. On a more abstract, scientific level, this unit encourages consideration of cause/effect thinking.

Each unit is devoted to a specific domain of cognitive functioning, describes the goals that parents should have in mind introducing new activities to their children, details instructions of what to do and what to say when presenting a new activity, and contains the actual description of the activities. Each unit is accompanied by a vocabulary list of suggested words for parents to use in the course of the activities.

The major difference between the SmartStart and the traditional remedial methods lies in understanding the specificity of internationally adopted children. The restoration or building from scratch of the basic cognitive capabilities is a prerequisite for successful remediation in the academic domain. The program is available free of charge at http://www.bgcenterschool.org/CourseLibrary/SCL1M.shtml. At this time, there is no research evaluating the effectiveness of this program for IA children, although we have numerous positive responses and reviews from adoptive parents and therapists who work with international adoptees. Here are some samples of activities presented in the SmartStart program:

Teach the child to recognize parts of a whole:

- Begin with objects. Identify and name the parts of each object and discuss the function of each part in relation to the whole (a bicycle, a telephone, a can opener).
- Show incomplete objects and call the child's attention to the missing part and its functional relationship to the whole (toy car without wheel, shirt without buttons, bell without clapper).
- Cut out pictures of objects and mount them on poster board or index cards. Cut the picture into two pieces, being certain that one picture is identifiable as "what is missing" from the other picture: a tree cut into trunk and branches.
- Have the child experiment to discover which of his/her body parts are most important in various activities (throwing a ball, picking up a paper clip).
- Progress to puzzles that have pieces that will form a picture. Help the child use clues rather than random attempts to fit pieces together. (Puzzles that form a pattern, not a picture, have fewer clues and are much more difficult. These can be introduced once the child has been successful with picture puzzles.)
- To make picture puzzles: cut out a picture from a magazine and mount it on a square of poster board or cardboard. Cut it into two pieces. Make other puzzles: three, then four, and five pieces. Cut vertically and horizontally before using diagonal cuts or odd size and shape pieces. Remove a piece from a complete picture puzzle and ask what is missing.
- Eventually progress to letters and numbers. Begin with felt pieces that can be put together to form the whole number or letter. Progress to pencil and paper tasks.
- Provide drawings of common objects with one part missing. Have the child draw in the missing part (hand on a clock, sleeve on a shirt, tail on a dog).

Teach the child problem solving while introducing appropriate words and expressions

Provide practice with classification. Deciding how to organize (classify) objects is the first in a series of steps that lead to the ability to organize new information by relating it to a concept or idea learned earlier. Information is not readily recalled if it is not related to something else in our thinking. Begin by sorting objects, then pictures of objects, and then move on to events and experiences.

- Begin with objects that can be easily classified into two groups according to an obvious attribute: color, size, shape, texture, and, later, function (use). Eventually, sort according to a concept (all furniture, food, animals, clothing, etc.).
- Progress to sorting one group of objects in several different ways (first by size, then by shape, etc.).
- Once objects are sorted, introduce new objects to be placed in the appropriate group. Have the child explain why he/she placed them there.
- Games such as Old Maid and Go Fish provide classification practice.

Teach the child association and generalization skills used in classification, which may need to be practiced in order to establish connections between objects and ideas. This is basic to developing skill in abstract thinking and the language to support it.

- Play "Twenty Questions" or its variation. Show the child how to ask questions in order to figure out an answer rather than just making wild guesses. Begin with several pictures of objects that you show the child. Turn them over; draw one. This way, the child sees a chance of figuring out the right answer through questioning. Do not accept guesses until after questions about its attributes are asked, and then only accept guesses that could have been arrived at because of the questions asked. Point out the connections that have been established as you go.
- Take turns describing something for others to guess. The guess must be based on the description. This builds vocabulary skills, reinforces expressive language development, and reviews attributes used in classification and later in compositions.
- Play "What's Wrong Here?" Find pictures or make up a setting with something included that shouldn't be or obviously excluded that should be present. For example, set the table correctly except for clothespins on a plate or without plates at all.

CCD Remediation and Special Education

Does CCD constitute a learning disability in a school environment? This is a complex question. We have to distinguish between the legal definition of learning disability and the actual functional symptoms of this educational handicap. The definition of learning disability formulated under IDEA explicitly says that "the term does not include children who have learning problems, which are primarily the result of . . . environmental, cultural, or economic disadvantage." As we know, CCD is mostly the outcome of complex childhood trauma, educational neglect, and cultural deprivation. Therefore, from a purely legal perspective, CCD should not be considered the basis for special education services. On the other hand, CCD functionally presents a psychoeducational profile typical for a learning disability (LD) condition, most certainly creates an educational handicap, and powerfully contributes to learning impediments. If an IA child is found to have attributes of CCD, cognitive remedial goals with appropriate remedial methodology ought to be a part of his/her Individual Educational Program (IEP). Below is an example of cognitive education goals formulated for the student's IEP.

Clinical case: Ben, a 9-year-old third-grade student in regular education class, was adopted from Rumania at the age of 6 years. His general cognitive abilities, as measured by the school psychologist, are in the low average range with clear-cut symptoms of CCD.

Needs and goals #1. Ben will learn systematic note-taking to enhance organizational skills and bolster recall. **Methodology:** Ben will be taught how to use flow charts and diagrams, how to develop superordinate and subordinate grouping strategies, and how to condense information, "chunking" it into manageable units. Repetition is to be built into the lesson plan, particularly for new information being taught. Ben will be helped to develop rehearsal routines, in which he pairs new information with over-learned skills and knowledge. **Means of accountability:** A brief teacher's report on the progress and difficulties; work samples.

Needs and goals #2. Ben will improve verbal comprehension of complex instructions and questions, particularly those carrying multisequential information. In presenting verbal information to Ben, such as instructions or directions, a "verbal bracketing" approach is needed – a clearly defined set of instructions in a simple sentence structure. **Methodology:** The following strategies should be used by his classroom teacher and the teacher's aide:

- Stop your instructions at key points to check for comprehension.
- Give your instructions in more than one way, verbally and visually.
- Have Ben repeat the questions or instructions verbatim.
- Slow your tempo and wait for Ben to process and organize a response.
- Use gestures and visual signals; exaggerate the signals when the message is important.
- Recognize that Ben may misunderstand complex language (e.g., negatives, passive verb constructions, etc.).

- Ben will retell the instructions as he understood them, and then the instructor will repeat them again, correcting the bits Ben did not process.
- Help Ben feel comfortable asking questions when he does not understand.

Means of accountability: A teacher's report on the progress and difficulties.

Needs and goals# 3. Ben learns and implements methods of self-regulating himself within a task. **Methodology:** Ben should have self-regulation strategies explained and modeled for him by his teacher; Ben will then be guided in using these approaches and strategies. The teacher should assist Ben in developing tools and strategies that will help him perform the task with minimized assistance and guidance. **Means of accountability:** The teacher's report and a checklist that reflects Ben's ability to perform different assignments using learned self-regulating skills. Practicing learned skills in real-life situations should be organized as a part of his learning experience.

In conclusion, the developmental aspect of the CCD in IA children still needs to be investigated; for example, what are the age-specific character-istics of CCD and what are the early "warning" signs of this phenomenon in preschool children? We are only at the beginning of understanding this phenomenon, and parents and educators alike are facing a new frontier. With the international adoptees who do have CCD, an age-specific, thoroughly planned, and persistent cognitive intervention should be applied to reverse the detrimental trends in their intellectual and academic performance.

Cognitive education, particularly in the field of remediation and special education, and specialized language therapies appear currently the most promising approaches in the educational treatment of cumulative cognitive deficit in international adoptees. Intensive focused research in this area is urgently needed to verify the effectiveness of these methodologies and guide our practical recommendations. In order to make remedial treat-ments more effective, the uniqueness of international adoptees should be taken into consideration, and existing methods should be appropriately modified and adjusted to meet the challenges presented by this group of students in our schools.

CHAPTER 6

Language Remediation of Internationally Adopted Children

Learning a new language is an inevitable part of being adopted internationally. For many IA children, this is a distressing experience related to an abrupt loss of the native language and a relatively slow acquisition of another language in a situation of ongoing stress of adjustment to a new physical and sociocultural environment. Early childhood is the most critical time for language development. Upon extraction from a birth language environment, every IA child goes through a radical change of the social situation of language development, and many IA children may need support and remedial services to help effectively develop the new language.

Language is a psychological function that mediates many other psychological competencies, such as perception, memory, cognition, social interaction, and goal-directed behavior, just to list a few. From the psychological perspective, there are four major domains of direct language application as a means of communication, behavior regulation, learning, and as a main medium of thinking/cognitive operations. Language is an effective psychological "tool" for addressing consequences of early and ongoing trauma, building cognitive capacities, and forming social competencies. It has multiple applications and must be considered in any therapeutic work and remedial programming for IA children.

Language can be acquired in a spontaneous and natural fashion; it can be learned in a systematic and planned way or can be mastered as a combination of both. The IA children master a new language as a by-product of life and shared activities with native speakers. They do receive formal instruction in their new language at school, but teachers are only one source of language acquisition, while adoptive parents, peers, media, and culture at large are the most influential facilitators of language learning. When IA children enter an unknown cultural and linguistic environment, learning a language for them is no less than a survival skill: they have to acquire communicative language for normal functioning as the entire process of adjustment is mediated by language. New language acquisition is the most crucial skill to be learned by IA children in their first year in an adoptive family.

A vast majority of IA children are not bilingual: they are monolingual on arrival, for example, as a 5-year-old girl with Chinese as her only language; and after several months, they are monolingual again, this time with English only. The IA children can be called "sequential" monolinguals because after a short period of transitional "bilingualism," they are returned to the status of monolinguals for all practical purposes.

The IA children are an extreme case of the so-called "circumstantial" language learning: they are forced by the social situation of development to acquire the language of their new motherland, and they do so in a context in which their own first languages have no use. The motivation to acquire a new language is much more intense in international adoptees than in bilingual children from immigrant families. The adoptive family is the primary source of patterns of proper English, while the same family cannot be a sustained source of the native language. Due to this situation, the native language of an adoptee quickly loses its functionality and personal meaning.

Language attrition in IA children is the process of losing their native language, which, if not in use, stagnates (it does not develop, stays "frozen" at the level of the initial entry to a new linguistic environment), the process of attrition begins and quickly speeds up; finally, the first language disappears for all practical purposes. In a few weeks in children younger than 4 and in several months to a year in children in elementary school, the native language loses its functionality and cannot be used for communication, behavior regulation, learning, and reasoning. The abrupt first language attrition has a set of negative consequences discussed below.

Social/communicative language and cognitive/academic language are two aspects of a new native language for IA children. Communicative language refers to the language skills needed for social interactions in everyday events within a practical and familiar context. It requires basic skills in pronunciation, vocabulary, and grammar. Communicative fluency is highly contextual and is supported by extralinguistic means, such as gestures, facial expressions, intonation, body postures, and so on. This aspect of language seems to be acquired naturally and without formal schooling.

Cognitive language refers to language as a tool of reasoning, a means of literacy, and a medium for academic learning. The mastery of cognitive language requires specific conceptual and semantic knowledge of the language itself. This language function emerges and becomes distinctive with the formal schooling and development of literacy skills. Communicative language forms first and serves as the base for cognitive language acquisition. In children adopted after the age of 5, the order of learning language skills is broken: soon upon arrival, they enter school and must learn the understanding, speaking, reading, and writing skills of their new language simultaneously.

In the context of international adoption, language as a behavior regulator presents an extremely important factor that explains many aspects of IA children's social functioning. Behavior regulation utility of language is responsible for the control and management of other people's actions, as well as self-regulation of a person's own behavior. Slow language development plays a role in behavioral difficulties, demonstrating high comorbidity of language impairment with behavior problems. Children who are unable to communicate effectively may not have the necessary skills to negotiate or resolve conflict and may have difficulties understanding and relating to others.

A nonstimulating environment of early language development in IA children makes them a high-risk group for later language disorders and delays. Thus, some of the most common notations in the orphanage-based medical records of children ages 5 and up are "delay in language development" and "speech and language disorder." Sometimes a specific diagnosis is indicated, such as *dysarthria* (faulty speech articulation) or stuttering (repetition of parts of words or prolongation of a sound out for a long time). With poorly developed native language, IA children face the challenge of learning a new one, as the initial delay in the first language means that a less supportive foundation for English language learning exists (Carter et al., 2005).

Confusion with the Assessment of Language in IA Children

The reported findings in the study of language functioning of older international adoptees after adoption are inconsistent and have a wide variability of outcomes. This situation poses a question about the standards that are appropriate and valid for identification of language problems in IA children. A separate issue is a differentiation between language impairment and temporary difficulties in a new language learning. In general, the results of the research on speech and language functioning of IA children are so divergent and conflicting that Glennen ends up with a call to better understand (Glennen, 2016, p. 148): "... who was assessed, what was measured, and the 'lens' used to view the results." Unfortunately, after many years of international adoption on a large scale, we still do not have a clear understanding of the nature of language problems in IA children.

One common ground is that the majority of specialists consider IA children to be an "at-risk" group for language development. As stated by Mason, Stallings, and Worthman (2000, p. 134), "nearly half of adoptees older than 3 years have language delays." The rate of referrals for speech and language services among IA children, after the English language became their only functional language, is statistically significantly above expectations for the population at large (Glennen, 2005; 2007a, 2007b; Eigsti, Weitzman, Schun, DeMarchena, & Casey, 2011; Gauthier & Genesee, 2011; Genesee, 2016). Even in children adopted from different countries before their second birthday and after living in the adoptive family for at least 2 years, the rate of referral for speech and language services was from 22 to 35 percent (Mason & Narad, 2005; Glennen, 2005; Geren, Snedeker & Ax, 2005). This is significantly higher than the 2- to 8-percent rate reported in the general preschool population, ages 3–6 (Glennen, 2007b). With "older" children, adopted at school age, the rate of referral goes as far as 30 percent to nearly 60 percent (Mcacham, 2006).

A major challenge for speech and language pathologists is the fact that IA children do not follow a typical pattern of language development observed either in monolingual or bilingual learners. As a result, standardized testing designed for these populations is not an accurate representation of language abilities in IA children (Scott, Roberts & Glennen, 2011). A skillful language pathologist would be able to differentiate signs of an emerging language in the English language learners from the signs of language disorder. However, it can be a challenge with IA students: at any point in the process of second language learning, an IA child may appear to be language-delayed or language-disordered due to nonlinguistic difficulties in mastering the new language. Thus, limited expressive and receptive vocabulary, odd phonology, incorrect syntactical and morphological structures, strange pragmatic skills, word-finding difficulties, and so on can be signs, which are common in both typical and language-disabled English language learners (ELLs). As found by a speech pathologist specializing in working with international adoptees (Glennen, 2008, 2009), "atypical" signs of language disorder in IA children may include a history of delayed language development in the native language, a slower rate of English acquisition in comparison with classmates in the ESL class, persistent problems with pragmatics (social language) even after more than 2 years of living in the English-only environment, persistent use of single words or short sentences responding to questions, and difficulty communicating with parents in the family.

Some IA children presented with an important phenomenon that has emerged rather unexpectedly for the parents and teachers: there was a noticeable decline in language capacities of IA students in the middle and high school. A number of research publications suggest that, while there are impressive advances in early language learning, delays may become evident when IA children must use their language to accomplish more complex academic and cognitive tasks (Gindis, 2004b, 2005, 2019; Goodman, 2013; Glennen, 2014a, 2015). This is a particularly typical trend for those children who were adopted relatively late, at school age (Hough & Kaczmarek, 2011; Scott et al., 2011).

The age of adoption has become a key factor in determining risks for language issues in IA children. Exposure to English before the age of 12 months is likely to result in minimal delays, according to Mcacham (2006). Language skills are strongly related to the age of adoption, with particularly important cutoffs at 12 months and 24 months; children adopted prior to 24 months have few delays, and children adopted later exhibit delays proportional to the length of time they were institutionalized (Glennen & Masters, 2002). For those adopted after 18 months, early expressive language predicts later language and cognitive abilities at 6 and 11 years (Glennen, 2005).

The older adoptees may experience significantly greater struggles in language learning. Overall, developmental outcome studies have been mixed (Scott et al., 2011). The preschoolers use language for everyday needs at home with caregivers, but as they reach the school age, language demands change in nature: the switch from social/communicative language to cognitive/academic one has to take place and many IA children reportedly have difficulty keeping up with this requirement despite their average conversational skills.

The Consequences of Abrupt First Language Attrition in IA Children

An abrupt first language attrition is likely to play a significant role in emerging English language delays and disorders, but this issue is the least researched aspect of IA children's language development. The potential harm that such rapid first language loss can cause is something that parents and educators alike need to be especially cognizant of. The swiftness with which IA children lose their native tongue and the profound nature of that loss are truly amazing.

In many parents' surveys and some research publications (Schmid, 2007; Pearson, 2008), the time frame of functional language attrition is tied to the age at adoption: the younger the child, the faster the attrition is completed. Our own study (presented in Gindis, 2019) of more than 700 children, ages 4–17, adopted from the overseas orphanages between 1990 and 2017 revealed a relatively consistent pattern of the functional language attrition for different age groups. Native languages in this study were Russian, Ukrainian, Chinese, Spanish, and Amharic (an official language in Ethiopia). The summary of these findings was presented in Table on page 22. Both processes, learning English and losing the native language, are the by-products of participation in a range of activities in the given social groups such as family, school, community, peers, and social media. In addition to age and the frequency of the native language use while living in an English-only environment, the initial low level of first language skills facilitates its rapid attrition in a situation when no practical need in keeping the language as a means of social interaction exists. It results in a lack of internal motivation to sustain the first language. There is one more powerful reason for a speedy native language attrition by international adoptees, which is practically never discussed – the trauma-related factor. The only exceptions are excellent works of Monika S. Schmid published in 2002 and 2012.

Indeed, this rather significant cause for a rapid loss of the first language, particularly in older adoptees, often stays under the scientific radar. The adverse trauma-related personal feelings and attitudes to a native language are essential to its maintenance or attrition. For an IA child, every aspect of life changes after the adoption: the food, the clothes, the language, the social milieu, and even something as personal as one's name could be changed. Language remains a single thread connecting adoptees to the past and often nightmarish memories of neglect, hunger, and abuse. The language is typically the only connection with those days of misery and suffering, and it needs to disappear as soon as possible because pain and sorrow are not the luggage one wishes to carry into the future. Subconsciously, language as the obvious link to the past is to be severed as soon as possible to preserve the mental health of the language carrier. Emotions are most likely a factor in any case of attrition, and they may play an even bigger role in language attrition than in language acquisition. Experts in the treatment of disorders stemming from traumatic experiences have long since identified language, even a mere sound of language, as a potential trigger of post-traumatic stress disorder (Schmid & Dusseldorp,

2010). This should not be a surprise because language is the single prevailing representation of a person's individual life history: it is the compelling link between the present and the past, and it is the most prominent "marker" of belonging to a certain ethnic and cultural group.

What are the psychological and social consequences of a rapid first language loss in IA children? The overall toll paid for the abrupt loss of the first language depends on the child's age and a host of individual differences. First and foremost, from psychological and educational perspectives, abrupt attrition of the first language is no less than an interruption in language development, when rapid attrition of the first language prevents transfer of basic linguistic skills from one language to the other. (See more on this subject in Linck, Judith, Kroll & Sunderman, 2009; Schmid, Köpke, & de Bot, 2012; Gindis, 2019.) For some IA children, an abrupt first language loss may intensify cognitive weaknesses and contribute to a cumulative cognitive deficit, discussed in the previous chapter of this book. Furthermore, language is a powerful tool for regulation of behavior, and when this tool is taken away abruptly, a set of inappropriate, regressive, immature, or clearly maladaptive behaviors can be observed.

It is important to understand from pedagogical, remedial, and psychological perspectives that the tempo of losing and of replacing language do not coincide in time: losing a language occurs much faster than mastering a new one. But the demand for major language applications – communication, behavior regulation, learning, and cognitive operations – remains as strong as ever. Problems with language are likely to have cascading effects on the academic and social functioning of IA children. That is why the rapid language attrition becomes a clearly trauma-producing factor, calling for systematic and appropriate help.

Due to the relatively slow emergence of functional English, adoptive parents are limited in their ability to regulate older IA children's behavior as they otherwise do for children, for whom language is a customary instrument of interpersonal interaction. For the school-aged IA children, lack of functional English in the first several months presents a significant educational challenge. It is manifested in numerous learning problems, showcasing cognitive weaknesses such as vanishing of basic cognitive skills with patterning, sequencing, discriminating, and so on; interruption in overall language development; and amplification of emotional and behavioral issues to the extreme. This leads to social and academic problems that could be addressed by educators and adoptive parents if the role of language as a regulator of behavior was properly understood.

Social/Communicative vs. Cognitive/Academic Language Acquisition

Eventually, all IA children – some sooner, some later – learn to communicate in English and master literacy skills to different degrees. Basically, the pattern of English language learning in international adoptees is the same as in other "circumstantial" English language learners: the communicative aspect of the language is acquired first and the cognitive/academic aspect develops later. However, the time frame and the overall dynamic of English language learning are quite different in IA children compared with their peers from immigrant families. Unfortunately, neither teachers nor parents realize that communicative fluency in adopted children in many cases is not transferable into cognitive language mastery, resulting in reading and writing problems years after the children are adopted.

Certain aspects of a language such as vocabulary and basic grammar structure are formed in IA students faster than comprehension of words with multiple meanings or mastery of age-appropriate reading and writing skills (Desmarais, Roeber, Smith, & Pollak, 2012). IA students showed impairments across several domains of language, particularly in the area of morphosyntax. Their utterances were shorter; their syntax was less complex as measured by several different methods, including the number of different complex structures produced. They also exhibited varied vocabularies, considering the set of distinct words they produced, as well as their use of pronouns. The finding confirmed in numerous publications is that the cognitive/academic aspect of a new language requires more time to attain and may present significant difficulties for the IA children. A deficiency in cognitive/academic language leads to learning problems with such subjects as reading, writing, and math that are heavily rooted in it. These difficulties may persist, failing to match comprehensive and relentless efforts of both adoptive parents and educational professionals to remediate such students.

English as a Second Language Methodology

From the sociocultural and educational perspectives, IA children belong to a large, mixed, and constantly changing group of population called English language learners (ELLs). This category of students consists mostly of children who were born outside of the United States and arrived in the country with their families, or were brought in by their adoptive parents, or were born to a language minority group in the United States and until school did not have much exposure to the English language. Most importantly, with the exception of internationally adopted kids, these children continue to use their first language in their families and sometimes in their neighborhoods. The majority of them are bilingual with one dominant language. The IA children, though a part of this diverse group, differ from the rest of the ELL classmates in many respects discussed above. But one common feature of all ELLs is that the members of this group are eligible for the English as a second language (ESL) instructions. Moreover, at present, English as a second language is a mandatory program for every non-English speaking child who enters the public school system in the United States (US Department of Education, 2020). Although IA children are automatically eligible for this educational service, their situation is radically different from other ESL students. Indeed, from the moment of the adoption, international adoptees live in monolingual (English only) families, not in the families where an "other-than-English" language is used. Actually, we have a unique and really paradoxical situation when students eligible for ESL have the English language as their sole home language! This changes the overall context of the second language acquisition and brings a possibility of enrichment at home and more active parental involvement in the process of new language learning. Probably for the first time in the history of ESL instruction, parents may act as teachers of and "language role models" for their children, with a home "follow-up component" of the classroom instruction possible. No wonder many adoptive parents demand that the ESL instruction for international adoptees be modified according to the special circumstances of their current situation. There is a call to create a developmentally appropriate and needs-specific ESL methodology for IA students that serves two concurrent purposes: to teach the English language and to remediate the deficiencies in language development itself (Gindis, 1998, 2004b, 2009). In other words, the ESL curriculum should be cognitive/academic and remedial at the same time: remediation should be intertwined with cognitive/academic instruction to compensate for language-related issues of IA children. The major issue, however, is that ESL teachers are not trained in remedial methods and speech and language teachers' involvement is needed (Gindis, 2004b, 2005).

Academic success depends on students gaining access to and comprehending the language of school discourse. In cognitive/academic language, used in the middle and high school, the vocabulary consists of words that are less frequent than those in everyday conversation, grammatical constructions are more complex because meanings must be made more explicit, and meaning is not supported by the immediacy of context and interpersonal cues (e.g., gestures, intonation). Therefore, the focus of ESL instruction for IA students should be on the cognitive/academic language and the specific preliteracy and literacy skills with less concentration on communicative aspects because these will be learned in the families through actual communication. If the ESL instruction assumes a remedial nature, the length of the program may be longer and the intensity of the instructions may be higher than in a regular ESL program. Following this logic, Chamot (2009, p. XVI) points to reasons for focusing on cognitive/academic language skills in the ESL classroom. Classroom teachers, she wrote, should not assume that ESL students already know appropriate cognitive/academic language when, in fact, ESL students have often acquired only social/communicative language skills. No wonder cognitive/academic language is not usually acquired outside of the classroom setting. Moreover, ESL students need assistance in using learning strategies with cognitive/academic language, just as they do with content knowledge and skills. For ESL students, the ability to use cognitive/academic language effectively is the key to success in grade-level classrooms: it provides the students with the tool of reasoning (cognitive operations).

As of now, ESL as an academic subject concentrates on teaching listening, speaking, reading, and writing skills (US Department of Education, 2017). However, after just one school year, the vast majority of IA students have fully functional social/communicative language. So, if an IA child after one school year in the ESL is not able to pass an exit ESL exam, it is very likely that this child needs remediation rather than continuation with the ESL in the next school year. After only one year in the English-only environment, the native language in the majority of IA students is not serviceable any more: the functionality of language as a psychological "tool" needed for social interaction, verbal communication, and learning has been shifted totally toward the English language. The continuation in an ESL class with a concentration on speaking and listening becomes a wasted time for students who already intensely practice these skills in their families. Moreover, ESL is usually provided on a pull-out basis, distracting IA children from other academic subjects. These children typically lack emotional stability and self-regulation to adjust to an additional distraction of being taken out of the general class and being singled out from their peers. We have to understand clearly that as of now ESL is not a special remedial service; it is an academic subject: it should not be used as a substitute for any special educational service or prevent the child from receiving such services. To rectify the problems arising in such situations, the parents should address them without delay. In practical terms, there are two consecutive steps here:

Get an affidavit: An adoptive parent should obtain a written note (affidavit) signed by a college-educated native speaker of the language. This can be a family friend (but not a relative), a teacher, a pediatrician, a therapist, and others. In this document, there is a statement that IA child's first language is nonfunctional any longer and cannot be used for school instructions, casual communication, or high-order reasoning and that the child has now only the English language available for all practical and educational purposes. Here is a sample of such an affidavit:

> *I, M. Johnson, a licensed chemical engineer, am a bilingual (Romanian/English) person with a native fluency and college-level literacy skills in Romanian language. By this written affidavit I confirm that Mihai, DOB: 3/31/2013, does not have a functional Romanian language. In no way can the Romanian language be considered as a means of communication, behavior regulation, or academic learning and remediation for this student. At this time, Mihai can be taught and tested psychologically and educationally only in the English language.*

Write a letter to your school principal with a request for your child to be removed from the ESL program.

Write a letter (always opt for a written documentation) to the principal of the school, where you introduce the IDEA's definition of "native language" as a qualifying basis to request a psychoeducational evaluation for classification of your daughter or son as a child with disability, eligible for special education services. I suggest that in a letter a parents quotes the following abstract from the IDEA-Part B Code of Federal Regulations, CFR (§300.19):

> *As used in this part, the term native language, if used with reference to an individual of limited English proficiency, means the following:*
>
> (1) *The language normally used by that individual, or, in the case of a child, the language normally used by the parents of the child, except as provided in paragraph (a)(2) of this section.*
> (2) *In all direct contacts with a child, including evaluation of the child, the language normally used by the child in the home or learning environment.*

Please indicate that in your situation, English satisfies both (1) and (2) of the code. So, even your child is a student of limited English proficiency (LEP), his/her native language is English.

In the same letter, request that your child be removed from the ESL program concurrently with the need for a psychoeducational assessment.

This step is necessary because of your child's obvious delay with the English language as compared with other monolingual children. Just dropping an ESL program might be not enough for your child's situation, as it will not automatically improve the grasp of the cognitive language, even being more consistently exposed to it during the academic subjects.

Special Education Assessments and Services

In order to qualify for speech and language services, a student must have his/her language skills evaluated. The problem for many IA children is that by the time school authority comes to the conclusion that the student needs language remediation, the child had already lost the first language and is not yet proficient in English (this situation is presented in Chapter 2). In other words, the IA child has no language to use for valid testing but needs to be tested in order to get services. The IA children of school age, if suspected of having language issues, must be tested within the first month on arrival. If the child is known to have language delays prior to adoption, the adoption documentation can be used to help qualify him/her for the immediate speech and language services upon entering school. If this did not happen and the first language is not functional and cannot be used for testing, then the school has to accept the situation of having the student with only one language who is at risk for learning failure.

Cognitive/Academic Language Learning Approach (CALLA)

The school-age IA students face a number of obstacles as they enter formal school in the United States. The major one is learning academic content in the new language, which implies understanding of academic discourse, writing coherently, and speaking at an advanced level. One of the most effective methodologies in building the foundation in cognitive/academic language in IA students is the Cognitive Academic Language Learning Approach (CALLA – Chamot, Barnhardt, El-Dinary, & Robbins, 1999; Chamot, 2009). In my professional opinion, although not designed for IA students specifically, the approach fits this body of students in our schools as no other remedial method.

Based largely on findings in cognitive psychology, the CALLA integrates cognitive/academic language development, content area instruction, and explicit directions in cognitive learning strategies for both content and language acquisition. CALLA offers detailed lesson plans that integrate academic content, cognitive/academic language, and learning strategies. These lessons rely heavily on scaffolding or the provision of instructional supports when concepts and skills are first introduced and modeled; the gradual removal of supports takes place as students develop greater proficiency, knowledge, and skills. Chamot and her colleagues have compiled extensive instruction materials and guidelines in the format of lesson plans and worksheets (Chamot et al. 1999; Chamot, 2009). CALLA was designed to meet the needs of ELLs who have developed social communicative skills through exposure to English-speaking environments but have not yet developed cognitive/academic language skills appropriate to their grade level. What is important to note, a minority of IA students with a history of formal education in their native countries may have acquired cognitive/academic language skills in their native language, but they need assistance in transferring concepts and skills from their first language to English – and CALLA delivers such provisions.

The CALLA model can best be described as having three goals and five stages in reaching these goals. The three interrelated components include (a) selected content topics, (b) development of cognitive/academic language based on the content, and (c) explicit instruction of learning strategies that aim at the content and the language. During the implementation of the CALLA model, instructors (e.g., speech pathologists) are expected to follow five steps: preparation, presentation, practice, evaluation, and expansion. Specific language development activities are selected from four types of tasks: (a) easy and contextualized, (b) difficult but contextualized, (c) context reduced but easy, and (d) context reduced and difficult. It is suggested that, depending on the level of the students' functioning, language development tasks should move from type (a) to type (d), which are cognitively demanding and context-independent tasks representative of mainstream content courses beyond the upper primary school levels.

What is really to be appreciated in CALLA methodology by everybody working on remediation of IA students is the learning strategies that are grouped under three headings: metacognitive, cognitive, and socio/affective strategies. Metacognitive strategies include strategies such as planning, selective attention, self-monitoring, and self-evaluation. These strategies (in fact, the self-regulation skills so needed by all IA students) are applied to both language per se and the subject-specific knowledge and skills. Instruction in metacognitive strategies is aimed to improve awareness of and control over the learning process. Through CALLA methodology, the students are explicitly instructed in metacognitive strategies that will give them the skills to utilize prior knowledge, organize information, retain and apply knowledge in various contexts, and reflect upon their own involvement in the learning process.

In fact, using CALLA methodology, IA students learn English as a by-product of studying an academic subject such as mathematics and social studies. The ESL teachers can construct language development activities based on the topics selected so that learners develop content knowledge and learn new concepts as they grow in their ability to use English as a learning tool. A major assumption underlying the CALLA model is that learning occurs through dynamic mental processes and should have practical orientation through the inclusion of a number of useful "psychological tools": tables, iconographic material, diagrams, charts, and lesson plans containing helpful information.

In my view, as a remedial specialist working with IA students, the GALLA methodology is a perfect blend of cognitive psychology, linguistics, and remedial teaching. It uses *scaffolding* (the five-stage model emphasizes a gradual shift of responsibility from the teacher to the learner); *flexibility* (the instructional sequence is flexible and occurs in cycles rather than in a fixed linear manner); *transference* (the students are systematically encouraged to apply what they learn to new tasks and new contexts); *overlearning* (the content, language, and strategies are presented in the cycle and are repeated); and *integration* (all the three components mentioned above are smoothly integrated: language and strategies are taught to learn the language for the specific content).

In conclusion, the language functioning of the IA children is significantly predetermined by the traumatic events of their past, the abrupt attrition of their first language, and a stressful situation of their new language absorbing. This is a unique psychological experience that is not fully researched and understood. For many IA children, difficulties with new language mastery result in cognitive, academic, and self-regulatory weaknesses. Remediation and scaffolding of language development are a necessity for many IA students. One of the best-proven remediation approaches in building cognitive/academic language in IA students is CALLA – a well-established methodology that went through several empirical and research verifications (Chamot, 2009).

CHAPTER 7

Academic Remediation of Internationally Adopted Children

In all modern societies, schooling is the main activity for children ages 5–18. School as an institution for academic learning and social ascertaining plays a major role in a child's life and powerfully influences all other domains of a child's existence. School years are expected to be a productive and content part of childhood, but in reality, school is often the main source of frustration and stress for a child. For students who are being disruptive, hurtful, or chronically conflicting, the schooling brings "toxic" stress. Education in our schools presents particular difficulties for internationally adopted children. They are not ready for this experience from many perspectives and are so emotionally fragile that they are traumatized when pushed by expectations beyond their reach. An academic "profile" of IA children adopted at school age (after their fifth birthday) includes many signs of learning impediments such as diminished or lack of intrinsic motivation for learning or achieving in learning activities; constant forgetfulness of learned material; difficulties with transfer of knowledge and skills from one situation to another; lack of age-expected learning strategies; immature self-regulation of learning behavior; poor concentration and limited attention span; and other learning predicaments described in dozens of research publications (Gindis, 1998, 2005, 2019; Dalen, 2001; Meese, 2002, 2005; Dole, 2005; Tirella, Chan, & Miller, 2009; Beckett, Castle, Rutter, & Sonuga-Barke, 2010; Julian, 2013; Zill & Bradford, 2018). These observable patterns of learning behavior often predefine academic failure, reinforcing low self-esteem, lack of interest in studying, and constant frustration associated with learning efforts.

Stating that school learning is the major activity in childhood and adolescent time, I am not diminishing the role of interpersonal interactions as a formative psychological factor in the adolescent period of development (ages 11–18). Moreover, this premise is at the foundation of the BGCenter four-level model. But in the case of international adoptees, who often lag behind at schools due to their background (neglect and trauma) and inability to fit in educationally, culturally, and emotionally in the school environment, for the majority of them, school and school-based learning are a constant source of failure and new traumatic experiences, which negatively affect their social life, peer interaction, and even mental/physical health. In other words, poor school performance and unsuccessful interpersonal interactions are closely connected and feed each other in a negative way.

The Overview of Academic Functioning of IA Children

In order to consider the academic functioning of IA children, we have to determine the criteria for judging academic performance. In the majority of research reports, the following benchmarks are used:

- Academic grades reported by teachers
- Results of standardized academic achievement tests in reading, math, and writing
- Number of referrals for special education academic services
- Special education placement according to educational classifications
- Retention or delayed entry to school due to "readiness" issues
- Teachers' and parents' surveys

This is a rather diverse set of benchmarks; therefore, one can expect a wide range of findings and judgments regarding the academic performance of IA children. Surprisingly, there is a relatively uniform conclusion that IA children perform significantly below norms for their grade and age when compared with nonadopted peers and they have substantially more school-related behavior problems. Thus, in the meta-analysis of over 70 studies, van IJzendoorn, Juffer, and Poelhuis (2005) found that about 13 percent of IA children in North America were referred for special education placement compared with five and a half percent among their nonadopted classmates. A number of other studies completed within the last 15–20 years in North America and Western Europe have found that by middle school, nearly half of international adoptees either had educational classifications reflecting their academic handicapping conditions or were placed into special education programs, or had, on average, 2–4 years of different special education services (Meese, 2005; Tirella et al., 2009; Zill, 2015, Thomas, 2016, Werum, Davis, Simon Cheng, & Browne, 2017). Teachers reported that IA children lag behind nonadopted classmates in academic achievements as measured by academic tests, capacity to learn independently, participate in school-based academic activities, and develop productive peer relationships (Zill, 2015; Helder, Mulder, & Linder-Gunnoe, 2016; White, 2017).

The Puzzle of the Middle School Academic Difficulties in IA Students

What is really unusual and so far not explained is the phenomenon of school problems of IA students surging in middle school, where IA children experience an increased stress from greater cognitive, academic, and behavioral demands as they advance up the grades. Zill (2016) called this phenomenon "a puzzle of the middle school," and this finding is supported by the existing statistics: a substantial number of international adoptees who did not have any diagnosed educational disabilities in the early grades were diagnosed with different educational problems in the grades six through eight (Dole, 2005, Welsh, Andres, Viana, Petrill, & Mathias, 2007; Welsh & Viana, 2012; Thomas, 2016; Zill & Bradford, 2018).

The consistent review of school performance of "older" international adoptees reveals that during kindergarten and first grade, sometimes even during the second and third grades, many IA children are not much behind their classmates. And then something happens that I termed as "the middle school academic plunge" (Gindis, 2005, 2009, 2019): the sudden drop in reading comprehension between grades six and eight and a further decline in all language-based subjects through the middle and high school. Thus, in the early elementary school grades, about 30 percent of adoptees need academic support, special education services, and special education placement. But by the middle school (eighth grade), a staggering 60 percent of IA students need educational support (Zill, 2015, 2016, 2017, Zill & Bradford, 2018).

One of the possible contributing factors to this phenomenon could be difficulties with cognitive/academic language described in the previous chapter. There is a longitudinal study, "The Reading Crisis: Why Poor Children Fall Behind" (Chall, Jacobs, & Baldwin, 1990), that describes the "grade 4 plummet" among students from the low socioeconomic groups. Chall and her associates have completed extensive longitudinal studies of various aspects of cognitive abilities as well as associated social factors to determine significant causal roots of this phenomenon and clearly pointed to insufficient cognitive/academic language as one of the major reasons. They wrote (p. 49),

> ... *the reading task changes around grade 4 from a focus on reading familiar texts where the task is one of recognizing and decoding words to one of comprehension of harder texts that use more difficult, abstract, specialized, and technical words.*

Thus, students who have developed fluent decoding skills can still experience changes from learning to read (grades one to three) to using reading as a tool for learning (grades four and up) (Cummins, 2003, p. 4). Anyone reading the book authored by Chall et al. (1990) will be amazed by the similarities between the students from disadvantaged families and international adoptees. But there is one huge difference: most IA children live in affluent families with educated and attentive parents who care about their health and school progress, who provide these children with massive remedial help, and who serve as models of standard English language. And still, by the high school, a significant number of IA students (more than half of this population) demonstrate both deficient cognitive/academic language and below grade placement academic achievement.

Causes of Success and Failure at School in IA Children

It would be practically important and scientifically instructive to find out why about one-third of international adoptees, presumably coming from the same damaging environment, have been doing well in school and socially mixed successfully with their classmates. Based on the existing literature, the following factors correlate with (but not necessarily are the cause(s) of) acceptable school performance.

Age of adoption: generally, the younger, the better, although adoption at a young age – before the second birthday – is not a guarantee of proper academic performance later. The decisive factor is that the time horizon for remediation is wider and the pattern of language learning is similar to population at large.

Country of origin: statistically, children adopted from China and South Korea performed academically better than same-age children from Russia, India, and Latin America. It is unclear why a vast majority of South Koreans were free from academic and cognitive problems (Seol, Yoo, Lee, Park, & Kyeong, 2016). The fact remains that the geography of adoption has relevance for proper academic functioning (Odenstad et al., 2008). It is possible that the quality of the orphanage system in the donating countries is a factor: this is particularly emphasized by some European researchers, who came to the conclusion that the better an orphanage system, the easier it is for adopted children to perform at school later in life after the adoption (Duszynski, Jonak, Garjaka, & Jankowska, 2015).

Gender: across the board, adopted girls performed academically better in school than adopted boys (Meese, 2005; Lindblad, Dalen, Rasmussen, Vinnerljung, & Hjern, 2009).

The question persists why so many IA children struggle so much in the Western school system although the adoptive parents and school personnel apply extraordinary resources, time, and patience to educate them. There were plenty of attempts to explain this phenomenon, and these explanations do make sense, to different degrees. Thus, a genetic endowment theory, supported by Miller (2005) and Zill (2015, 2018) and a number of other researchers, appears relevant. The parents adopting internationally cannot choose the genetic bequest of the children they adopt; most children available for adoption are likely to have a less favorable intellectual/academic potential than their adoptive parents. Significant intellectual stimulation and emotional encouragement provided by adoptive parents may not be able to overcome the limitations of the adopted child's genetic heritage.

The review of research literature (Gindis, 1998; Dalen, 2001; Beckett et al., 2010; Welsh & Viana, 2012), combined with parents'/teachers' surveys (Clauss & Baxter, 1997; Price, 2000; Hellerstedt et al., 2008), allows establishing the subjective and objective factors that negatively affect school performance of IA children. The subjective factors are as follows:

- Linguistic transition from one language to the other; weak native language foundation, followed by its abrupt attrition that negatively affects the cognitive and academic functioning (see Chapter 6)
- Limited or complete lack of academic readiness due to neglect/deprivation (see Chapter 7)
- Cumulative cognitive deficit in older adoptees (see Chapter 5)
- Maladaptive behaviors instilled by trauma and institutional life (see Chapter 1)
- Lack of motivation to achieve academically (see Chapter 5)

These factors are the consequences of educational neglect and repetitive stressful events that affected all domains of an IA child's life, including learning in school. Trauma affects learning through a number of venues. Thus, orphanage background shapes behavior through its impact on a child's aspirations, sense of efficacy, and personal standards of achievements. Many of the difficulties IA students encounter in school are closely connected to beliefs they hold about themselves and their place in the world: self-perception as "incapable" and school-related anxiety constitute significant obstacles for their successful learning. The desire to be on known and manageable "turf" rooted in their early childhood experiences of insecurity is typical for many students with post-institutional backgrounds. This is an obstacle in the learning process: to be a good learner means to take risks, to step into unknown territory, to be sure of one's own ability to cope, and to be ready to accept help from an adult or more competent peer. Thus, emotional functioning can strongly affect the children's ability to concentrate on classroom work, to stay alert during lessons, to follow classroom routines, and to participate in classroom activities along with their classmates.

The objective factors for school difficulties of IA children are related to our schools as educational institutions: the presence of damaging misconceptions about IA children and their unique educational needs, inappropriate school placement, a continuous dilemma of providing remediation vs. mainstream education for IA students, and other issues discussed below. Aggregated, these objective factors constitute no less than an extension of traumatic experiences in IA children.

Academic Readiness in the Context of International Adoption

Readiness for school experience is one of the key issues in international adoption. School readiness is a structured set of competencies relevant to societal expectations for a certain chronological age (Kaufman & Sandilos, 2017). Readiness is always a range of competencies that may be roughly described as "deficient," "below average," "average," or "above average" in relation to the majority of a child's peers. Readiness is typically considered in relation to school entry of a young child (Duncan, Claessens, & Huston, 2007). However, in the context of international adoption, readiness really needs to be examined for all age levels as the "school-age" IA children are adopted from 5 through 17 years.

According to the "apple-or-coin" test used in the Middle Ages, children were to start formal schooling when they were mature enough for delayed gratification (self-regulation factor) and had the abstract reasoning involved in choosing money over a fruit. Since the Middle Ages, not much progress has been made in this domain: there are no selection criteria, universal tests, or even commonly agreed-upon set of standards that allow parents and professionals to decide whether a child is ready for formal schooling. Legally, the only requirement for academic placement in the United States is the chronological age of the child; thus, children must be 5 years old by September 1 (or January 1 in some states) for kindergarten entrance, 6 for first grade, 7 for second grade, 8 for third grade, and so on.

The concept of academic readiness is inherently controversial because children learn and develop at a different pace. For example, clear articulation may be achieved by some children by the age of 4, and others have it only by the age of 8, while the majority will speak clearly by the age of 6. All this is still considered normal by most speech pathologists (Bernthal,

Bankson, & Flipsen, 2013). The same goes for many self-help skills, decoding of printed words, following multiple directions, and so on. No wonder we see children with wide variations in their school-related skills in typical kindergarten through third grade.

There are four intertwined but still distinct domains of child's functioning playing a role in school readiness: (1) language as a means of regulatory function and the mediator of literacy skills, (2) cognitive ability to learn specific skills and knowledge, (3) academic or pre-academic skills and knowledge, and (4) social and emotional capacity to function in school as an institution and to participate in shared activities with peers. These four factors of school readiness, being powerful inhibitors or facilitators of learning, do not always develop in harmony: a child may be ready cognitively or language-wise but be very immature socially, or vice versa.

A vast majority of international adoptees, who joined the adoptive families after the age of 5, are not ready for school experience in all major domains of school readiness, such as general health and physical growth, gross/fine motor skills, language, cognitive abilities, pre-academic or academic skills, social skills and adaptive behavior, emotional self-regulation, and school-related motivation.

Language-wise, their readiness for school functioning is significantly below the age expectations. As presented in Chapter 6, remediation in academic/cognitive language deficit should go hand in hand with the process of second language acquisition in international adoptees.

Social skills and the ability to participate in shared activities are important indicators of readiness. The capacity to initiate, respond to, and maintain social interaction is a must in school due to the very nature of the school environment. With its emphasis on collaboration, teamwork, and project-based activity, school places a high demand on a child's social skills. In addition, a teacher–pupil interaction comes into play: social skills are needed to interact with an adult in a teaching position. Self-regulation becomes a major part of social/emotional competency: this is the basic requirement for functioning at school and an indication of the child's emotional and social maturity. Socially as well as academically, self-regulation is needed for what is called "goal-directed behavior." As presented in Chapters 1 and 8, emotional vulnerability in international adoptees in the school context makes them less able to tolerate stress as expected for their age, less capable of self-regulating their goal-directed behavior, and less self-sufficient in overcoming the emotional strain while competing in school (Julian & McCall, 2016).

Cognitive competence includes fundamental processes, such as classification, pattern detection, comparison, association, concept formation, detection of similarities and differences, regulation of attention, and so on. Many basic cognitive skills in typically developing children are formed in their preschool years through direct and mediated learning. These cognitive competencies further develop during school-based learning and form the base for math, writing, and reading proficiencies. However, in many school-age IA children, this foundation has not been formed due to educational neglect and deprivation in their preschool and elementary school years, and it is much more difficult for them to master literacy skills. Limited cognitive readiness affects the overall school readiness (this theme is discussed in Chapter 5).

Academic and pre-academic skills, as a component of school readiness, are usually measured by a wide range of standardized educational tests, with all their possibilities and limitations in terms of psychometric properties and practical utility. Clinical practice (see argumentation in Chapter 2) shows that these tests are grossly inappropriate for IA children: by default, children with an institutional background have a huge disadvantage compared with their counterparts living in middle-class families. As a result, they are delayed in regard to many pre-academic and academic skills and accomplishments.

Academic Placement of IA Children and the Concept of Bidirectionality

All adoptive families who brought home a child older than 5 face the issue of proper school placement. Inappropriate initial classroom assignments may have devastating consequences, both academic and emotional. A suitable classroom, on the other hand, is the basis for effective remediation, productive learning, and successful adjustment and socialization. In terms of older adoptees, some of them, even if they are 7 or 8 years old, might not have been exposed to formal schooling in their native countries. On the other hand, many of those who are older than 8 and who have had at least 2 or 3 years of formal schooling in the native country may have functional literacy in their native languages and may even be advanced in certain academic skills (e.g., math, as often seen in adoptees from Russia and China). General information in science, humanities, and so on may be limited or just different from American teachers' and parents' expectations. Graphomotor skills may be limited due to the lack of practice or may be age-appropriate or even advanced. Language development, as a rule, is delayed. Social skills, motivation, and emotional self-regulation are, typically, immature. Cognitive skills may be age-appropriate or delayed. Loss of native language, communicative vs. cognitive language dilemma in learning English, cognitive problems related to losing one language and acquiring another, and behavior/emotional problems related to adjustment – all these issues are typical for this group of internationally adopted children.

Creation of recommendations for proper school placement is a highly individualized process, based on the result of initial assessment, school resources, and child's mastered skills and personality. The school system has only one criterion for grade placement: the child's chronological age. School personnel argues that this standard has been working just fine for many decades with children from immigrant families. However, the nature of IA children's lack of readiness is very much different from what one can observe in children from immigrant families. The arguments of school personnel for the age-appropriate classroom placement usually can be reduced to a few related concerns. Thus, the school believes that the children must be with their peers because of social reasons: they need to have a role model of age-appropriate behavior. It would be difficult for IA children to get along with classmates who are 2 or more years younger, particularly in the middle and high school years. The school personnel speculate that there is no purpose in holding IA and immigrant children back from where they ought to be chronologically, as they may not do well that first year or two, no matter what the placement is. The more sophisticated school administrators use this argument: "Why artificially lower the requirements for a child who has already lowered expectations for himself/herself in an academic setting?"

On the other hand, the arguments for below age-grade placement are usually promoted by the adoptive parents. Based on their experience living with adoptees, they reason that IA children demonstrate delays and distortions in cognitive abilities, emotional development, and self-regulation. A post-institutionalized child of a certain chronological age may be much younger developmentally and functionally. Many of them behave like younger children, regulate their emotions and motivation like younger children, and have cognitive skills and academic knowledge below their chronological age expectations. The parents believe that their children should be placed at school with their real, not "ideal," cohort. In order to recommend and create an optimal learning environment, we have to match the child's actual readiness with the level of instruction and social requirements of the school grade. Therefore, considering an appropriate educational program for IA children, we have to take, as a reference point, their actual level of functioning. If this level is below their chronological age, they are to be placed accordingly to ensure a positive school experience, which is the prerequisite for long-term school success. IA children, due to their past history, are particularly vulnerable to stress associated with school performance. Exposing them to this stress on a level that they are not able to handle may result in emotional/behavioral problems that adversely affect the whole family. A mismatch between the child's learning capacity and academic placement is a recipe for a traumatic school experience. It is not right to start the life of a child newly arrived in America with frustration and failure.

Current options for the IA children who are "not ready" for the age-appropriate school experience, in their parents' and teachers' opinion, include delayed entry to kindergarten or first grade, retention for another year in the same grade, lower-grade attendance, enrollment into an "inclusion" or "transitional" class, or special education placement.

The major pitfall of the current school readiness practices in relation to IA children is rooted in the belief that readiness is totally within the child, and he/she is required to demonstrate readiness before entering the school system or a specific grade. When the parents and educational professionals decide that the readiness resides solely in the children's properties, and if the age-appropriate placement is clearly unsuitable, they have to restrict themselves to the three options mentioned above: delayed entry (for preschoolers), below the age-appropriate grade placement, or special education arrangement.

However, there is another perspective on the issue of school readiness, discussed in the Winsler and Carlton (1999) publication, which is very relevant to the situation of international adoptees in our schools. The paradigm is called the "bidirectional approach," implying that readiness resides in the child–school interconnectedness. Within the bidirectional approach, a child and a school are considered as an interconnected entity adjusted to each other. Let us consider the criteria for such interconnectedness in the context of IA children's readiness.

Child-referenced criteria may include chronological age, which is an important but not a decisive factor; general health; language development; social skills and ability to participate in shared classroom activity; self-regulation; age-appropriate cognitive competence; and specific school-related academic or pre-academic skills.

School-referenced criteria may include experience with international adoptees, quality of the ESL program, support services within regular education, availability of remedial programs outside of special education, range of special education programs and services, and, last but not least, the willingness of the administration and teachers to accommodate an IA child's unique needs.

School professionals and adoptive parents are to consider all these factors in their mutual relevance: placement decision needs to be based on careful consideration of all elements listed above in the context of child/school interconnectedness. For many IA children, particularly those adopted at school age, academic placement below chronological age in combination with remedial programming (in or outside of special education) is the right way to go: we have to restore the foundations before proceeding to teach more advanced academic skills to reverse the damage done to IA children's learning capacity in the past. Many, if not the majority of IA children adopted after the fifth birthday, require remediation before entering the mainstream education classroom.

The Issue of Retention

Still another emotionally charged dispute between the schools and adoptive parents is the issue of retention. There are no research-based published studies about international adoptees and grade retention, but according to a number of parents' surveys and clinical practice reports, it appears that IA students are retained significantly more often than their nonadopted peers.

There is comprehensive research on the topic of "retention" vs. "social promotion" in population at large, and the objective findings favor neither retention nor social promotion: both have advantages and disadvantages. The Light's Retention Scale – Fifth Edition (2015) (LRS-5) is often used to assist parents and school professionals in making decisions about promoting or retaining a child. As a practitioner, I found this questionnaire useful and helpful for the IA students. The easy-to-use form identifies specific areas of concern, including the child's age, emotional maturity, life experiences, level of intelligence, behavior, and more. The Light's Parent Guide includes a concise statement of important factors used in decision-making. The administration of LRS-5 helps adoptive parents carefully review their arguments and judgments in retention decisions; this instrument is designed specifically to be used as a counseling tool during parent/teacher conferences.

Specifically, the LRS-5 data can help the adoptive parents to formulate their arguments in obtaining approval for retention by the school authority. These data may show if their child belongs to the "at-risk" category, and proposed retention would serve the goal of preventing the development of a full-fledged educational handicapping condition. Some IA children may need extra time to create the foundation in basic cognitive processes and academic skills that make possible their progress in the mainstream curriculum on the next grade level. Another argument may be made about the IA children's emotional vulnerability, which typically transpires in LRS-5 data. An extra year in the grade would promote the IA child's emotional maturity and self-regulation. What is crucially important is that, in addition to retention per se, IA children must have a comprehensive and structured scaffolding system to address the emotional fragility. They should not be exposed to undue stress facing a challenge that is beyond their actual readiness as their progress in social and emotional functioning is as important as in the academic area. The more positive the school experiences are, the greater the chances for long-term school success.

The decision about retention must always be highly individualized as potential negative effects may outweigh positive outcomes. Retention should be considered as a "strong medicine": it should be considered only in the instances where there is a solid likelihood that the child will benefit academically, socially, and emotionally. And the most important is this request: in order for retention to be as helpful as possible, it must be accompanied by supportive remedial services, obtained either through the special education department or within the general education.

Retention vs. Special Education

In many cases, the issue of readiness for an appropriate school experience is confused with the issue of eligibility for special education services. There are cases when an international adoptee may not benefit from mainstream age-appropriate schooling due to a specific learning/language disability or pervasive developmental delay. Under these circumstances, being delayed entering kindergarten, being held back in the same grade, or being placed in a lower grade may lead to many negative consequences. Merely retaining a child with a genuine educational disability may not help at all. Too often, parents and school districts alike prefer to use a notion of being "developmentally not ready" instead of a classification for special education. The "wait-and-see" position is typical for many school districts in relation to testing international adoptees for special education services. We have to realize that if a child has an educationally handicapping condition and no remediation, it is, in fact, a continuation of the same educational neglect that this child was exposed to before adoption. In other words, although entry to formal schooling (kindergarten) may be postponed for some solid reasons (health, severe language delay, etc.), this "readiness" option must be contingent on the availability of an extensive system of remedial services. There is no "one-size-fits-all" recommendation, but the general rule of thumb is the following: if a child is functioning more than 3 years below his/her chronological age or a child has a specific identifiable disability, this child may need special education services rather than retention or other "readiness" options.

Damaging Misconceptions about IA Children in School

The promotion of a bidirectional approach in developing the academic readiness of IA children requires that school personnel be properly informed and liberated from many misconceptions about IA children. Here are just a few major notions that are common for the general public and school personnel but have no basis in reality:

- IA children are considered similar to children from recently immigrated families and therefore should be educated the same way, placed academically according to their chronological age, and taught English as a second language the same way. Parents would be generally advised to "wait and see" how their children adjust to the new social/cultural and school environment.
- IA children are seen by the school personnel as "bilingual." This leads to many unfortunate consequences in terms of remediation, when ESL instructional services are considered as the means, often the only one, of addressing IA children with language and learning issues. School staff continues to believe that IA children "keep" their language and fails to consider that an abrupt language loss and its cognitive and academic consequences lead to an educational handicapping condition in some children.
- School personnel often think that no psychoeducational testing should be done before an IA child learns English. This is in direct contradiction to the major educational law, IDEA-2004 (34 CFR 300.532(a)(ii), that states that "tests and other evaluation materials used to assess a child are provided and administered in the child's native language."
- There exists a widespread belief that difficulties, both academic and behavioral, are solely due to the IA children's institutional background and no learning or other disability exists, rather than the consequences of being raised in an orphanage. Loving families, good nutrition, and consistent schooling are all these children need for recovery.
- The IA children adopted at school age should continue their education from the grade level they were in their native countries. This specific

misconception is particularly damaging because it leads to a grossly inappropriate school placement. The grade placement in the country of origin should not serve as a base for the school placement in the United States/Canada educational systems. It is likely that adopted children have significant gaps and breaches in their academic knowledge base, assumed to be present in children of their age who were raised in a biological family. No significant transfer of academic skills from the native language curriculum to the American curriculum should be expected. In my clinical experience, providing psychoeducational testing of internationally adopted children from Eastern Europe and the Russian Federation, in particular, I found that too many of the school-aged children in reality performed from two to four grades below their claimed grade placement in their native countries when tested against the standard curriculums in these countries. Several years of deprivation and educational neglect result in the majority of IA children having an astonishing lack of age-appropriate academic skills and the ability to regulate their internal psychological processes. These children are very much in need of remediation along with education, and it is often a big mistake to decide on their school placement based on the placement in the country of origin.

Abovementioned false assumptions are truly damaging for internationally adopted post-institutionalized children, depriving them of needed help and support in education. All children who fall behind age-expected norms in school functioning deserve immediate intervention, but for IA children, it's crucial: only a few of them can catch up on their own. For most of them, early intervention is the only thing that will keep them moving along; without such a scaffold, they are doomed to failure.

Academic Remediation for IA Children: Math, Reading, and Writing

In this chapter, the focus will be on academic remediation, which is designed to scaffold a student who lacks basic learning skills and academic knowledge to achieve expected competencies for continuation in the mainstream educational process. Remedial programs are not the same as special education programs. Remedial programs are suitable for students who do not have an identifiable learning disability, while special education is designed to meet the needs of students with the diagnosed educational handicap. Students, who did not learn the material the first time it was taught, may need a reteaching, or an alternative approach, or modifications to the lessons, or just more time to complete assignments. Federal law (IDEA-2004) strongly supports remediation within the general education settings (34 CFR Sec. 300.116(e)).

There are two attributes that are common for the remedial and special education programs: (1) both require specialized instructions that are different from mainstream teaching and (2) both are taught by specially trained teachers. Remedial education teaches the material in a different way from how a student was taught the first time around by including pre-teaching, repetitions, practices, and instructions in a small group setting, thus providing for more individual attention (Ehri, Dreyer, Flugman, & Gross, 2007; Slavin, Lake, Davis, & Madden, 2011). Effective remedial programs in schools often include extended school year (ESY) instructions. Although the ESY option is designed for special education students, remedial services during summer vacation prove to be extremely useful for IA students.

There is a widespread professional judgment, which I fully support, that remediation for the IA children is to be multisensory, that is, visual, auditory, and tactile-kinesthetic (Snowling & Hulme, 2012). Multisensory teaching/learning theory states that students learn more productively if they are taught using more than one sense (sometimes called "modality"), such as visual, auditory, kinesthetic, and tactile, to enhance learning. Presented below are the specific remedial techniques and recommendations used for more than two decades at the Center for Developmental and Cognitive Assessment and Remediation, known as BGCenter New York and Arizona (www.bgcenter.com), for the IA children ages 5 through 17.

Remediation in Math

One of the methods proven to be successful with IA children is Stern Structural Arithmetic (Stern & Gold, 2007). Educational practice has shown that the application of Stern Structural Arithmetic leads to positive results because the dependence on the abstract concepts is kept to a minimum and most learning is achieved through a direct multisensory experience. The teacher is provided with a wealth of different tryouts and games from which to choose, according to the individual needs of the child.

There are other multisensory methodologies, such as Touch Math (http://www.touchmath.com/), Hands-On Manipulatives (http://www.hand2mind.com/resources/why-teach-math-with-manipulatives), and the Math Perspectives curriculum (http://www.mathperspectives.com/) that have proved their effectiveness in remedial work with IA students. All these methods, in addition to being multisensory in nature, use the "scaffolding" approach, which is the most appropriate for IA students. Both automaticity and processing speed of math operations in IA children could be successfully trained through the Kumon methodology (McKenna, Hollingsworth, & Barnes, 2005, see also http://kumongroup.com/eng/about-kumon/method/). Learning basic arithmetic facts to the point of full automaticity is a prerequisite for successful math remediation of IA children.

Mathematics has its own vocabulary that is truly "terra incognita" for many IA students even after more than 2 years of attending the school. The words and their meanings need to be specifically taught as an IA child is unlikely to learn them incidentally. Teaching key math terms as a specific skill rather than an outcome of basic math practice is essential for an IA child. Math terms may include words such as "sum," "difference," "quotient," "proper fraction," and so on and should be listed and displayed in the classroom to help jog an IA child's memory during independent assignments. For an IA child, it may take repeated teacher's modeling, patient reminding, and much practice to utilize these techniques.

The IA students should not work on a large number of math problems without feedback from the teacher prior to completion and without a period of guided practice. They need regular reviews of the previously covered material. The modeling should be present in steps designed to increase skill in comprehending a computational process. The teacher should demonstrate how to solve a problem while verbalizing the keywords associated with the step, and the IA student performs the step while verbalizing the keywords and looking at the teacher's model. After that, the student completes additional problems with the teacher's model still available.

Remediation in Reading

Based on parents' and teachers' reports, different reading remedial programs centered on the Orton–Gillingham approach (Sayeski, Earle, Davis, & Calamari, 2019; see also https://www.ortonacademy.org/resources/what-is-the-orton-gillingham-approach/) proved to be the most effective with the IA students. The contemporary versions of the Orton–Gillingham methodology are multisensory, structured, sequential, cumulative, and rather flexible in their application. The Orton–Gillingham teaching sessions are action oriented with auditory, visual, and kinesthetic elements reinforcing each other for optimal learning (Shaywitz, 2003), which is essential for the IA students.

The most well-known Orton–Gillingham-based remedial reading program is the Wilson Reading System (WRS, Harrison, 2015). It is a twelve-step remedial reading and writing program for individuals with language-related learning difficulties. It directly teaches the structure of words in the English language, so the students master the coding system for reading and spelling. In WRS, the rules of reading in English are presented in a very systematic and cumulative manner, and it is manageable for the majority of IA students. Visualization techniques are used for comprehension (see more at www.wilsonlanguage.com). Fluency and comprehension of reading/writing skills are emphasized in WRS, and criterion-based assessment, built into the program, tracks the student's progress. Reading comprehension skills include summarizing, paraphrasing, predicting, and drawing inferences. In this method, spelling is taught through specially arranged dictations, in which students practice encoding of the spoken language. WRS provides explicit teaching of the rules of the language that are necessary for comprehending, remembering, and communicating academic and social information. This remedial approach provides not only direct remediation in basic academic skills but is concurrently aimed at developing organizational skills, work habits, and regulation of attention. In my clinical practice, I have found WRS to be one of the most efficient for IA students: all BGCenter reading tutors were Wilson-certified teachers.

There are other multisensory remedial programs that proved to be successful with IA students (Ehri et al., 2007; Slavin et al., 2011), among them:

- *Project Read* (http://www.projectread.com), which teaches reading and writing concepts and skills to adolescents in the mainstream classrooms as well as in special education using multisensory methods.
- *Specialized Program Individualized Reading Excellence* (also known for its abbreviation S.P.I.R.E.; http://www.epsbooks.com/SPIRE). It is a multisensory intervention reading program for struggling readers in grades K through eight based on Orton–Gillingham philosophy.
- *Slingerland Multisensory Approach* (https://slingerland.org/Home) is, in my opinion, probably the most "orthodox" adaptation of the Orton–Gillingham approach. It is used today both as a preventive and remedial methodology. It is practiced in small groups and in one-on-one setting with students ranging from primary grade children to adults. Simultaneous, multisensory teaching strategies are incorporated into every facet of the lesson. All the language arts skills – oral expression, decoding, reading comprehension, spelling, and written expression – are taught with the one integrated direct instruction approach.

Students are given guided practice in the functional use of these skills with the goals of independent reading and writing.

- *Sonday System* (https://www.winsorlearning.com/sonday-system-1) presents systematically structured detailed lesson plans for both remedial reading intervention and intermediate/advanced reading instruction based on the Orton–Gillingham approach. This methodology was used mostly in our Arizona center and proved to be very efficient with older IA students.

Remediation in Reading Comprehension

Reading comprehension is often understood as a process, which integrates (1) decoding skills, (2) vocabulary knowledge, (3) prior knowledge of the topic at hand, and (4) relevant strategies to make sense of a text (Kintsch & Kintsch, 2005). Thus, reading comprehension remediation is traditionally presented as a set of mental strategies that can be practiced and mastered (Wanzek & Vaughn, 2007; Hulme & Snowling, 2013).

Problems with reading comprehension are typical among older IA children. Comprehension difficulties usually emerge around the second grade and are magnified in the fourth to fifth grade or later. This often comes as a surprise for the families, as these children do not show any noticeable reading skills deficits up to this moment. In my view, the roots of their reading comprehension problems can be traced to four major issues:

1. Lack of cultural context awareness. The context awareness is a function of the length of exposure to the new international adoptees' culture. This process takes time and is subject to individual differences.
2. Lack of or ineffective deployment of strategies (cognitive processes and skills) necessary for a speedy reading understanding.
3. Emotional problems related to developmental trauma that block cognitive processes involved in reading activity.
4. Individual differences in cognitive and language development (e.g., learning disability) that may require different types of instructions for reading comprehension.

A lot more research would be required to quantify and describe the interrelations between these aspects of the IA student's reading skills development, but in practical terms, the separation of these aspects may help approach each of them via specific methodologies that already exist.

My observation of reading issues in older IA children is that while the minority may be poor decoders (and without speedy and accurate decoding, no effective comprehension is possible), the majority of those IA children with reading comprehension problems are functional decoders but still fail to understand what they read or what they hear during classroom instructions.

What is important to understand is that when IA students do not know the meaning of the words, they cannot figure it out from the context as many of their classmates routinely do. What is even more important is that they fail to identify implications or make conclusions from the text. Inferences are important because practically any text omits certain information that is assumed to be known to the reader. Here is a good example offered by Willingham (2017, p. 2):

> *Take a simple sentence pair like this: "I can't convince my boys that their beds aren't trampolines. The building manager is pressuring us to move to the ground floor." To understand this brief text the reader must infer that the jumping would be noisy for the downstairs neighbors, that the neighbors have complained about it, that the building manager is motivated to satisfy the neighbors, and that no one would hear the noise were the family living on the ground floor. So, linking the first and second sentence is essential to meaning, but the writer has omitted the connective tissue on the assumption that the reader has the relevant knowledge about bed-jumping and building managers.*

I came to the conclusion that the major means of reading comprehension improvement is in the overall cultural education – the familiarity with general cognitive context and the context of a specific subject, like chemistry or history. Without such prior knowledge, an IA child will not be able to understand the text even with the help of cognitive techniques. Cognitive skills in reading comprehension are mostly effective when the general context is readily available to a student. Stating this, I by no means deny the usefulness and effectiveness of comprehension strategies tutoring. (See Oakhill & Cain, 2016 for a comprehensive review; Willingham, 2017.)

Remediation in Writing

Among many interventions in writing techniques tried at BGCenter from 1996 to 2016, the Self-Regulated Strategy Development (SRSD) (Graham, Harris, & Troia, 2000) appears to be the most productive for the IA students grades four through nine. With SRSD, students are explicitly taught writing strategies and self-regulation procedures such as goal-setting, self-monitoring, self-instruction, and self-reinforcement.

The objectives of the SRSD approach are to assist students in mastering the cognitive processes of planning, producing, revising, and editing written text; to develop the ability to monitor and manage their own writing; and to form positive attitudes toward writing and themselves as writers. The sequence in presenting the SRSD methodology includes the following components:

- The teacher and the IA student discuss the strategy. This includes providing the rationale for the strategy, explaining each step, and pointing out mnemonics. For example, on an opinion essay, the child may plan what to say using the **TREE** strategy – **T**opic sentence, note **R**easons, **E**xamine reasons, and note **E**nding.
- Using the SRSD methodology, the IA student will employ the strategy and self-regulation procedures in the process of his/her independent writing.
- The teacher provides as much support as needed at each step, from initial modeling to final observation of the student's independent performance. The teacher needs to be flexible: the child may progress at his/her own pace. The teacher should offer encouragement and point to evidence of the child's progress in writing. SRSD is not a "prepackaged" model: it can be individualized for each IA child.

Classroom Accommodations

As I mentioned before, remediation goes hand-in-hand with compensation. One of the most popular compensations is different forms of classroom and testing accommodations. The goal of classroom accommodations is to introduce as much individualization and structure into the classroom environment as possible in order to reduce performance-related anxiety and to organize effective learning processes. An accommodation does not entail changes in the curriculum for an IA student. It changes the way the teacher presents information and the student practices new skills, or the way the teacher tests the student. An accommodation makes it possible to succeed in learning, but it does not guarantee it for the student; however, an absence of an accommodation or inadequate one could make success difficult or impossible. Classroom accommodations are a useful means of adapting the general classroom environment toward the child's needs and should be consistently implemented. The accommodations have to be written into the child's IEP or

504 Plan. Here are sample classroom accommodations for Maria, an 11-year-old IA student.

- Maria has to gain bi-sensory attention. Therefore, it is important to gain Maria's visual and auditory attention before speaking with her. Emphasize important information using intonation and stress. Repeat important words when necessary.
- It is beneficial to work out a cueing system to help Maria become aware of times when she is not paying attention. These "pre-tuning" techniques help focus Maria's attention on the upcoming subject. Use words such as "listen," "ready," and "remember this one." Before giving instructions, stand close to Maria, use Maria's name, and gently tap Maria's shoulder, or use another cue to make sure you have Maria's attention.
- Mark transitions between activities by clearly identifying the new activity by naming and explaining the sequence of steps needed to accomplish the task. A clear completion of an activity may be accomplished by briefly summarizing what Maria should have achieved before transitioning to the next activity.
- Provide preferential seating, placing Maria near the teacher and away from competing or distracting noise sources (windows and doorway), and provide a quiet study/work area, such as a study carrel for individual work, testing, or tutoring. This helps minimize Maria's problems in foreground/background discrimination.
- Repeat a direction and allow ample response time. It may be necessary to repeat each step of the instruction and allow time between each step for Maria to process the information.
- Emphasize keywords when speaking, especially when presenting new information. By substituting words and simplifying the grammar, the intended meaning may be conveyed and understood more easily. Encourage Maria to ask for clarification. It may be necessary to rephrase the information to ensure that Maria has fully comprehended the task.
- Have Maria repeat the content of the instructions to provide comprehension feedback. This technique allows the teacher to see which parts of the instruction need to be corrected or repeated. Ask for verbal accounts rather than a "yes" or "no" response. Reinforce listening for *meaning* rather than *exact repetition*.
- Maria should be given adequate time to comprehend and complete tasks. Avoid giving penalties for not completing assignments in the

prescribed classroom time. Whenever possible, give Maria additional time in the resource room to complete the assignment. It may be necessary to allow Maria more time to formulate responses to verbal questions, especially questions that include comparisons, generalizations, and explanations requiring lengthier and more complex language organization.

Testing accommodations are the alterations in the way a test is administered or the student responds. The Individualized Education Program (IEP) team makes decisions about which test modifications are appropriate for a student. Test accommodations may include changes in the time allocation for the test, or when and where the test is given, or how the assignments are presented. In general, no test accommodation should be recommended for an IA student unless he/she has had an opportunity to use it during the instruction. To be fair to an IA child, and to get the best measure of proficiency, the instructional and test-taking accommodations should correspond. Test modifications have to be introduced, periodically reviewed, and adjusted by the IEP team as needed. Please see more on this subject in Gindis (2007).

Special Education Options for IA Children

An IA child may have any of the thirteen educational classifications listed in the major federal law IDEA-2004 (Individuals with Disability Education Act, reauthorized by the Congress in 2004), or a combination of two or more of those conditions. According to BGCenter statistical data, the educational classifications, most often received by the IA children, are in descending order: Other Health Impaired, Speech/Language Impaired, Learning Disabled, Emotionally Disturbed, Multiple Disability, and Autism (Gindis, 2009, 2019).

Special education provides specialized placements and related services designed to meet the unique needs of students with disabilities. The continuum of special education services in public school – from less to more restrictive – is based on the degree and specifics of the child's disability. Following the comprehensive and focused psychoeducational or neuropsychological assessment, the following specific questions about an IA child's educational needs ought to be answered:

- Does the child qualify for educational classification?
- What is the most appropriate educational placement?
- What are the goals of remediation?

- What are the methods of remediation?
- How should progress be measured?

Proper understanding of the answers to these questions is the basis for the organization of the needed support system for the IA children at school. The school's legal obligations to children with any of the recognized educational handicaps must be spelled out in the child's Individual Educational Program (IEP). IA students with the recognized special education needs may remain in a regular education class with so-called supplemental special education services, such as speech-language therapy, counseling, physical or occupational therapy, orientation and mobility services, school nurse services, assistive technology services, and other appropriate developmental or corrective support. Please see more on this subject in Chapter 3.

In conclusion, one of the lessons learned within the 30 years of international adoption on a wide scale is that many, likely the majority of IA children, need remedial instructions; a significant minority that has educational handicapping conditions needs special education services; and some need special education placement and services. Intensive, focused research in this area is urgently needed to verify the effectiveness of existing remedial and special education methodologies to guide our practical recommendations for IA children. In order to make remedial treatments more effective, the uniqueness of international adoptees should be taken into consideration, and the existing methods should be appropriately modified and adjusted to meet the challenges presented by IA children.

CHAPTER 8

Creation of Social and Cultural Competence in Internationally Adopted Children

Maintaining Cultural Heritage in IA Children – Myth or Reality?

It is great to have roots, as long as you can take them with you.
Gertrude Stein

"Being proud of cultural heritage and maintaining first language" in IA children is one of the controversial, issues. As it often happened to other "obvious" things in human societies, there exists neither a commonly accepted understanding of what "culture" we are talking about nor a clear vision of its influence in the process of international adoption. Before discussing this issue in the context of the mental health of international adoptees, I would like to clarify some notions and terms, often found in the domain of "culture acquisition" and "culture keeping."

There are many definitions of culture, but for the sake of clarity, let us agree on the understanding of culture as a man-made environment (Vygotsky, 1987–1998) that has many different elements and presents individuals' and groups' way of life, such as customs, values, arts, religion, cuisine, folklore, fashion, holidays, aspirations, attitudes, and so on. For our purposes, it is important to understand that culture serves as a regulator of behavior; we act and judge the conduct of others according to certain cultural norms. On the one hand, culture creates a "template" of our own behavior with many automatic elements that we often do not consciously recognize. On the other hand, culture creates the "lenses" through which we perceive the world, and it gives meaning to everything we experience. As the *Concise Guide to Cross-Cultural Psychiatry* (Gaw, 2001, p. 5) says:

> *Culture defines the guidelines that provide a contextual basis for our lives. It is through this cultural lens that our own as well as other's thoughts, feelings and behaviors are interpreted and shaped. Culture acts as a buffer of meaning ... provides a great storehouse of ready-made solutions to problems.*

For the public at large, the word "culture" has a mostly positive connotation, with a few exceptions, such as "prison culture," or "gang culture," or "orphanage culture."

In the case of older international adoptees, adoptive families and children initially represent different cultures, and their relationships will be affected by these differences. During the adjustment period (from several weeks to several months, depending on the child's age at adoption), these cultural differences are very noticeable. It is up to the adoptive parents to understand them and not to allow them to undermine the relationships. Older adoptees may experience no less than a culture shock – a sense of confusion and uncertainty resulting in anxiety that may affect their perception of a new and alien, for them, environment. Cultural shock is likely due to the encountered new language, overload of information, technology gap, the old skills and knowledge not being applicable in a new environment, and many other reasons. Cultural shock in the adoptive parents is typically caused by certain cultural expectations and cultural differences found in the following:

- *Expression of emotions:* Giving hugs and saying casually "I love you too" is almost an automatic behavior in many families in the United States. Not so for children from other countries, where reservation and timidity in expressing feelings is a normal and expected behavior. To say "sorry" and "excuse me" when you unintentionally push someone is also culturally determined behavior; a child from overseas may express his/her feelings in a different way, for example, saying "oi" and giving you a "guilty" look. In general, the expression of feelings is more controlled and contrived in many foreign countries.
- *Interaction with adults:* In children coming from countries of Eastern Europe and China, there is a strong understanding of the "social distance" between an adult and a child. A child should never treat an adult as a peer and is expected to always maintain this distance by understanding the roles and responsibilities.
- *Interaction between genders:* The notion of gender equality may not be an everyday reality to some foreign children. Certain expectations and "roles" could be attached to "male" vs. "female" behavior.
- *Manners and mannerisms in everyday life:* The way people eat, take bath, talk, accept help, or express disgust is different in different cultures; so, before being upset with the child's behavior, try to understand the cultural component of it.

Walking a Thin Line: Preservation of Cultural Heritage and Language

About cultural differences: "In Germany, unless something is permitted, it's forbidden. In the US, unless something is forbidden, it's permitted. In Russia, unless something is forbidden, it's compulsory."

In the United States exists a popular idea of preserving one's culture and heritage. Multiculturalism has become one of the stereotypes of modern society, competing with the old notion of a "melting pot," where various customs mix together and produce the American way of life. One popular slogan is that of a "gorgeous cultural mosaic": the idea that one must both keep one's own customs and acquire the new traditions (https://sites .google.com/site/sheilasanchez900/english-11/-cultural-mosaic-vs-melting-pot). The idea that the IA children should keep their original culture and language in addition to acquiring the new language and cultural customs is, of course, a variation of the same popular mantra.

Most IA children were quite young when they were adopted, and they don't really have a "cultural heritage" beyond their orphanage experience. It is most confusing for them to be urged to keep something "alive" that really was not in the context of their lives there and isn't in their life in the United States either: on arrival, they are definitely "culturally deprived" children (Gindis, 2019). They've lived in poverty, in dreadful conditions, and in orphanages. They did not have positive role models and normal childhood experiences; they had been ignored or harshly regulated during all their lives. Such cultural "basics" as to how to sit at a table with a family, or how to come to parents for help, or how to behave in a store is terra incognita for the newly adopted children.

The adoption of a child older than 5 denotes the start of new socio/cultural imprinting while trying to erase the previously absorbed socio/cultural/personality experiences. A peaceful coexistence of two cultures in an adopted child is a myth: learning a new language in the process of the first language attrition is a good model of cultural "retraining": new culture enters the psychological space not to exist peacefully with the old culture, but to aggressively push it out, wipe it out, and delete it. Just as it takes time to learn a new language, it takes time to understand and adjust to a new culture – not on the surface, but internally, and most of the IA children will do it eventually.

As for the "keeping culture" paradigm, the reality is that the parents of international adoptees will never be able to reproduce the cultures these children had lost (Jacobson, 2008). There is absolutely no way to provide the kind of cultural authenticity and intensity they would have had in functional families in the countries where they were born. With the exception of living after the adoption in a thriving ethnic community, where cultural tradition and identification are authentic and consistent, there is no way to make up for the loss of cultural environment for the IA children.

Orphanage Culture: Do We Need to Cherish and Retain It?

In the context of adoption, we must clarify what "culture" we are talking about. There is a particular "orphanage culture," which is a breeding ground for a specific orphanage behavior, attitudes, and personality's traits. The orphanage represents a microculture that exists within the macro-culture of the donating country. This micro-to-macro interdependency includes a number of intermediate subcultures of a particular region, ethnicity, age group, and so on. Adoptive parents may think about the great Chinese culture, but their adopted children experience a specific culture of their regional orphanage; the remainder of the orphanage life may be painful, bringing to memory suffering, hunger, and abuse. Life within the orphanage culture facilitates the development of specific survival skills, reflected after the adoption in the post-orphanage behavior of the child (Gindis, 2019); it also forms certain attitudes and moral norms, hardly compatible with family life. As an example, let us take the phenomenon of "entitlement," which is a product of orphanage culture and reported by many adoptive parents.

The dictionary defines the word "to entitle" as to "furnish with a right or claim to something." A sense of entitlement is normal for a child at a certain stage of human development: when a 15-month-old demands whatever he/she sees around for his/her possession, it is a natural and passing stage of his/her growth. However, for a 9-year-old, it is not appropriate developmentally: a child should have learned by this time to balance taking and giving. Typically developing child by a certain age should learn that desirable goods (e.g., toys) normally come as rewards for achievements or presents given for certain events (birthday, Christmas, graduation, etc.) and not just because the "thing" exists and "I want to have it." When a child whines and screams, demanding a new toy advertised on a TV ad or new pair of sneakers he/she observed his/her classmates wear, this is an incident of entitlement-driven behavior. The children raised in orphanage culture have this feeling of entitlement on a much greater scale and much longer in life. Due to the very nature of life in orphanage, when goods and services are coming from "out of the blue" and are distributed seemingly evenly to all only because they belong to the group, it produces in orphanage inmates the feeling of entitlement. They are used to the notion that if one member of the group has something (say, is given a pencil and a notebook), the other members of the same group are supposed to get the same, and it does not matter if they need it or deserve it. While a sense of entitlement is the unfortunate result of poor parental techniques in children raised in the families, in the orphanage residents this is a survival skill predetermined by the very nature of institutional care. While a child raised in the family sooner or later will understand that a "thing" in his/her possession is earned or given as a good will gesture from parents/relatives/friends, an orphanage-raised child perceives it as something he/she is entitled to possess and therefore must have it. It is only one small step from the feeling of entitlement to obtain a thing through theft, robbery, or deception.

There are many other artifacts of orphanage culture affecting post-orphanage behavior of a child, such as "self-parenting," "hypervigilance," "proactive aggressiveness," "extreme attention seeking," and "indiscriminate friendliness with strangers," which are described in the literature (Gindis, 2019). To be fair, there may be certain positive features in a child's attitudes and behavior, stimulated by the orphanage culture as well, such as the higher value of self-help skills, motivation to please adults, and being highly accustomed to the order and routine. Former orphanage residents are often good at helping adults with home chores. They usually accept the routine in the house when it is timely and firmly established. Moreover, the lack of routine may be upsetting for them.

"Does My Past Have a Future?": International Adoption and Cultural/Language Heritage

The intentions behind "keeping the child's culture" are noble: diversity leads to social tolerance. Still, this is a rather controversial recommendation from the perspective of cultural adjustment and the mental health of an adopted child. What is the cultural identity of a Gypsy child from a Romanian orphanage who was mistreated just because she was a minority? Or a 9-year-old, neglected in an Estonian orphanage simply because he was ethnically Russian? Or a Tatar boy from the Ukrainian orphanage, teased for his almond-shaped eyes and dark skin? For an American social worker and for most adoptive parents, a Romanian Gypsy is a Romanian.

The same goes for the Estonian and Ukrainian children, even though these children themselves are acutely aware that they are not welcomed in those countries because they are "different" from the "natives." What "culture" should be saved and reinforced in the ethnically Russian children adopted from Kazakhstan, who speak mostly Kazakh, but who were made very aware that they are not Kazakh people? When adoptive parents consider teaching their child about cultural issues, they have to understand the entire subject first and foremost from their child's perspective and weigh the consequences for their child's mental health and emotional well-being. Consider this parent's testimony:

> My adopted son Gregory is a Kalmyck, which is yet another ethnic minority from the Caucasus area in Russia. He looks Asian, but came from Russia at the age of 7. He fiercely resists when people call him Russian. He said he was teased and beaten up by older children in his orphanage because he was not Russian. I told him, just before his Bar Mitzvah, that he should be proud of who he is and he should love his Russian heritage. He got immensely upset and said 'It is not a good thing. I am American and I am Jewish.' My rabbi (we belong to a Reformed synagogue) keeps telling us that we have to respect his heritage and his culture. I am confused, indeed, because Gregory refuses even to hear about all this cultural stuff.

I remember a passionate plea from a 13-year-old girl adopted from Russia at the age of 9. She had quite a mature personality and a set of views along with a number of learning and social issues. "All I hear from them (the adoptive parents – BG)," she told me, "is Russian this and Russian that, how great is Russian language and literature. How many times do I have to explain them that I'm a gypsy? In Russia they treated me as dirt. Why the hell are they pushing it down my throat?" A situation like that creates hazardous grounds for mental health maintenance. This is the case when the parents' ideology conflicts with the mental health of the adopted child.

In general, the opposite point of view to keeping culture can be formulated this way: adoptive parents should be respectful of the child's cultural background but concentrate on the cultural traditions and norms of the country where the child lives now. That's what an IA child needs to understand to internalize productive socialization and peer acceptance. "Cultural camps" and "trips to the country of origin" are a mixed blessing, to say the least (Quiroz, 2012). They can be a trigger for psychological trauma and do not help in socializing here and now. The inept attempts of parents to keep the original culture of adopted children can be an obstacle to their children's current acculturation. The appeal to honor internationally adopted children's heritage and their sense of identity sounds nice, but the problem is that neither the children nor the parents can pinpoint, let alone keep and support, this elusive identity. Based on my 30 years working with international adoptees from different countries, I fully agree with the statement of Quiroz (2012, p. 542) about this faulty "culture keeping" practice that she sardonically called "cultural tourism":

> . . . cultural tourism results in "staged authenticity" or the misrepresentation of culture. Staged authenticity threatens the development of a healthy identity. The transnational profile can rarely be applied to adopted children who are unlikely to maintain ongoing contact with their communities of origin . . . . Consequently, the culture of origin of adopted children remains distant at best, replaced by a set of cultural productions that fail to capture the identity of origin.

"Forced Bilingualism" from the Mental Health and Educational Perspective

Preservation of the first language in an internationally adopted child is a "hot" topic for many adoptive families. The stories, like the one below, are very typical:

> We adopted our 8-year-old daughter Katerina from Russia two months ago. The question is: what can we do to help Katerina keep and develop her Russian language skills? No one in our family speaks Russian. This weekend, when our Russian baby sitter came over and helped her write letters back to her former orphanage, she noticed that Katerina was already starting to lose her recollection of written Russian: she was using English letters rather than Russian, and mixing them up. Obviously, my first priority is that Katerina becomes proficient in English, but if there's any way to keep her Russian as well, I'd love to do that. Any advice? Can we wait on Russian until she has English under her belt?

From the developmental and educational perspective, bilingualism is a two-edged sword: it may be a blessing for some and a curse for others. Generally speaking, for the healthy, well-adjusted, normally developing children, dual language mastery may facilitate their cognitive, language, and social capacities. In a child with developmental delays, language impairments, a background of educational neglect, cultural deprivation, and possible emotional trauma, second language learning may inhibit and complicate adjustment to the new family and society.

An IA child lives in a monolingual English-speaking family, not in a bilingual immigrant family, and in the vast majority of adoptive families, the native language will not be used by the adoptive parents. But the same family will provide this child with patterns of proper English. For most adoptive families, preservation of the first language is not a major priority: on the child's arrival, the concerns are about learning English, child's health, attachment, initial adjustment, education, and remediation, if needed. There is no place for preserving the native language as the first-order priority. By the time when adoptive parents are ready to take care of this issue, the native language is gone. This is a typical scenario for most adoptive families.

The exceptions may occur without special efforts, and sometimes they may be the results of planned and well-executed heroic efforts. For adoptees who are older than 8 at the time of adoption, are physically healthy, have age-appropriate language development and grade-appropriate literacy skills, have a positive attitude toward their native language, and have an opportunity to use it for practical purposes and receive an encouraging recognition of their special skills from their family and peers, the maintenance and development of their native language are possible, and bilingualism is a viable option. But that is an exceptional case, and exceptions only confirm the rule: in general, bilingualism and international adoption are not compatible. In a child who has language delays, is emotionally and behaviorally immature, or has learning disabilities of any sort, and, most important, has lived through severe adverse childhood experiences during his/her early formative years, the attempts to forcefully preserve the first language may lead to an undue strain and emotional and behavioral problems. The external reinforcement of the native language in a child who has a negative attitude toward that language, who resents the status of a "foreigner," and who has no need for this language for immediate survival purposes may be a recipe for a disaster.

Sometimes a sincere desire to preserve the native language and native country's cultural affiliation in their children motivates the adoptive parents to think about hiring a tutor or a native-speaking au pair to maintain the language. While in the majority of cases, these attempts are doomed to fail anyway, the issue persists, as the whole idea is very tempting: why to lose a skill that takes a great effort to build? Judge for yourself reading this real-life story.

A 40-something-year-old couple had adopted two girls from Guatemala: 7- and 8-year old, respectively. Within the first week, the parents hired a live-in native Spanish-speaking nanny, also around 40. From day one, the girls felt more at ease with their au pair: she served as a mediator between them and the parents. On the one hand, the girls clearly understood who their parents were. On the other hand, the mother–daughter bond formed with their Spanish-speaking nanny – their point of contact for all problems and the path of least resistance. Why struggle with English when the nanny understood them so much better? They came to her for permissions, thanked her for the cake, and hugged her good night. Not immune to warmth, the nanny developed feelings for the girls. And, as a good person as she was, she couldn't help changing this pattern. The help of a native-speaking caregiver definitely made life easier for this adoptive family in the short term, but this arrangement complicated life immensely in the long run. The live-in nanny took over the basic functions of a parent, without malicious intent, of course. Parents and only parents must be a source of comfort, security, and information for an adopted child from the very beginning and for many years to come. By placing another adult between themselves and their newly adopted children, the parents had invited serious problems with attachment.

The best course of action is to go together with the adopted child through the difficult phases of adjustment and language learning and to emerge from this period with the strengthened attachments and naturally acquired language skills in English, rather than attempting to "save" the first language. The bottom line is that bilingualism is not an option for the majority of internationally adopted children. It is more productive to concentrate on developing and facilitating mastery of their newly found mother tongue – the English language.

Culture and Trauma: How Native Culture and Language Serve as Post-traumatic Trigger

The road to hell is paved with good intentions.

Every social worker molded by the American education system says like a prayer that we must embrace and accept our cultural heritage, incorporating it into our everyday life. On paper, these ideas do look just fine, but I must admit that in many cases, I witnessed this approach is detrimental for the mental health of international adoptees. Cultural artifacts along with native language can be, potentially, a post-traumatic stress trigger for many IA children. Even toddlers associate their pre-adoption language with the orphanage and English with their family life. The memory of the orphanage with its rules and patterns of behavior and poorly understood remote regional customs is not necessarily something an adoptive family needs to cherish to help their child fit in their new sociocultural milieu. In the pre-adolescent time and particularly during adolescence, there is a great desire to merge with the mainstream and be like peers; any deviation from mainstream leads to isolation and an inner sense of inferiority and shame. A natural desire in such cases is to hide all differences and erase every indication marking an adolescent as an outsider. I already mentioned the native language as a possible trigger for a post-traumatic reaction. It is a well-known fact that adoptees from practically any country (with the possible exception of Latin America) often bluntly refuse to speak their native language or, at least, are not comfortable when they hear their native language. There are, of course, some individual differences and exceptions. Below are a few parents' testimonies, who adopted their children from Eastern Europe, which was for almost 14 years the second-largest source of international adoption in the United States. From a parent's e-mail message:

> *Neither of my children will speak Russian. My youngest, 12 was adopted at age 5 and has forgotten he ever lived in Russia. My oldest, 16, adopted age 9, has always refused to speak Russian. We even have friends with 3 adopted siblings the same age as my children. From the beginning, my daughter would answer in English, when spoken to in Russian. I was told by the professionals that she has too many bad memories of Russia, so don't push her. I haven't although it would be nice for her to be bilingual but her emotional well-being is more important. I think it is very common for many of our Russian adopted children to decide very quickly on arrival to renounce all painful conflicts over their dual-identity by rejecting Russian.*

From a parent's e-mail message:

> *We found out quickly that there is a very negative association with anything Ukrainian and our daughter wants to be as far from it as possible. I was disappointed in this finding because I thought it would be a really neat thing to be a Ukrainian girl and speak the language, but realized that was MY thinking and not HER experience or what SHE felt or needed. Bottom line, she's an American and why not completely embrace her being an American?! Being that she is an ethnicity that is not particularly embraced by the Russian/Ukrainian culture, gives even more understanding as to why our daughter had/has this reaction. Also, she, like any kid, does not want to be "different" and though we, as adults, think it is unique and special and wonderful, they as kids see and feel it much differently.*

From a parent's e-mail message:

> *My daughter is 11. I have a book about Kazakhstan where she is from and about her ethnic background and wanted to go over with her and read and show pictures. She could not care less. She said, I don't look like Kazakh or like those people in the book. She wants to be like any girl that lives around here and wants no part of her past. She rolls her eyes and throws temper tantrum when*

we try to teach her about her culture. She hates to be associated with her birth country and yells every time I say she is Kazakh girl: "I am an American girl, leave me alone". My question is: when would be a good time to get her into counseling to make it less painful for her to accept her culture? Should it be now or wait? Our social worker said we have to work out on this issue and make proud of her cultural heritage.

From a parent's letter:

I've decided for now to close the door on Russian culture, music, language, cartoons, food. My children were adopted at ages 6 and 8, in 2004 and 2005. I put a lot of efforts into keeping their cultural roots alive, going to festivals, buying CDs and books, etc. This I thought was important to their self-esteem and identity. I tried to keep their Russian language alive, and some acquaintances tried to give me a guilt trip that not enough effort was put into this intellectual luxury. Well, you know what, my children want nothing more to do with Russia. Russia was a place of sadness and hunger to them. They really don't want to be reminded, and they want to focus on life and success now. I am sharing this, so parents won't be surprised, and so they won't burden themselves with keeping up on this stuff if the desire or timing or interest is not there.

To conclude, for foreign-born adoptees, the notion of their cultural background is strongly linked to their experiences of past abuse, deprivation, and neglect. It is a controversial component of their struggle for identity in their new motherland. It is a part of their thoughts about the adoption itself and their relation to their biological family and their loyalty to the new parents and siblings. Those adoptive families who are eager to embrace the child's native culture and would try to learn the language, eat the food, and fill the house with the ethnic knickknacks should be careful with this endeavor not to trigger the unhealthy traumatic memories. With adopted children, even as young as toddlers, the language can be the link with the painful past, which most of the children would be more than happy to forget. Families should be aware of the fine line separating the need for preserving of cultural identity and the need for healing and moving on.

Social Competence and the Deficiency of Social Skills in IA Children

The age-appropriate and functional social skills are at the core of competence in interacting and communicating with other human beings. Social skills include a significant nonverbal component. The process of learning and interiorizing social skills is called socialization. Lack of such skills can cause social awkwardness, and children with poor social skills tend to have more behavior problems as they lack the tools that enable them to communicate, ask for help, have needs met in appropriate ways, get along with others, develop healthy relationships, protect themselves, and be able to interact with peers and adults age-appropriately (Tarullo & Gunnar, 2005; Palacios, Moreno, & Roman, 2013).

Social/emotional disturbances are among the most established and persistent socio-emotional sequelae of institutional rearing (Shannon, van Dyke, Hongjun, Vigil, & Walton, 2004; Tarullo & Gunnar, 2005). The surveys of adoptive parents (McCarthy, 2005; National Survey of Adoptive Parents, 2009) and research (Meese, 2005, Gindis, 2006, 2015, 2019; Juffer & van IJzendoorn, 2005; Gunnar & van Dulmen, 2007, Bruce, Tarullo, & Gunnar, 2009) suggest that a disproportionally large number of internationally adopted children fail to establish and maintain age-appropriate social relations during their pre-adolescent and adolescent years. Difficulties with peer relations are, in a certain way, their "trade-mark": teachers, parents, and international adoptees themselves uniformly report that too many IA children are less socially successful than their peers.

In all periods of childhood, but particularly during the pre-adolescent and adolescent years, peer interactions constitute the core of socialization and provide a feeling of belonging and self-validation, a context for self-disclosure and emotional security (Ryan, 2000, Thompson & O'Neill, 2001). Peer friendship is a form of attachment, while peer rejection and bullying are psychologically traumatic. Inadequate socialization causes adjustment difficulties, emotional instability, and anxieties (Cogen, 2008). Rejection by peers has a negative effect on a child's self-esteem and contributes to the development of loneliness and gloominess. Rejected children often gravitate toward one another, thus escalating each other's depressive or acting-out behavior. International adoptees have a tendency to associate with younger children, children with learning or behavior issues, and those who are the least popular (Shannon et al., 2004; Julian & McCall, 2016). If this issue is not properly addressed, the experiences of rejection may accumulate and form a foundation for emotional and behavioral problems. While international adoptees show at times amazing catch-up in many domains of adaptive behavior and learning, the socialization domain and social skills development are often remained substantially delayed or impaired. As presented in a number of reviews (Julian & McCall, 2016; Wolfgang, 2011), IA children have lower levels of social competence in comparison with parent-reared children. Social difficulties of adopted children may last into adulthood.

Caregiver–child relationships and interactions during the first several years of a child's life form the foundation of future social behavior. According to Julian and McCall (2016), children adopted before their second birthday have better social skills than those adopted after this age. Girls adopted as adolescents have particularly poor social skills (Julian & McCall, 2016). It was found that a later age at adoption is associated with a variety of social difficulties, such as interfamily relationships, disinhibited social behavior, lack of age-appropriate social skills, and poor peer interaction (Gunnar & van Dulmen, 2007; Merz & McCall, 2010).

Expert consensus in a number of research publications points to a so-called "latent period" in developing social problems: international adoptees tend to have social difficulties in adolescence more often than in preschool and early school years (Merz & McCall, 2010; Colvert et al., 2008). The adolescent time in IA children is characterized by a "step-like" increase in their rates of social and behavioral problems (Barcons et al., 2012). Parents, teachers, and service providers should be aware that social and behavioral problems may emerge during adolescence, even in those IA children who had problem-free childhood. I mentioned a "cumulative social deficit" phenomenon in a number of my publications in the past (Gindis, 2006, 2019): social problems may remain unnoticed until the adolescent time when hormonal changes cause traumatic memories and experiences to reemerge. Adolescence is the time when social and behavioral demands and expectations heighten, adolescents become more independent, and adults tend to pull back their support. The problems in the adolescent years reflect underlying deficits in certain basic skills, immature executive function, and emotion regulation problems that only become evident in behaviors that emerge later in development (Julian & McCall, 2016). Although there is a time span between the adolescence and pre-adoption traumatic experience, social/behavioral issues are the legacy of early childhood trauma.

The Causes of Peer Rejection: Subjective and Objective Factors

Peer rejection of an IA child may occur for a variety of reasons that could be grouped as mostly subjective (personal attributes of a specific child) and mostly objective, such as a lack of age-appropriate language skills and cultural marginality. The first group of factors is produced by complex childhood trauma and includes such psychological characteristics as mixed maturity in self-regulation, chronic hyper-arousal or dissociation, emotional fragility, and the learned survival post-institutional behavior. These personal attributes are deeply ingrained into an IA child's psychological makeup and require, in many cases, external help to overcome these traits after the adoption. As noted by their parents and teachers, the common base for rejection of IA children by their peers is their overt behavior, typically described as "aggressive," "quirky," or "inconsistent." Because of their immature and, at times, challenging behavior, IA children may require more supervision and thus are less likely to be invited to their friends' houses. Adoptive parents, in turn, are concerned about their child's behavior when they cannot monitor it, so they are also reluctant to permit play dates away from home. Rare after-school contacts do not facilitate companionship and offer no opportunities to develop the closeness between friends that encourages self-disclosure and the provision of emotional support.

Lagging social language development

For international adoptees, learning English is a survival skill. In less than 2 years after joining the adoptive family, most of the later-adopted children don't seem to differ from their peers in terms of their communicative language. They can chat about everyday subjects, and it appears as if they've managed to move on with their lives and blend into the new lingosphere. Alas, that is true only at first glance. A review of the recorded conversations of adopted children with their peers and parents (Gindis, 2019) reveals a lack of age-expected language mastery: their speech is full of circumlocutions, with at times wrong grammar; the content is supplemented with frequent fillers; word meaning comprehension may be extremely literal, and so on. (See Chapter 6 for more detailed analysis.)

In typical development, social interaction skills are mastered during the process of maturation without any conscious effort or formal instruction. Comprehension of the language of communication comes to native speakers simultaneously with the "reading" of nonverbal clues (facial expressions, body language, tone of voice, etc.) and the understanding of the context of communication (previous knowledge of the subject of conversation). There are, of course, individual differences in the level of proficiency and sophistication of a child's mastery of communicative skills, but there are certain societal expectations as well: we have different expectations for a 4-year-old and a 9-year-old, and we may easily recognize "immature" or "advanced" social language skills in a particular child.

Communication with peers increases dramatically during pre-adolescence and the adolescent years. The content and dynamic of verbal exchange are characterized by rapid topic changes, slang expressions, subtleties of irony and sarcasm that infuse peers' conversations, and, of course, by rich non-verbal language cues. Adolescents with limited language skills cannot efficiently participate in the rapidly changing, emotionally tense social language processes of peer groups (Turstra, Cicia, & Seaton, 2003). On the other hand, having well-developed, age-appropriate language proficiency highly correlates with successful peer interactions and friendship. An adolescent with good language skills is successful in detecting and using humor, sarcasm, persuasion, deceit, empathy, and flattery. In negotiation or conflict situations, the speakers can understand their partners' motives and collaborate to achieve a mutually acceptable outcome (Ryan, 2000). Unfortunately, too many IA adolescents lack exactly these social language skills.

Differences in cultural background and values

An older IA child's arrival to a new country is typically accompanied by confusion and anxiety. The children are often disoriented and overloaded with information they cannot process: a classical "cultural shock," full of misinterpreted social patterns and confusing situations. Their perception of basic social and cultural conventions can differ from their parents' and peers' perceptions. Cultural stereotypes are ingrained so deeply that both adopted children and adoptive parents don't perceive them as culture-specific but as a hindrance in interaction and communications. This process of entering into the family and peer group implies accepting, either consciously or subconsciously, the values, attitudes, norms, social roles, and manners of interaction that are prevalent in the targeted group (Ryan, 2000). It takes time to get rewired for the new cultural norms, and the duration of transition depends on age, social conditions, and individual factors, but eventually most adopted children do transition. However, cultural differences may affect peer relations months and years after adoption.

What Is to Be Done?

Basically, there are three ways to help IA children with socialization: direct teaching, mediated teaching (modeling), and the organization of the environment.

Pragmatics Development

Pragmatics (social language skills) is introduced through direct teaching and practicing: the IA child's parents and teachers should talk to him/her, explaining and practicing the use of double meaning expressions in everyday life (e.g., playing word-based games with the child), making sure the child indeed understands those expressions correctly. There are a number of special educational programs that facilitate social and cognitive language development. One such program, called SmartStart, was created specifically for IA children (see Chapters 5 and 6: http://www.bgcenter.com/smartstart.htm). This program stresses the utmost importance of adult mediation that the adopted children lacked in their early stages of learning.

Direct Instruction in Social Skills

It is necessary and possible to increase social interactions for international adoptees by explicitly teaching them specific, new, and culturally different social skills and values, raising their awareness of the need to see another person's perspective. Parents, teachers, and therapists may consider these methods:

- Taking the role of an instructor in friendship "know-how" by modeling, explaining, and practicing specific social skills such as greeting, parting, welcoming, declining, and so on according to the child's age. Model appropriate behavior when the child has classmates or neighbor's kids visiting him/her at home.
- Selecting skills valued by peers increases the odds of their use and reinforcement. Special attention is to be paid to social skills that are of critical importance, such as sharing, accepting criticism, giving and receiving compliments, taking conversational turns, respecting others' personal space, following directions, controlling anger, and so on. Skills teaching can be embedded into everyday life activities or become "special sessions" during "quality time" at home and in counseling sessions at the school or private office.
- Modeling how to be emotionally aware of another person's feelings by recognizing the child's emotions, listening to them empathetically, and trying to understand the situation from his/her perspective. Validating the child's emotions does not signify approval, just understanding. The appropriate interpretation of the emotions and the causes of these emotions could be instructive educationally and healing therapeutically.
- Teaching the child how to deal with bullies. Despite the schools' effort to prevent bullying, harassment can be subtle and still painful. Many typically developing children experience the stress of bullying and rejection; it is a part of normal maturation. The IA children, however, experience this stress to a much higher degree than can be considered "normal" (Bruce et al., 2009).

- Attempting to provide social skill analysis at an age-appropriate level, discussing with the child after the fact what the child did, what happened when the child did it, what the outcome was (positive or negative), and what the child will do the next time.

If an IA child has an IEP at school, social skills improvement goals should be clearly formulated and included in it. For example,

- John will understand and respond appropriately when others accidentally or intentionally do something he doesn't like (e.g., talking loudly, touching his things, etc.).
- When frustrated, John will choose and apply one of several prior scripted strategies of self-regulation and self-calming.
- When wanting the attention of another person, John will wait for the appropriate time to speak.
- John will share a preferred object or activity with peers upon request with minimal adult prompting.
- John will be taught how to understand and respond appropriately to unkind jokes.

On the Internet, there are many specialized social skills curriculums of rather high quality, applicable in the school, family, or community settings. Here are references to some of them:

- Social Skills Curriculum available at https://study.com/academy/lesson/what-is-a-social-skills-curriculum.html for students of all ages and developmental levels. The topics include communication, being part of a group, expressing feelings, caring for oneself and others, social problem solving, managing conflict, and listening.
- *TeachTown Social Skills* curriculum available at http://web.teachtown.com/clinicians/teachtown-social-skills/.
- *Social Skills Curricula & Programs* available at https://k12engagement.unl.edu/strategy-briefs/Resources%20for%20Social%20Skills%20Curricula%209-22-2014_0.pdf.

Although direct instruction in social skills could be provided by the parents, another option is a specialist (e.g., social skills coach), with parents performing follow-up activities at home.

In schools, there are different social skills training groups and social skills "curriculums." For many IA children, these are much-needed services. Such training should target responses to the social overtures of other children and adults, initiating social behavior, minimizing aggressive and annoying behavior while using a flexible selection of responses, and self-managing new and established skills.

Playgroups, visual cueing, social games, and video modeling are the age-appropriate techniques to be used. In addition, there are many interactive, developmentally appropriate computer programs that aim at developing social skills. A good example is *101 Ways to Teach Children Social Skills: A Ready-to-Use Reproducible Activity Book* by L. Shapiro, 2004. Some of these programs, like the *Anger Control Games* at http://www.roundgames.com/onlinegame/Anger+Management, have been highly praised by many parents of internationally adopted post-institutionalized children I have worked with.

Culture Familiarization

Systematic, reflective, and congenial familiarization of adopted children with the American culture, particularly those who arrived after their fifth birthday, will help these children tremendously in their integration into the social environment. Parents and teachers should try their best to close cultural gaps using books, stories, games, songs, sayings, jokes, and so on, which internationally adopted children missed by arriving into the adoptive family at a later stage. This will help them with a better and quicker understanding of various cultural references used by peers. The parents should go culturally to the beginnings; everything that surrounds a child born into this culture has to be introduced into IA child's life and reinforced through multiple repetitions and references. It is just as important as learning literacy skills.

Organization of Environment and Specialized Help

Parents can help initiate and promote friendships by creating social opportunities for the child to be involved in different activities such as sports, arts, dance, craft and so on. The goal is to select the right activity and lead the child to at least a modest success, in which they can showcase their skills and be appreciated by their peers. Every child must be successful in some activity, experience pride, and be recognized as an achiever in something. This will build the platform for productive peer interaction. The parents could use their immediate surroundings: neighborhood, local organizations, and other gathering places to introduce the adopted child to different social activities: enrolling the child in the age-appropriate out-of-school organizations or having them involved in different volunteer work. Cross-gender and cross-generation interactions should be a part of the adopted child's social experience. In any social setting, an IA child needs to be sure that when his/her own capacity to cope with the fear and stress break down, an external source of help (a parent, a teacher, a counselor, a more capable peer, etc.) is readily and permanently available to maintain safety, predictability, and protection. Traumatized IA children feel much safer in situations with established rules, regulations, clear limits, and a sense of predictability.

Mental health professionals, therapists, counselors, and adoption agency workers are powerful sources of building social and cultural competence in international adoptees. Adoptive parents need access to cultural/social services (consultation, guidance, and attendance at specialized workshops and different community resources). Some families may benefit from connecting with a mentor parent with a similar background (e.g., children of similar ages or cultures) (Kittle & Reed, 2020).

In conclusion, although many IA children adopted at different ages show remarkable recovery in their physical health and academic functioning, their social and emotional difficulties often persist and sometimes even increase over time, particularly in middle adolescence and young adulthood. Institutionalized children seldom have access to the experiences they need to acquire joint attention skills, pretend play, attachment, and secure social interactions. To compensate for early childhood losses, the older IA children have to be specifically trained in maintaining positive peer and adult relations. Their participation in shared and socially meaningful activities under the leadership of a competent and committed adult to facilitate this socialization is especially important. We know that early social deprivation consequences are not easily reversible and have far-reaching corollaries for socio-emotional functioning. Remedial interventions for the improvement of social skill competence are no less urgent than academic remediation.

CHAPTER 9

Therapeutic Parenting as a Major Force in Rehabilitation and Remediation of Internationally Adopted Children

The internationally adopting parents, either as a married couple (73 percent) or a single household, are described in a number of research publications (Zill, 2015, 2017; Foli, Hebdon, Lim, & South, 2017; Zill & Bradford, 2018; Leon, Steele, Palacios, Roman, & Moreno, 2018). On average, adoptive parents (APs) belong to a middle class; an overwhelming majority of them have college education. APs went through a home-study process – a state-regulated procedure for determining fitness for adoption, including health, criminal records, financial status, and so on. Practically all APs had some parental training provided by their adoptive agency and other relevant institutions. In about half of adoptive families, the adopted child is the first and only child with first-time parents. The rest, however, have biological children in the family, and those children are mostly older than the adopted child. The mean age of adoptive parents is higher than the average for biological parents in general population. In terms of race and ethnicity, whites make up the majority of adoptive parents (Zill, 2016). In sum, individuals and couples who adopted internationally are a mature, well-educated, financially well-to-do, and strongly motivated group. One more specific feature of adoptive parents is that they are especially anxious about and sensitive to their children's well-being and are forceful in obtaining diagnoses and related treatments for them, seeking out expert care at the earliest sign of trouble (Hamilton, Cheng, & Powell, 2007). In terms of the amount of time, energy, personal involvement, and material resources these parents put into caring for their internationally adopted children, they demonstrate advantages over all types of families, including a two-parent biological family. Elevated sensitivity to their children's real or perceived needs forces adoptive parents to make a tremendous parental investment to rehabilitate and remediate their adopted children. On average, they start their parenthood with a greater commitment and more preparation (Zill, 2016). According to the results of more than one national studies, adoptive parents not only spend more money on their adopted children, but they invest more time together, reading to children, or eating meals together (Hamilton et al., 2007; Gewirtz, Forgatch, & Wieling, 2008; Whitten & Weaver, 2010).

Adoptive parents face problems and challenges unknown to the non-adoptive families, and parenting international adoptees in many cases is different by comparison with nonadoptive families (Petersen, 2012; Werum, Davis, Simon-Cheng, & Browne, 2017). Adoptive parents are often confronted with the trauma consequences and delays of age-appropriate functioning that may test their parenting abilities. Adoption is not a miracle that can automatically cure all problems of post-institutionalized children. Adoption itself comes with its own challenges, emphasizing the need for support to adoptive parents. After a long, sometimes arduous process of applying to adopt and waiting for a placement, the parents need help in adjusting to the everyday realities of raising a child (*Therapeutic Parenting Journal*, 2015). Tensions also may surface in the marriage as a result of difficult parenting. Whether these difficulties result in elevated risks of abusive parenting is a largely unexplored area (Miller, Chan, Reece, Tirella, & Pertman, 2007; Lawson & Sibla, 2016).

External Supports and Services Available for Adoptive Families

Complaints of insufficient post-adoption support and services are not rare among adoptive parents (Cogen, 2008). The problem is that the availability of post-adoption support is unevenly presented in the United States, concentrated mostly on the East and West coasts. On the other hand, a lack of information about such services may be a cause of the feelings of "isolation" and "helplessness" reported by some adoptive parents. An adoption-oriented medical management and individual and family psychotherapy, as well as educational services in school and support groups, are available at many locales in the United States (National Council for Adoption, 2019).

Medical Management

In the United States, there is a wide-ranging network of medical services specializing in international adoption: one of the many comprehensive listings of international adoption clinics and doctors could be found at https://www.bbinternationaladoption.com/adoption-medicine. There is a subdivision on Adoption and Foster Care within the American Academy of Pediatrics that services physicians who provide care for adoptees.

Specialized medical services are available now for those who need them before, during, and after adoption. These services include pre-adoption consultations to prepare families for medical issues that commonly occur among children adopted from certain regions. The consultants may review the pre-adoption medical documentation from the native country of a child. Comprehensive post-adoption medical evaluations are available by a pediatrician specializing in adoption issues. Usually, these medical assessments are performed according to the guidelines developed by the American Academy of Pediatrics (Miller, 2005). Ongoing medical monitoring is available on demand by local medical staff for practically all adoptive families.

Psychotherapy

A well-known and popular type of professional support is individual, group, and family psychotherapy, provided by a licensed social worker, psychologist, and sometimes a psychiatrist. Psychotherapy is a wide field with many different theoretical approaches and techniques. Each theoretical perspective acts as a roadmap, so it is important to find the right match between a therapy in question and an adoptive child's issues. An additional requirement in this match is the psychotherapist's experience with treatment of international adoptees. Not every competent therapist is a good match for every family; the "chemistry" between a therapist and a patient is the crucial component in any psychotherapy. The search can be complicated by restrictions imposed by insurance companies or health management organizations (HMOs).

Selecting and Working with a Psychotherapist

By the time of the first appointment, the parent usually knows about such public information as how long has the therapist been in practice and what degrees, licenses, or certification he/she possesses. The following questions, developed at BGCenter (Gindis, 2019), can be asked in the process of selection of the right therapist. (Please note that some questions can be asked after an initial assessment session but before a commitment to the therapist):

1. What is the therapist's general theoretical orientation? If the answer is "eclectic," ask about the base for a theoretical framework that determines the therapy.

2. How much experience does the therapist have with post-institutionalized, internationally adopted children and how often does he/she treat children from this group?
3. Does the therapist have experience with transracial adoption?
4. Has the therapist attended additional training on the issues related to international adoptees?
5. Did the therapist receive specific training for trauma-related issues in children?
6. What kind of support would the therapist provide to the parents? Does he/she work only with the children?
7. How does the therapist address emergencies if they occur? Is the therapist accessible outside of session time in such cases?
8. Can the therapist estimate a time frame for the course of therapy?
9. Will the appointments interfere with school attendance?
10. Will the therapist be working collaboratively with school and be available (at least by phone) for the appropriate school meetings?
11. What is the cost of therapy and when is payment expected (after each session, at the end of the month)?

More valuable information on this topic can be found at Child Welfare Information Gateway (2012). A review of the most effective individual and family psychotherapeutic methodologies for internationally adopted children and their families is presented in Chapter 4 of this book. It is to be clearly understood that the family's involvement is critical to a positive outcome of the therapy. Although the adoptive family, in most cases, is not the cause of the adopted child's trauma, healing from the trauma will take place within the adoptive family. Unfortunately, many therapists who are new to the treatment of adoption issues may perceive the adoptive family as a dysfunctional unit that causes the child's problems. These professionals may not fully understand the nature of pre-adoption traumatic experience and not fully include the adoptive family in the process of healing. Adoptive parents should be open with the therapist about what is going on at home. Parents are to be decisive, if needed, to change a provider if the therapy does not appear to be progressing appropriately.

Parental Counseling

Counseling in parental techniques is different from psychotherapy and may complement the therapy or be used separately. Its goal is to modify the specific patterns of behavior in the parent in order to resolve practical day-to-day problems that can cause difficulties with the management of the child. Parental techniques for an adopted child often differ from those required for a biological child (see more discussion below). Thus, the adopted child may need help in establishing meaningful relations with the members of the family; he/she needs social skills training and enhancement in communicative skills with peers and adults. An experienced counselor will recommend how to modify some typical parental requests and attitudes in contentious situations, what to say, how to feel, and how to react while working on these tasks. Real hands-on experience is a must for a counselor as is a detailed and open presentation of the specific situations on the parent's part.

Psychiatric Hospitals and Residential Treatment Centers

The need for an intensive treatment outside of the family, often on an emergency basis, happens more often in international adoptees than in their peers in the population at large (National Council for Adoption, 2019). Basically, two major options are available in this case: residential treatment centers (RTCs) and inpatient, residential, and outpatient psychiatric facilities.

Hospitalization is particularly necessary if the child becomes suicidal or dangerous to others. The psychiatric admission evaluation and a short-term treatment plan are usually readily available for adoptive parents to review. Most local psychiatric hospitals have emergency admissions for child and adolescent services. Long-term psychiatric facilities include psychiatric residential centers for patients with a chronic psychiatric disorder that impairs their ability to function independently. In most cases, an international adoptee may not need a long-term psychiatric hospitalization but in need of firm limits and a structured environment, which residential treatment centers are expected to provide. These facilities are extremely expensive, and adoptive parents often have to find funds through their insurance, local school district, or court. The number of international adoptees in residential treatment centers (RTCs) is significant, although no reliable statistic is available (Brown, LaBrenz, & Fong, 2018). There are several RTCs specializing in domestically and internationally adopted children.

Some residential programs use relationship-based treatment, which promotes healing through the relationships that the child or youth establishes with staff and not just through changing behaviors. Family connections are critical to help children remain connected and aware of their relationship with their families. The ongoing family relationships also remind children that they have not been abandoned. The more connected that children are to staff in a residential facility and to their parents, the greater the chance for healing and for improving enough to return home.

Internet-Based and "In-Person" Adoptive Parents' Groups

Parents' groups are popular and useful resources of information and motivation. These groups promote camaraderie and moral support, organize petitions, protests, and so on, and mobilize the "grassroots" movements. The experience of those who have "been there, done that" is a great value for a novice in the group. The range of interests of these groups is really without borders. Most of them are selective in their membership. For example, there are groups of single parents, parents adopting from a particular country, parents having children with certain handicapping conditions, and so on. But some are with a rather broad base, like Families for Russian and Ukrainian Adoption, Eastern Europe Adoption Coalition, Families with Children from China, and Latin America Parents Association. No less popular are in-person adoptive parents' groups that exist either by themselves due to the enthusiasm and leadership of particular individuals or under the auspices of the adoption agencies. These groups may meet at public facilities, libraries, or private homes.

Informal support includes social networks of other families with internationally adopted and community agencies that provide training, respite, social events, and recreational activities. Formal support includes publicly funded, state-administrated programs such as early intervention, special education, and respite services. Each state organizes its services and membership differently, and the adoptive parents should learn their own state's unique rules to access support by contacting the state or county offices of the Department of Health and Human Services. Adoptive parents should not feel to be left helpless: these services and support are to be accessible for them at any time and in any place in the country. Adoptive parents should use them freely and productively.

Therapeutic Parenting

It's a slippery slope finding the best name for the sort of parenting needed for international adoptees. There is a number of practical and effective parental models with different "tags" attached, like "dyadic developmental parenting" by D. Hughes (Hughes, 2011), "integrative parenting" by Wesselmann, Schweitzer, and Armstrong (2014), "parenting beyond consequences" by H. Forbes (2010), and so on. I prefer the name "therapeutic parenting" (TP), although this "brand" is claimed by attachment therapies and used in a rather broad sense. My understanding of this unique kind of parenting is based on what is presented in the famous Patty Cogen's book, *Parenting Your Internationally Adopted Child* (Cogen, 2008). Dr. Cogen writes about accurate attunement to a child's inner fear, resulting from the internal perception of the world as an unsafe and dangerous place to live; modeling of physical and emotional regulation for a dysregulated child; organization of home environment in a certain way; and setting clear, developmentally appropriate limits and consequences to help a child develop and maintain self-control. I would add to Dr. Cogen's model the direct and mediated instruction in language and social skills as presented in "SmartStart methodology" (Lidz & Gindis, 2000) and R. Green's "rules of engagement" and collaborative problem-solving methods (Green, 2006).

Therapeutic parenting is a specific way an adoptive family brings up their adopted children with development mediated by trauma. There is significant literature devoted to parenting children with adverse childhood experiences (see reviews in Wesselmann et al., 2014; Leon et al., 2018; Lange, Callinan, & Smith, 2019). To summarize, parenting children with adverse childhood experiences is an amalgam of structure and discipline, love and nurture, which allow a child with deep-seated complex trauma to feel safe and cherished with the goal to overcome and compensate for traumatic experience and scaffold to the age-appropriate flow of development. Although many findings could be applicable to international adoptees, parenting of IA children is as specific as children themselves.

There are certain specific parental techniques (discussed below) that prove to be therapeutic in nature. However, therapeutic parenting is not only a set of "techniques" but also the state of mind and personality of the parents: to develop effective self-regulation is possible only through modeling the parents' own self-regulation, honesty is taught through honesty, love to music only through the parents' own love to music, and so on. In summary, therapeutic parenting is a blend of state of mind/personality and techniques/methodology. Amazingly, some parents are born with this quality, some are completely deprived of it, most have it to some degree, and many can be taught how to provide therapeutic parenting.

Parenting traumatized adopted children can be a traumatizing experience by itself: these children often do not trust that adoptive parents will be different than those adults that hurt them or were negligent to them in the past. That is what their "internal working model" of the world tells them. It is precisely this fear of trusting a caregiver and intense need for safety that makes the balance between structure and nurture so important.

Therapeutic parenting means having realistic expectations for the child. Children who have been abused or neglected in early life may not be functioning at their chronological age in terms of their physical, social, emotional, and cognitive skills. They may also be displaying unusual coping behaviors. Thus, a traumatized child can be unresponsive to affection, be socially inappropriate for his/her age, have difficulty controlling emotions presenting with frequent tantrums, be emotionally withdrawn, and so on. Therapeutic parenting (TP) means commitment, patience, and perseverance in parenting a needy and difficult child who may progress slowly and regress often. It is important to understand that most changes and improvements in behavior and emotional control are not immediate; they are rather incremental, requiring more time.

In some aspects, TP is not a typical, culturally approved, "commonsense parenting" (Petersen, 2012) with "natural" means of parenting. TP is an intentionally created specific method in use, not a "spontaneous" parenting. In some ways, TP may be counterintuitive and controversial, as seen from the passage below (Krause-Grindlay, 2019):

> Therapeutic parenting in action can look very different for each family and each situation, and is often counter-cultural. This approach can sometimes look, to an outsider, like too much leniency or overly firm boundaries. Therapeutic parenting could mean the parent calmly offering food to a child who has just hurt someone or acted disrespectfully, because the parent suspects he is hungry. Once he has calmed down, it could then mean walking him through fixing his mistake with a "redo," something that will likely have a more lasting impact than dealing with the issue when the child is dis-regulated. The fundamentals are that the parent is tailoring the response towards the child in order to best facilitate his healing.

TP uses "time in" instead of typical "time out" as a means of discipline. Other alternatives to "time out" could be used as described in the book for parents written by A. Brill (2014). TP needs to show love and compassion, even though the parent does not like what the child did or said: "I do not like what you have done, but I love you because you are my son/daughter."

TP is a "proactive," not a "reactive," model of parenting. The major principle of proactive parenting is to create situations in which, paraphrasing the famous expression of William Gladstone, "it is easy to do right and difficult to do wrong." As Dr. Cogen puts it, proactive parenting is "as if" parenting: internationally adopted children of different ages often do not communicate their needs clearly and parents must behave "as if" the child has expressed those needs distinctly. The essence of proactive patenting is in the preventive care-giving response, anticipating the child's distress.

In Dr. Cogen's book, one can find a number of clever techniques, mostly in the form of games and shared activities that are essential in proactive parenting. Such techniques need to be developmentally sensitive: what is appropriate for a 5-year-old may not be relevant for an 8-year-old.

TP concentrates on forming social connectedness, which is one of the main objectives in bringing up an adopted child. A therapeutic parent models how to be emotionally aware of other people's feelings by recognizing the IA child's emotions, listening to him/her empathetically, and trying to understand the situation from the child's perspective. Validating the child's emotions does not signify approval, just understanding. The parents' interpretation of the child's emotions and the causes of these emotions could be instructive educationally and healing therapeutically.

TP implies willingness and ability to accept help and create a support system. As a part of preparation for international adoption, the prospective adoptive parents should create a functional model of three layers of support. The first layer is the immediate family and close/trusted friends. The second one consists of fellow adoptive parents, professionals from the adoption agencies, and online support groups that are mostly composed of adoptive parents, but some professionals may also participate. The third layer includes specialists in the field of international adoption: medical doctors, psychologists, therapists, and educational lawyers.

TP includes skillful advocacy for children's needs outside the family – in schools and communities. TP is about learning and expending the parental techniques. Some techniques could be learned from other parents, some from parenting resources, education, or even media, while others may have been purely intuitive. There are resources online, parenting classes, and counselors who can help. What follows is a set of evidence-based effective parental techniques proven to be effective with internationally adopted children. Therapeutic parenting is not a "one-size-fits-all" approach. Therefore, there are general principles, and there are specific techniques. For example, "children need to feel safe" is a general principle, but how this is achieved may be different for different children and in different families.

Samples of Therapeutic Parenting Techniques

The Structure of Daily Routines

Daily structure is based on a few simple rules for the morning, midday, and evening routines in the family, like brushing teeth, coming to the dining room at a certain time, bedtime, and the like. Daily routines give IA children a sense of security and control over their lives: repetitive events and actions make them feel calmer and safer. Care and nurturing should be a foundation of structure to promote safety. When accepted, routines eliminate power struggles in the family as knowing what comes next makes the transition easier for the child and allows parents to maintain consistency in their expectations. Daily rules should be presented to the child and consistently maintained.

Behavior Contract

A behavior contract is essentially an agreement between the parents and the older (ages 5 and up) children about certain behaviors. There are only a few things in life that must not be negotiated with the children, such as safety, health, and school attendance. All the rest can be negotiated through behavior contracts, presented on paper, or even hung on the walls for visual cues. There exist even printable forms of various behavior contracts at http://www.freeprintablebehaviorcharts.com/behavior_contracts.htm.

Consequences

Consequences have to be associated with each positive and/or unacceptable behavior. The consequences should be as close to a natural continuation of the situation, both in time and meaning, as possible to help the child develop "cause-and-effect" thinking. The best way is to develop in consultation with your counselor or therapist, if needed, a "schedule" of consequences for poor decisions and contrite behavior as well as for good decisions and positive behavior. A consequence should be for every kind of behavior. The enforcement of consistent natural consequences for the actions is the way for an IA child to learn responsibility and develop "cause-and-effect" thinking. For example, attention and "quality time" with parents could be used as a reward (Bernstein, 2015; Jewells, 2020).

Handling of Temper Tantrums

A child's tantrum is an emotional outbreak with crying, screaming, hitting, throwing things, angry ranting, and resistance to attempts at pacifying. In many cases, a tantrum is a reaction to a situation that has no acceptable solution in the child's view, causing extreme frustration and emotional shutdown. In internationally adopted children, tantrums could be a learned orphanage behavior: they might have observed it in the orphanage, they might have reacted like this before, and in the absence of any other coping mechanisms, tantrums became their default reaction. The initial stages of life in the family are very stressful for these children, so tantrums may occur rather often. A dysregulated child is more prone to tantrums and more easily slips beyond the point of no return in tantrum development.

The IA children may experience frustration at school, and though they are able to contain themselves there, they release tension at home through tantrums. Addressing the school problems may decrease the frequency of tantrums at home. Tantrums typically parallel sleep deprivation, inconsistent daily routines, too many distractions during the day, prior stressful situations, bouts of anxiety, and so on. Many IA children have sensory disintegration issues: too much stimulation makes them nervous and even more dysregulated. The understanding of the need to avoid tantrums and the acquisition of appropriate skills to divert them are a part of the TP "tool bag":

- **Create "emergency preparedness" plans and diffuse explosive anger before it starts.** Identify the triggers for anger. The parents do not have to like the IA child's expression of anger or agree with the reason for it, but they should not ignore or dismiss it. Show the IA child how to redirect himself/herself away from anger-producing situations. It is good to have a special place in the house where the child can go when he/she is angry and where he/she can calm down without anyone bothering him/her.
- **Explain the *HALTS* acronym.** When we're hungry (**H**), angry (**A**), lonely (**L**), tired (**T**), or sick (**S**), we need to halt and take care of those needs. Snacks, naps, break time, and a fun activity – these can ward off temper tantrums.
- **Stay calm and lead by example.** Model healthy anger management strategies for the IA child. Let him/her see you work through frustrating situations positively. If you exploded, apologize and explain where you went wrong.
- **Identify and then teach the IA child simple methods of self-regulation and self-calming,** such as counting, walking, changing body position, and so on. Suggest strategies, such as taking a shower or taking a few deep breaths. Get physically active, especially outside; teach the IA child to channel their anger into productive avenues like physical work, exercise, or sports. Physical activity redirects explosive

anger, and fresh air – as long as it's not too hot – is great for neutralizing anger, too. Avoid digital gadgets as much as possible: digital interaction can distill negative emotion without providing a physical outlet.

- **Set ground rules.** Consider tackling the issue of tantrums when the IA child is in a good mood and open to talking. Use a "safe word" during disagreements: "If either one of us says it, that's going to be a signal that we need to take a step back and calm down." Together, choose a word that you can use to communicate warnings of impending anger storms.

- **Communicate clear expectations and be consistent.** The IA child should have a clear understanding of what is expected of him/her in various situations. Telling IA children what they should not do doesn't help to know what to do. Instead of saying "Don't yell!!" TP parent should say: "You need to talk in a quiet voice." Often parents will deliver consequences only when they have reached their limit of frustration and therefore give an overly severe punishment (Bernstein, 2015; Jewells, 2020). Always follow through. Only threaten a consequence that you can actually deliver. For example, don't say you are going to take away TV for a month when you know that is not realistic.

- **Offer a choice.** If a parent finds that the IA child is becoming defiant or the family is at the beginning of a power struggle, it is useful to give a child some control back by offering a choice which would be acceptable for the parent (Taylor, 2001; Jewells, 2020). For example, after asking the child several times to clean up the room, the parent may say: "Here is your choice: you can either clean up your stuff now or when your favorite TV will start; which do you choose?" If the child continues to ignore the request, the parent should say: "If you do not make a choice, I will choose for you." With consistency, the child will begin to understand that it is better to have some control than none.

In the midst of a tantrum, certain behaviors of the parent will not work and may create an even more frustrating situation (Barkley & Benton, 2013):

- Don't do a lot of talking in general because this will send the IA child a message that tantrums are a good way to get the parent's attention.
- Don't ignore the IA child completely: that's a sign of disrespect and could be dangerous for his/her safety.

- Don't restrain the IA child unless you feel that he/she or someone else is in immediate physical danger or there is going to be significant destruction. In that case, safety has to be the parents' priority.
- Don't reward the IA child after the tantrum has ended by giving in to his/her demands. This only serves to reinforce tantrums as a method of reaching his/her goals (Jewells, 2020). Praise the child for calming down and then resume regular activities.

No family-based management plan for an older child can be a "silver bullet" for immediate improvement of the situation. Behavior patterns do not change overnight; only consistent, long-term hard work on the parents' part may help.

Please note that these recommendations were written at BGCenter based on clinical experience and information contained in the following sources (see in References for more details): *The Explosive Child* by Green and Ablon (2006), *From Defiance to Cooperation* by Taylor (2001), *Your Defiant Child: Eight Steps to Better Behavior* by Barkley and Benton (2013), *The Defiant Children – Tips for Parenting* by Jewells (2020), and *Ten Days to a Less Defiant Child* by Bernstein (2015).

Therapeutic Parenting and the Parent's Burnout

Adoptive parents are human beings who must also work, take care of the rest of the family, and so on. Therapeutic parenting is a formidable load that may end up in parental burnout. Parents' fatigue is defined as a context-specific syndrome resulting from enduring exposure to chronic parenting stress (Mikolajczak & Roskam, 2018; Mikolajczak, Gross, & Roskam, 2019). Its primary symptom is overwhelming exhaustion relating to one's role as a parent. Other symptoms include emotionally distancing from children, feeling fed up with parenting, losing one's sense of accomplishment from parenting, and feeling defeat in the parental role. As Harriet McCarthy (2017) writes about this phenomenon in adaptive parents:

> *Parent burnout is a legitimate and very real concern for those who have children with any kind of challenging issues. Frequently, parents of children with special challenges will complain that they feel trapped, disappointed, over-committed, and increasingly unable to cope. They seem to have lost any satisfaction in the job of parenting their special-needs child. They can't find ways to relax and renew their energy for what is acknowledged by all to be a very difficult job. Parents are understandably exhausted when they find themselves with children*

so needy or so difficult to handle that they require constant monitoring. Especially at risk are those parents who have poor or nonexistent support systems. They can't seem to imagine any options for easing the constant pressure of their obligations and run the real risk of becoming more and more isolated. For those who are parenting the poorly attached or unattached child, the lack of emotional reciprocity makes things doubly difficult.

As the means of recovery, McCarthy suggests doing a re-evaluation of the parents' expectations, as unfulfilled expectations will only compound the feelings of being trapped and dissatisfied, and to get rid of preconceived notions of what should or may happen in the future. The goals of parenting have to be realistic and constructive. There is another effective anti-fatigue method that McCarthy calls "self-preservation action." She writes that the adoptive children's mental and physical health and their overall progress depend on the adoptive parents' emotional stability and level of functioning as a family. Self-preservation requires developing a plan for parents' own well-being and for finding time away from the child to do something for themselves. In other words, TP should follow the "aircraft safety rule": in the case of emergency, first put the gas mask on yourself and after this on your child. The parents must find ways to take care of themselves both physically and emotionally to be able to take care of the child.

TP is difficult. However, for internationally adopted children, TP is not an option, but a necessity.

CHAPTER 10

Transitioning to Adulthood Using the Individual Transitional Plan

Transition from childhood to adulthood (from schooling as the major activity to after-school education or employment as the major activity) is not easy for even typically developing individuals, but for many international adoptees, it is a formidable task that requires thoughtful, well-planned scaffolding. Most adoptive parents are aware that their adopted teenagers need guidance to transition successfully from high school to the next phase of young adulthood. However, not all parents have a vision of concrete steps that must be taken to guide and prepare teens for adult life. Parents may be faced with numerous legal, organizational, financial, and parenting questions dictated by the degree of support their children need in the transitional period. Without such a road map, no effective scaffolding is possible. Individual Transitional Plan (abbreviated as ITP further in the text) is such a road map. ITP is a must in a case when an IA adolescent or young adult has handicapping condition(s).

In order to create the functional ITP, adoptive parents need to give realistic and practical answers to the following questions:

- Will my child receive a regular high school diploma or a substandard document of educational attainment?
- Should my child receive more academic instruction or turn to occupational training?
- What occupational training programs are available locally and at what cost?
- Will my child be able to get a paid job?
- Will my child be able to live independently?
- Which public benefits will my child be eligible for?
- What supports are available for a person with my child's specific disabilities?
- Which state and local agencies shall I apply to for help in creating and implementing workable ITP?

The public benefit system in the United States for adults with disabilities includes many provisions (e.g., social security, vocational rehabilitation, Medicaid waivers, etc.) and is not easy to navigate. The youngster and the parents should consult with professionals specializing in this area, such as independent educational consultants, psychologists, or lawyers to ensure they have maximized all possibilities for a brighter future for their internationally adopted children. Based on the determined level of support needed, an ITP can be presented on one of the three levels of scaffolds:

- *Minimal support* is needed for IA youngsters who could choose a college, vocational school, or competitive employment with some accommodations as a postsecondary goal. They are expected to live independently with minimal initial guidance and supervision.
- *Moderate support* is needed for IA youngsters who will be trained for nontechnical jobs such as manual labor, possibly having supported or sheltered employment and semi-independent living as postsecondary goals.
- *Significant support* is needed for IA youngsters who end up in sheltered workshops, attending a day program for adults and living in group homes with daily supervision.

The Structure, Content, and Goals for Individual Transition Plan

ITP is a document with a coordinated set of actions that creates a bridge between school life and after-school life for students with disabilities aged 16 through 21. There is an *Updated Transition Guide* (2017), published by the Office of Special Education and Rehabilitation Services (available at https://www2.ed.gov/about/offices/list/osers/transition/products/postse condary-transition-guide-may-2017.pdf), which is "must" reading for everyone involved in the creation of the transition process. School districts are responsible for the education of students with disabilities through the age of 21 unless a youngster graduates with a regular diploma before this age. ITP is a part of an Individual Educational Plan (IEP) and should be based on the student's personal needs, strengths, skills, and interests. It has to identify and develop goals to accomplish during the remaining school years to assist the student in making his/her post-high-school adjustment. IDEA-2004 states that an IEP team must begin focusing on transitional planning by the time a child turns 16 or earlier (14 years in some states) if the IEP team decides so.

There are only general legal requirements for how the ITP should be written in terms of its structure and content. Based on many years of working with international adoptees who are adolescents or young adults with disabilities and their adoptive families, school systems, legal professionals, and related state agencies, I have developed a workable (but not ideal, of course!) model of ITP for international adoptees that includes the following elements:

1. Legal foundation for ITP based on federal laws and regulations with specific states' variations and additions.
2. Developmental history.
3. Results of the latest psychological, educational, and specialized assessments.
4. Family's and student's vision statements for the after-school life.
5. Results of a functional vocational evaluation and the related vocational or college education goals.
6. Adaptive behavior and independent living goals.
7. Level of academic attainment and associated goals.
8. Accommodations and related services while in school.
9. Accommodations and supportive services to be transferred to Section 504 if college or occupational training is planned.

Keep in mind that an ITP is a flexible document, and the structure, content, and goals in particular are subjects to change based on the student's progress or the lack of progress.

Legal Foundation for ITP and Specific States' Modifications

According to the IDEA, 2004 revision (Section 300.43, FR Doc 06-6656, Federal Register: 8/14/2006, Volume 71, Number 156), an ITP for a person with a disability:

> (1) *Is designed to be within a results-oriented process, that is focused on improving the academic and functional achievement of the child with a disability to facilitate the child's movement from school to post-school activities, including postsecondary education, vocational education, integrated employment (including supported employment), continuing and adult education, adult services, independent living, or community participation;*
> (2) *Is based on the individual child's needs, taking into account the child's strengths, preferences, and interests; and includes:*
> *   *Instruction;*
> *   *Related services;*

- *Community experiences;*
- *Development of employment and other post-school adult living objectives;*
- *If appropriate, acquisition of daily living skills and provision of a functional vocational evaluation.*

Transition services for children with disabilities may be special education, if provided as specially designed instruction, or a related service, if required to assist a child with a disability to benefit from special education.

The variations in the requirements for an ITP exist in practically all states. Thus, the federal law requires that ITP be established by the age of 16, while in several states, the age may vary between 14 and 16. In some states, the federal law and regulations are considered as a minimal base, and more specific additions are created. The states are also different in the range and quality of the support systems in implementing ITP (Neubert & Leconte, 2013; Caverdish & Connor, 2018). The legal aspect of ITP is comprehensively presented in a number of current publications, such as Hamblet (2017), Kirchberg (2017), and WriteLaw website available at http://www.wrightslaw.com/idea/art/defs.transition.htm.

Developmental History

This part of an ITP is crucial for internationally adopted youngsters because many causes of neurologically based disabilities along with social and emotional problems are rooted in their developmental histories. This information is important for understanding both current levels of functioning and future performance. In some cases, neurological impairment(s) related to pre- and post-birth adversity (e.g., fetal alcohol syndrome) could be the major cause of disability. In other cases, a generalized weakness of the central nervous system of an internationally adopted youngster reveals itself in sensory-motor disintegration, emotional reactivity and rigidity, dysregulated attention and concentration, and a host of "soft" neurological signs (Marlow, 2005). For many international adoptees, repetitive traumatization in early childhood may have accumulated to socially induced emotional trauma that predisposes them to a combination of delays in social/emotional maturity, self-regulatory capacity, cumulative cognitive/academic deficit, and emotional fragility. Parents should not discount their adolescent's persistent self-perception as a "rejected" and "unwanted" person, which may result in low self-confidence, low self-esteem, and complicated interpersonal relationships. Last but not least, the abrupt loss of their first language and their specific mode of English language learning may contribute to both academic and social difficulties. Therefore, the proper understanding and interpretation of international adoptees' developmental history must be the foundation of their ITPs.

Results of the Latest Psychological, Educational, and Specialized Assessments

Each person is different, so there are no required tests that must be included in an ITP (Walker, Kortering, Fowler, & Rowe, 2010); still, the most recent assessments in several domains are needed in the creation of the original ITP and modifications during the annual reviews. These are psychological assessments with cognitive and social/emotional component; educational evaluations based on major achievement tests (please note that educational assessments cannot be more than two semesters old); and any specialized assessments, if needed, such as speech and language, occupational or physical therapy, or the evaluation of the need for an assistive technology. Accurate interpretation of the assessment results leads to an effective and realistic ITP.

The Family's and Student's Vision Statements

In order to focus the ITP process on future needs, both the parents and the teenager ought to formulate what is known as "postsecondary vision statement." ITP is to create a foundation for IA adolescents' and young adults' base for their future independent or semi-independent life, gainful or supportive employment, and, most importantly, the emotional stability and social connectedness, which is at the base of "a normal" life. That is why it is advisable to have an elaborate vision statement. The postsecondary goals should reflect the vision statements of both the parents and the student.

For example, Mr. and Mrs. G. formulated the vision statement for their son Jose to include as goals: "emotional stability, independent living, and gainful employment." The parents stated that they are open to various forms of training for their son: from vocational school to onsite learning/ apprenticeship to community college. In their view, "Jose's strengths are good physical health, near average intelligence, age-appropriate communicative language proficiency, interest in auto-mechanic technology, and competence with certain phone and computer applications." They see Jose's weaknesses "in immature social skills, delayed academic skills, poor self-regulation, and emotional fragility due to elevated anxiety with distinct depressive qualities."

The adolescent's own expectations for life after school should also be as specific as possible: Thus, Jose wrote in his vision statement: "I would like to make enough money to live on my own, do a job I am good at, preferably car repairs, have friends and a girlfriend, own a car. I am willing to continue education beyond high school, either part-time or full-time. I prefer to stay at home with my parents and continue with my post-school education and employment in my state."

Occupational Evaluation and Development of Vocational Goals

In order to create a functional ITP and its core – vocational and future occupation educational plans and goals – an IA youngster should take an occupational assessment. This evaluation can be done at school or privately and has to be based on occupational tests, questionnaires and inventories, interviews, and the analyses of related documents. Here are a few recommendations for the most reputable and useful instruments.

Interest inventories will help an IA youngster identify what he/she might be interested in doing as a career. An example of interest inventories is the Strong Interest Inventory (Blackwell & Case, 2008), known as *Strong*, which gives lists of jobs that line up with a person's interests, pointing out clusters of jobs to explore. The parents and teachers should be aware that adopted children may choose a career goal that will be difficult to impossible to achieve because of their disability, level of functioning, or emotional instability. However, interest inventories such as Strong can help the ITP team to identify a different job in the same or similar field that is acceptable for this particular youngster. For example, a 17-year-old girl wants to be a veterinarian, but due to her severe learning disability (she reads on the sixth-grade level and her math is on the fourth-grade level), this is not a realistic option. The question is if she wants to be only a veterinarian or she simply wants to work with animals. Would she be happy working as a caregiver to animals at an animal hospital or animal shelter?

Personality tests measure motivations, needs, and attitudes. They may help to discover whether a particular person is suited for a certain career or not. An example of a personality test that is often used in association with the Strong Interests Inventory is the Myers–Briggs Type Indicator (Quenk, 2009).

Career development scales help determine if an adolescent has the ability to perform a particular job and its required tasks and thus help formulate specific career goals (Multon & Lapan, 1995). Self-determination assessments are designed to measure an adolescent's abilities in goal setting, problem-solving, self-advocacy, self-evaluation, persistence, and self-confidence (Wehmeyer & Fied, 2007).

Please note that all the above-mentioned instruments are designed for nondisabled typical adolescents and young adults. In relation to IA adolescents, these methods have serious validity limitations and can only serve as a "navigation tool." Using assessment tools as guidance, the school-based counselor and parents, along with the youngsters themselves, can formulate the school-to-work transition program goals and objectives to be included in the ITP. Here are some examples of the goals:

Goal: Sam will explore his interests, skills, and capacities related to employment as follows:

- Use interest inventories to identify a number of occupational fields for exploration.
- Describe the importance of individual characteristics in getting and keeping a job.
- Explore the educational requirements of various occupations.
- Demonstrate the use of resources to gather information about careers.
- Demonstrate knowledge of how occupational skills and knowledge can be acquired.
- Explain how employment opportunities relate to education and training.

Goal: Anna will complete a variety of real work tasks to explore her vocational potential in the chosen areas of work. She will:

- Apply her job readiness skills to internship, shadowing, and/or other work-related experiences.
- Evaluate the relationship between her individual interests, abilities, and skills and the requirements of a chosen job.
- Demonstrate knowledge and application of safety standards to the work setting.
- Apply job readiness skills to seek real employment opportunities.

Various transitional goals are formulated and available at https://www.parentcenterhub.org/transition-goals/ and in the comprehensive book published by the Council for Exceptional Children (Hamblet, 2017).

Adaptive Behavior and Independent Living Objectives

An important part of an ITP for an IA adolescent with a disability is the question of the type of living arrangement the young adult is expected to have in after-school life. The independent living skills are everyday things that adults do, such as preparing meals, doing laundry, maintaining good personal hygiene, traveling around town, shopping, and so on. The ITP team must think about how the presence or absence of these skills in adolescents relates to their postsecondary goals in education, vocational training, and employment. This aspect of ITP should be based on the administration of such instruments as the Adaptive Behavior Assessment Scale, third edition (Harrison & Oakland, 2015) and several focused interviews with the parents and the student. This part of the ITP is particularly important for Level 3 (significant and multiple support) of the transitional plan. The goals and objectives for this section of the ITP may look like this:

Goal: Sam will develop independent cooking skills. He will:

1. Pack his lunch independently by January 15th.
2. Prepare his breakfast independently by February 1st.
3. Independently cook one hot meal using the microwave by June 1st.
4. Make macaroni and cheese for dinner using a gas stove by June 15th.
5. Make dinner for himself three times a week by September 1st.

Goal: Anna will travel to and from work by herself, using the town bus system. She will:

1. Learn to read the bus schedule and walk to the bus stop from home with assistance by the end of the first quarter.
2. Learn to board the bus and signal the bus driver for her stop by the end of the second quarter.
3. Learn to walk from the bus stop to her job by the end of the third quarter.
4. Learn to take the return trip home by bus by the end of the fourth quarter.
5. Take the bus to and from work by herself by next year.

Services, Accommodations, and Support

In this section of the ITP, the appropriate support, services, and different accommodations should be listed and explained. These may become a contentious issue between the family on one side and the educational or training institutions on the other. A number of transition-related service providers that are available to a student with a disability in high school include guidance counselor offices and career centers. The following major transitional services offered by them should be considered in an ITP:

- *Academic Instruction.* The higher the IA students with disabilities will climb up on the academic skills and knowledge ladder, the more perspective they will have on their vocational horizon and the better off they will be with vocational training and college education. The IA students should receive remedial education, when needed, to enhance their reading, writing, and math skills as deemed necessary to prepare them for postsecondary education (more information on this topic is available in Chapter 7 of this book).
- *Related Services.* These may include occupational therapy, physical therapy, speech/language therapy, counseling, special transportation, and travel training.
- *Community Experience.* It includes community work experience, recreation/leisure activities, tours of postsecondary educational settings, residential exploration, driver's education and practice, and membership in a team/club/organization.
- *Employment.* This service may include career planning, job shadowing, occupational guidance counseling, testing of interest inventories, help with job placement and internship options, and on-the-job training. It may also provide situational work assessments, work samples, work adjustment programs, aptitude tests, and a series of job tryouts.
- *Adult Living Skills.* This service provides referrals to vocational rehabilitation centers available in all states in order to find out about social security benefits and work incentives, explores residential options for the disabled, and trains in renting an apartment and in personal home management. Daily skills may include self-care, health and wellness training, independent living, and money management training.

Contributing Agencies in ITP Implementation

While the IEP is implemented at school only, the ITP should be implemented at school, at home, and in the community. Most important, some of ITP goals can be reached only by cooperation between the family, school, state agencies, and community. The parents should not expect the school to do it all alone: there are about 112 waking hours in a week; 35 hours are spent in school and 77 at home and community. Thus, an ITP should indicate the organizations and individuals to be involved in helping IA adolescents to attain their postsecondary goals.

School District

Adoptive parents need to be fully aware of the available options and what their children are entitled to in our educational system. The school's special education staff is mandated by the law to provide students with counseling, help identify vocational interests, participate in educational and vocational planning, and help with goal setting, prevocational skills training, academic support, and enrolment of their students in specific programs and services. The school has the major role not only in creating and implementing the ITP but also in the referral of the IA students and/or students' parents to a governmental agency for services. The school district is responsible for contracting with community agencies that need to be involved in the IA adolescent's ITP – for example, for job or career exploration, job training, and so on. A school-based counselor should play an important role by assisting in locating the funding for programs that support education or vocational training.

Intermediate Agencies

These are state organizations or community-based establishments that provide postsecondary education and training for students with disabilities by offering an exploration of career options from volunteer work to local internships and apprenticeships, such as youth employment programs, transition partnership programs, local vocational centers, and so on. All states in the United States have vocational programs designed for individuals with a disability; these programs employ vocational counselors to help students with ITP to make the transition to postsecondary education or training more efficiently. The IA adolescents with disabilities need to register in one or several such intermediate agencies. The students' ITP has to be clear about which member of the IEP team is responsible for coordination and communication with state or community agencies. Intermediate agencies may be helpful in providing such direct passages to the trade training.

- *Internships* offer hands-on work experience and mentoring, providing students with a real sense of what full-time work is like and the accommodations they'll need. Internships usually last a few weeks to a year and could be paid or unpaid.
- *Apprenticeships* can be a good option for teens who want to learn a trade through hands-on experience. Apprentices are trained by workers in skilled trades such as carpentry and plumbing. These are mostly unpaid volunteer jobs.

Family

Adoptive parents should begin preparation for transitioning of their IA adolescent to adult life early on, probably as early as the age of 14. The parents must set the stage for transition, working on developing the necessary interests and skills from early adolescent time. The family plays a decisive role in developing such crucial adult life qualities as self-regulation, self-confidence, and self-advocacy.

Self-confidence develops only when there are actual achievements to base it on, and those, no matter how small, come through consistent and intense learning, training, and the acknowledgment of success. Early on, IA children need to be led into activities where they will be reasonably capable of success and perseverance. They can't be left to the task of selecting such activities by themselves later – that is the responsibility of their parents.

Self-advocacy is the ability to understand and effectively communicate one's needs to other individuals. It implies understanding one's own strengths and needs, and it is socially acceptable and effective when a person has a realistic understanding of what help or adjustments will address these needs. Self-advocacy should be a written goal for an IA adolescent's IEP; still, the parents should not rely solely on the school in developing this social skill. They need to be sure that their child fully understands his/her disability and is able to explain it and request due help and support. The parents should talk to their teenagers about their strengths and the extent of their disability and teach them via direct instructions, role-playing, and other methods the words to use about what they can and cannot do. Self-advocacy implies knowing when a person can benefit from asking for help, learning to tell others what's needed, asking for help in different ways from different people, and thanking people who help along the way. It is one of the most important "transition" skills a student can learn in the family and school. With enough proper practice, IA adolescents will learn to speak from a position of strength, not embarrassment, and they will communicate with confidence. The benefits of self-advocacy go beyond academics into the domain of socialization. It is a dynamic and ongoing process as the individual changes over time (Gindis, 2015). Here are samples of self-advocacy goals to be included in the IA youngster's ITP.

- Maria will be able to communicate her accommodation needs to employers and service providers.
- John will learn how to identify the authorities (e.g., supervisor, human resources person, administrator, etc.) to whom he needs to address his requests for accommodations.

- Viktoria will learn how to file a complaint if she meets an obstacle getting her accommodations; she will learn through documenting communications and interactions in a journal and keeping copies of all letters, e-mails, policies, and procedures.

Adoptive parents should understand and manage educational documentation. All students with special needs get either a standard diploma or a certificate that has different titles in different states. The parents of an IA adolescent should do their best to avoid getting only a certificate if the family and the youngster plan on postsecondary occupational training or college, as a high school diploma is needed for practically all forms of postgraduation training. In particular, the parents need to have a clear understanding that IEP ends with the high school graduation ceremony: colleges and trade schools accept only Section 504 plans as a major document for continued support and accommodations. Assuming that the IA adolescent graduates with a regular diploma, carefully examine his/her most recent IEP to see how to convert it into a workable 504 Plan. This is the most practical way to ensure that accommodations continue in the postsecondary environment under the protection of the Americans with Disabilities Act, Amended Acts of 2008 (https://www2.ed .gov/about/offices/list/ocr/transition.html).

The creation of Section 504 Plan has to be done while the IA student is still in high school prior to graduation. Before taking the IA student with a disability off the IEP, the parents should request a document called a *Summary of Performance* (SoP). This record is required under IDEA-2004:

> ... *for a child whose eligibility under special education terminates due to graduation with a regular diploma, or due to exceeding the age of eligibility, the local educational agency shall provide the child with a summary of the child's academic achievement and functional performance, which shall include recommendations on how to assist the child in meeting the child's post-secondary goals.* (20 USC 1414(c)(5)(B)(ii), https://www.wrightslaw.com/info/trans .sop.htm)

This document is a brief but still all-inclusive presentation of the student's strengths and weaknesses at the moment the IEP ends and the accommodation plan of Section 504 begins.

Special Role of Social/Emotional Behavior Goals in ITP

There should be a separate and clearly articulated section in ITP for an IA adolescent because emotional stability, motivation, and social functioning are the most vulnerable aspects of these youngsters' development. Here are a few related samples to be considered for an ITP:

Goal 1: Pamela will demonstrate increased self-control with mood and emotional regulation implementing self-calming methods to cope with heightened emotions; increasing verbalization of how she feels as opposed to acting out; engaging in counseling and being open to learning relaxation techniques and modulation skills; complying with recommended medications, if any are prescribed; and using her personal safety plan.

Goal 2: Pamela will demonstrate improved impulse control, judgment, and decision-making while in the learning environment (school setting or occupational training site) complying with existing rules, regulations, and policies; completing school and work training assignments on a regular, consistent basis; verbalizing connections between impulsive behavior and consequences; increasing verbalization of acceptance of responsibility for misbehavior; decreasing the frequency of impulsive, negative, and disruptive interactions with staff and peers; identifying triggers that increase impulsivity and identifying what need is met by acting-out behaviors; and identifying constructive ways to utilize energy and healthy physical outlets to safely expend energy.

Goal 3: Pamela will develop and maintain appropriate staff and peer relationships establishing a positive self-image and feelings of self-worth; avoiding negative peer influences, terminating involvement with negative peer groups; demonstrating a leadership role and not following her peers' negative behaviors; taking ownership of her behaviors; developing appropriate boundaries with her peers and the staff; developing positive social skills necessary to establish healthy, appropriate peer and staff relationships; and achieving a sense of belonging by consistently engaging in socially appropriate behaviors.

ITP and Postsecondary College Education

This part of an ITP is an exploration of the possibility and necessity of continued postsecondary education on different levels and in various forms. The selection of postsecondary education needs and possibilities is to be practical, realistic, and connected with the other aspects of the transitional plan of an IA youngster. IA high school graduates with educational handicapping conditions may plan to continue postsecondary college education. Preparation for this should start with the beginning of high school and be fully reflected in ITP.

Every college in the United States that is getting federal funds in any form or amount is required to have an office to provide services and accommodations to students with disabilities. The exact name of this office varies (Education and Disability Resources, Disability Support Services, Center for Student Success, etc.), but all such offices have the same legal responsibility to provide accommodations and support to students with disabilities. Moreover, currently there are more than 20 colleges that specialize in working with students with different learning disabilities (see https://www.bestvalueschools.com/rankings/students-with-learning-disabilities/). Selection of the right college, among other things, will depend on the "fit" between the specific youngster's need for support and the accommodations the college is able to provide.

Some students with documented disabilities are eligible for accommodations on college board exams. Students cannot take the SAT, SAT Subject Tests, PSAT/NMSQT, PSAT 10, or AP Exams with accommodations unless their request for accommodations has been approved by Services for Students with Disabilities. The accommodations for students with disabilities on SAT are provided by the College Board's Services for Students with Disability. To obtain accommodations, the proof of disability is to be provided. Adoptive parents can obtain useful information on this subject at https://accommodations.collegeboard.org/. Please note that the acceptable documentation must meet several criteria; for example, evaluators' professional credentials are clearly established, the most current diagnosis is clearly stated in the context of educational, developmental, and medical history, the functional limitations are described, and recommended accommodations are justified. Psychological and medical tests ought to be no more than 3 to 5 years old.

The accommodations available in most colleges include the following (Hamblet, 2017):

> *Reduced course load; Priority registration for courses; Help with study skills and time management; Extended time on papers and projects; Course waivers and substitutions; Alternative exam formats (extended time; oral rather than written exams, others); Private dorm room; Extended time for exam; Reduced distraction site for exam; Preferential sitting; Permission to record classes; Use of laptops for tests and exams; Use of calculators for tests and exams; Note-taking services and smart pens; Use of assisting technology (voice recognition software, text-to-speech computer programs; etc.).*

See more on this topic at https://www.wrightslaw.com/info/sec504.college.accoms.brown.htm.

Note that school-based accommodations have nothing to do with College Board Accommodations, although the fact that the student had school-based accommodations is useful in obtaining them in college. The fact that a student had accommodations (spelled out either in IEP or 504 Plan) does not guarantee that the same accommodations would be available in a college. IA adolescents are to be educated on how to register for accommodations at college while still in high school. More information about the required documentation for specific disabilities may be found at https://accommodations.collegeboard.org/documentation-guidelines/disabil ity-documentation. The time lines for submitting the Student Eligibility Form are available at https://accommodations.collegeboard.org/#dates. More tips on how to avoid typical mistakes when applying for accommodations are provided at https://accommodations.collegeboard.org/tips-faqs/ faq. I highly recommend the book authored by E. Hamblet (2017) as a comprehensive and up-to-date guide in this rather complicated for parents and even school personnel domain.

In conclusion, internationally adopted children have experienced many transitions in their lives. As we know now from experience, the transition from adolescence to adulthood is a major challenge for IA individuals. In the field of international adoption, there is a growing understanding that for many IA individuals, an adolescent period extends beyond 18 (the age of legal majority) well into the early 20s. As observed by Blaustein and Kinniburgh (2015), many IA late adolescents may operate as "almost adults" in appearance but still need support to navigate both their internal and external worlds successfully. One of the means of scaffolding this difficult move is an Individual Transitional Plan, which should be created early and be realistic, effective, and highly individualized to meet the family's and the youngster's vision for the future. It is likely that many students with disabilities and backgrounds in international adoption will continue to need accommodations and support beyond high school, be it in college education, employment, or vocational training. Creation of ITP at the age of 14 to 16 enhances the identification of the areas of personal strength and weakness; development and reinforcement of skills applicable to future job training or college education; reinforcement of emotional self-regulation and self-confidence; and training in self-advocacy. With more time for maturation and continued support and accommodations, IA youngsters with disabilities gain the capacity to be successful in all major aspects of their postsecondary life. Time is precious in relation to creation and implementation of ITP, and success is contingent upon timely delivered, intense, focused, and specialized remediation.

Conclusion
The Art of the Possible – Recovery after Trauma

Like any complex human endeavor, international adoption carries opportunities and risks. The truth of life is that although a lot of international adoptees have remarkably good outcomes, too many suffer from complex early childhood trauma in different degrees, and a sizeable minority has lifelong negative consequences of early childhood adversity (E. Donaldson Adoption Institute, 2010). Resurgence from prolonged trauma of early childhood and dire consequences of adverse childhood experiences throughout the rest of life are among the major themes in the study of human development. Our understanding of this matter has scientific importance: just think of a centuries-long dispute of nature vs. nurture or the role of early childhood experiences in the lifespan of individuals. It also has tremendous practical significance for the mental health of our fellow contemporaries. So many questions ought to be answered. Is it possible to recover from the adverse childhood experience completely, or to some extent, or practically never? How does an abrupt change in the social situation of development affect childhood development? What is to be done to address trauma-related issues? The list of questions goes on and on.

International adoption, as a "natural experiment," gives us a unique chance to gain valuable knowledge about human development in the context of adverse early childhood experience. International adoption revealed the new aspect of what was known for centuries as "human resilience to adverse circumstances of life." Indeed, while resilience after trauma is traditionally considered a personal attribute (Clarke & Clarke, 2003), international adoption points to the significant, if not decisive, social factor of this phenomenon. International adoption clearly demonstrates that resilience is to be understood as the product of the interaction of a person's individual characteristics and sociocultural settings this person is developing within. Adoption means a dramatic change of social situation of development, and the chance for a child to recover depends on the degree and quality of social scaffold and input. The very diversity of the adoption outcomes points to the contribution of the child's own biological and psychological characteristics and a variation in quality of their socio-cultural rehabilitation, remediation, and support. Our experience with international adoption teaches us that the recovery from adverse childhood experiences based on the child's own capacities is rather an exception than a rule, the "wait-and-see" position is wrong, and "a good breakfast every morning, hug at night, and love for the rest of the day" are not merely enough.

While overall international adoptions have declined since 2007, the percentage of adoptees from age 5 to 17 consistently climbed (The AFCARS Report #27, 2020; Adoption Statistics 2020, US Department of State). An increasing number of families are considering adopting older children (Child Welfare Information Gateway, 2015). An adequate prep-aration for adoption of "older" post-institutionalized children is the most urgent issue of the contemporary phase of international adoption (Kittle & Reed, 2020). The "late adopted" child has a chance to succeed if the parents and support specialists (teachers, therapists, service providers) will be armed with specialized knowledge and skills about the most adequate and effective remedial and rehabilitative methodologies and technologies.

The list of interventions is rather long. It can be preventive or proactive, such as pre-adoption counseling or initial remedial education. It can be corrective or reactive, such as behavior modification or psychotherapy. In real life, preventive and corrective measures are closely intertwined. The issue of methodology in rehabilitation and remediation is crucial at this stage of existence of international adoption, where now older children constitute the majority.

There is a widespread opinion that due to their pre-adoption adversity, all internationally adopted children are special-needs children. It could be argued that if delay in development is recognized as a special need, and practically all international adoptees do have delays to different degrees, then indeed all international adoptees are in need of special services, medically, psychologically, and educationally. With the current changes in international adoption described in the Introduction of this book, the percentage of older and disabled children increases dramatically, and rehabilitation and remediation of them emerge as the major attribute of international adoption.

In one of the most influential publications in this field, the author (Compton, 2016, p. 151) wrote: "One key area for future research is the area of intervention ... effective treatment approaches for families ...."

The description of such treatment methodologies, aimed at neurophysiological, psychological, educational, and social restoration of neglected and traumatized children, is the substance of this book. These methods are verified through research and clinical practice within the last three decades and attempt to answer the typical questions: how (what means?), why (this particular method/technique?), who (apply these methods: health professionals, parents, teachers?), when (on what developmental stage?), and so on. This book accumulated research findings and clinical experience of a large group of dedicated adoptive parents and professionals.

One of the lessons that we learned from the three decades of massive international adoption is that the recovery from adverse childhood experiences is contingent upon effective and focused scaffolding efforts from the "village" of parents, teachers, community helpers, and mental health professionals working as a team. Indeed, the art of the possible – recovery from severe early childhood trauma – depends on the degree and quality of social scaffold and input. The desired outcome of research in the field of international adoption is to provide the proper means of scaffolding former institutional residents to the status of productive, self-sufficient, emotionally stable, and law-abiding members of our society.

Appendix

Developmental Trauma Disorder Questionnaire for Adoptive Parents (DTD-Q-AP)

Please read the statements below and specify if, to the best of your knowledge, the child has experienced traumatic events described as:

I. Total abandonment at birth by biological parents

1. Definitely No
2. It is not known

3. It is likely (alleged or suspected, but not documented)
4. Definitely Yes

Could you indicate the age as: 0–3, 3–6, 6–9, 9–up?

Comments:

II. Repeated abandonment (frequently left alone for many hours and days) during early childhood

1. Definitely No
2. It is not known

3. It is likely (alleged or suspected, but not documented)
4. Definitely Yes

Could you indicate the age as: 0–3, 3–6, 6–9, 9–up?

Comments:

III. Death, severe mental/physical impairment, or prolonged unavailability of the principal caregiver due to alcohol or drug abuse

1. Definitely No
2. It is not known

3. It is likely (alleged or suspected, but not documented)
4. Definitely Yes

Could you indicate the age as: 0–3, 3–6, 6–9, 9–up?

Comments:

(cont.)

IV. Repeated change/separation from caregivers due to multiple placements

1. Definitely No
2. It is not known

3. It is likely (alleged or suspected, but not documented)
4. Definitely Yes

Could you indicate the age as: 0–3, 3–6, 6–9, 9–up?

Comments:

V. Failed adoption or foster care (disruption) in the native country or in the United States

1. Definitely No
2. It is not known

3. It is likely (alleged or suspected, but not documented)
4. Definitely Yes

Could you indicate the age as: 0–3, 3–6, 6–9, 9–up?

Comments:

VI. Extreme physical discomfort: hunger, cold, dehydration, etc.

1. Definitely No
2. It is not known

3. It is likely (alleged or suspected, but not documented)
4. Definitely Yes

Could you indicate the age as: 0–3, 3–6, 6–9, 9–up?

Comments:

VII. Extreme neglect of the child's basic physical and emotional needs, if reported or documented

1. Definitely No
2. It is not known

3. It is likely (alleged or suspected, but not documented)
4. Definitely Yes

Could you indicate the age as: 0–3, 3–6, 6–9, 9–up?

Comments:

VIII. Physical abuse: beating, torturing, etc. by caregivers

1. Definitely No
2. It is not known

3. It is likely (alleged or suspected, but not documented)
4. Definitely Yes

Could you indicate the age as: 0–3, 3–6, 6–9, 9–up?

Comments:

(cont.)

IX. Witnessing violence, physical assault, murder, beating, drinking, and/or sexual orgies

1. Definitely No
2. It is not known

3. It is likely (alleged or suspected, but not documented)
4. Definitely Yes
Could you indicate the age as: 0–3, 3–6, 6–9, 9–up?

Comments:

X. Chronic illness, physical impairment, injury, or dysmorphic features (e.g., cleft palate)

1. Definitely No
2. It is not known

3. It is likely (alleged or suspected, but not documented)
4. Definitely Yes
Could you indicate the age as: 0–3, 3–6, 6–9, 9–up?

Comments:

XI. Placement in an institution (orphanage or hospital) and transfer between institutions

1. Definitely No
2. It is not known

3. It is likely (alleged or suspected, but not documented)
4. Definitely Yes
Could you indicate the age as: 0–3, 3–6, 6–9, 9–up?

Comments:

XII. All kinds of abuse by peers (from bullying to rape) in the orphanage

1. Definitely No
2. It is not known

3. It is likely (alleged or suspected, but not documented)
4. Definitely Yes
Could you indicate the age as: 0–3, 3–6, 6–9, 9–up?

Comments:

XIII. Adoption to a foreign country: sudden loss of language, racial identity, cultural and physical environment

1. Definitely No
2. It is not known

3. It is likely (alleged or suspected, but not documented)
4. Definitely Yes
Could you indicate the age as: 0–3, 3–6, 6–9, 9–up?

Comments:

(cont.)

XIV. Adjustment to new social, cultural, and physical environment: family life, new ethnic or racial community

1. Definitely No
2. It is not known

3. It is likely (alleged or suspected, but not documented)
4. Definitely Yes
Could you indicate the age as: 0–3, 3–6, 6–9, 9–up?

Comments:

XV. Negative experiences at school in the new country

1. Definitely No
2. It is not known

3. It is likely (alleged or suspected, but not documented)
4. Definitely Yes
Could you indicate the age as: 0–3, 3–6, 6–9, 9–up?

Comments:

XVI. Traumatic experiences within the adoptive family: death, severe illness, life-threatening accidents (e.g., fire, car crash, etc.), divorce, home violence, community carnage, frequent change of place of residents, etc.

1. Definitely No
2. It is not known

3. It is likely (alleged or suspected, but not documented)
4. Definitely Yes
Could you indicate the age as: 0–3, 3–6, 6–9, 9–up?

Comments:

XVII. Traumatic experiences related to race, ethnic belonging, or national identity of the adopted child in relation to his/her adoptive family and community

1. Definitely No
2. It is not known

3. It is likely (alleged or suspected, but not documented)
4. Definitely Yes
Could you indicate the age as: 0–3, 3–6, 6–9, 9–up?

Comments:

XVIII. Other traumatic events, please specify:

References

Abrines, N., Barcons, N., Brun, C., Marre, D., Sartini, C., & Fumadó, V. (2012). Comparing ADHD symptom levels in children adopted from Eastern Europe and from other regions: Discussing possible factors involved. *Children and Youth Services Review, 34*(9), 1903–1908.

Almas, A. (2012). Effects of early intervention and the moderating effects of brain activity on institutionalized children's social skills at age 8. *Proceedings of the National Academy of Sciences, 109*, 17228–17231.

Arvidson, J., Kinniburgh, K., Sinazzola, J., Strothers, H., Evans, M., Andres, B., Cohen, C., & Blaustein, M. (2011). Treatment of complex trauma in young children: Developmental and cultural considerations in application of the ARC intervention model. *Journal of Child & Adolescent Trauma, 4*(1), 34–51.

Bakermans-Kranenburg, M., Steele, H., Zeanah, C., Muhamedrahimov, R., Vorria, P., Dobrova, K., & Gunnar, M. (2011). Attachment and emotional development in institutional care: Characteristics and catch-up. *Monographs of the Society for Research in Child Development, 76*(4), 62–91.

Bakermans-Kranenburg, M., van IJzendoorn, M., & Juffer, F. (2008). Earlier is better: A meta-analysis of 70 years of intervention improving cognitive development in institutionalized children. *Monographs of the Society for Research of Child Development, 73*, 279–293.

Barcons, N., Neus, A., Brun-Gasca, C., Sartini, C., Fumado, V., & Marre, D. (2012). Social relationships in children from intercountry adoption. *Children and Youth Services Review, 34*(5), 955–961.

Barkley, R., & Benton, C. (2013). *Your defiant child: Eight steps to better behavior.* New York: Guilford Press.

Barroso, R., Barbosa-Ducharne, M., Coelho, V., Costa, I., & Silva, A. (2017). Psychological adjustment in intercountry and domestic adopted adolescents: A systematic review. *Child & Adolescent Social Work Journal, 34*(5), 399–418.

Beckett, C., Castle, J., Rutter, M., & Sonuga-Barke, E. J. (2010). Institutional deprivation, specific cognitive functions, and scholastic achievement: English and Romanian Adoptee (ERA) study findings. *Monographs of the Society for Research in Child Development, 75*, 125–142.

Beckett, C., Maughan, B., Rutter, M., Castle, J., Colvert, E., Groothues, C., & Sonuga-Barke, E. (2006). Do the effects of early deprivation on cognition persist into early adolescence? Findings from the English and Romanian adoptee study. *Child Development, 77*, 696–711.

Behen, M., Helder, E., Rothermel, R., Solomon, K., & Chugani, H. (2008). Incidence of specific absolute neurocognitive impairment in globally intact children with histories of early severe deprivation. *Child Neuropsychology, 14*, 453–469.

Benjet, C., Borges, G., Mendez, E., Fleiz, C., & Medina-Mora, M. (2011). The association of chronic adversity with psychiatric disorder and disorder severity in adolescents. *European Child & Adolescent Psychiatry, 20*, 459–468.

Berlin, L., Bohlin, G., & Rydell, A. (2003). Relations between inhibition, executive functioning, and ADHD symptoms: A longitudinal study from age 5 to 8 1/2 years. *Child Neuropsychology, 9*, 255–266.

Bernstein, D., & Fink, L. (1998). *Child trauma questionnaire manual.* San Antonio, TX: The Psychological Corporation.

Bernstein, J. (2015). *Ten days to a less defiant child.* Boston, MA: Hachette Books.

Bernthal, J., Bankson, N., & Flipsen, P. (2013). *Articulation and phonological disorders.* New York: Pearson.

Bick, J., Zeanah, C., Fox, A., & Nelson, C. (2018). Memory and executive functioning in 12-year-old children with a history of institutional rearing. *Child Development, 89*(2), 495–508.

Blackwell, T., & Case, J. (2008). Test review – Strong interest inventory, revised edition. *Rehabilitation Counseling Bulletin, 51*(2), 122–126.

Blaustein, M. (2012). Factsheet: Attachment, self-regulation, and competency: A comprehensive framework for intervention with complexly traumatized youth. Retrieved from www.nctsn.org/sites/default/files/interventions/arc_fact_sheet.pdf

Blaustein, M., & Kinniburgh, K. (2010). *Treating traumatic stress in children and adolescents: How to foster resilience through attachment, self-regulation, and competency.* New York/London: Guilford Press.

(2015). When age doesn't match stage: Challenges and considerations in services for transition-age youth with histories of developmental trauma. Focal Point: Youth, Young Adults, and Mental Health, 29, 17–20. Portland, OR: Portland State University.

Bodrova, E., & Leong, D. (2007). *Tools of the mind: The Vygotskian approach to early childhood education* (2nd ed.). Upper Saddle River, NJ: Pearson Merrill/Prentice Hall.

Bonanno, G. (2004). Loss, trauma, and human resilience. *American Psychologist, 59*, 20–28.

Bowlby, J. (1980). *Attachment and loss*, vol. 3. New York: Basic Books.

(1988). *A secure base: Parent–child attachment and healthy human development.* New York: Basic Books.

Brigance, A. (2004). *Brigance diagnostic inventory of early development (IED-II)* (2nd ed.). North Billerica, MA: Curriculum Associates.

Brill, A. (2014). *Twelve alternatives to time out: Connected discipline tools for raising cooperative children.* Scotts Valley, CA: CreateSpace Independent Publishing Platform.

Brook, P., & Haywood, C. (2003). A preschool mediational context: The Bright Start curriculum. In A. Hoon, L. Hoon, & O.-S. Tan (Eds.), *Mediated learning experience with children: Applications across contexts*, 98–149. Singapore: McGraw-Hill Education.

Brown, K., LaBrenz, C., & Fong, C. (2018). From adoption to residential treatment centers. *Adoption Quarterly, 21*(3), 182–200.

Bruce, J., Tarullo, A., & Gunnar, M. (2009). Disinhibited social behavior among internationally adopted children. *Development and Psychopathology, 21*, 157–171.

Bruner, J. (1966). *Toward a theory of instruction.* Cambridge, MA: Harvard University Press.

Bureau of Consular Affairs (2020). US Department of State statistics (2020). Retrieved from travel.state.gov/content/travel/en/Intercountry-Adoption/adopt_ref/adoption-statistics.html

Calhoun, L., & Tedeschi, R. (2006). *Handbook of posttraumatic growth: Research and practice.* New York: Lawrence Erlbaum Associates.

Camelia, E., Hostinar, C., Stellern, S., Schaefer, C., Carlson, S., & Gunnar, M. (2012). Associations between early life adversity and executive function in children adopted internationally. *Proceedings of the National Academy of Sciences, 109*(2), 17208–17212.

Carter, J., Lees, J., Murira, G., Gona, J., Neville, B., & Newton, C. (2005). Issues in the development of cross-cultural assessments of speech and language for children. *International Journal of Language Communication Disorders, 40*, 385–401.

Caverdish, W., & Connor, D. (2018). Toward authentic IEPs and transition plans: Student, parent, and teacher perspectives. *Learning Disability Quarterly, 41*(1), 32–43

Cermak, S. (2009). Deprivation and sensory processing in institutionalized and post-institutionalized children: Part 1. *Sensory Integration and Special Interest Section Quarterly, 32*(2), 1–3.

Chall, J., Jacobs, A., & Baldwin, L. (1990). *The reading crisis: Why poor children fall behind.* Cambridge, MA: Harvard University Press.

Chamot, A. (2009). *The CALLA handbook: Implementing the cognitive academic language learning approach* (2nd ed.). White Plains, NY: Pearson Education.

Chamot, A., Barnhardt, S., El-Dinary, P., & Robbins, J. (1999). *The learning strategies handbook.* White Plains, NY: Addison Wesley Longman.

Child Welfare Information Gateway. (2012). *Selecting and working with a therapist skilled in adoption.* Washington, DC: U.S. Department of Health and Human Services, Children's Bureau. Available at www.ifapa.org/pdf_docs/FindingATherapist.pdf.

(2015). *Parenting your adopted teenager.* Washington, DC: U.S. Department of Health and Human Services, Children's Bureau. Retrieved from www.childwelfare.gov/pubPDFs/parent_teenager.pdf.

Clarke, A., & Clarke, A. (2003). *Human resilience: A fifty year quest.* London: Jessica Kingsley.

Clarkson-Freeman, P. (2014) Prevalence and relationship between adverse childhood experiences and child behavior among young children. *Infant Mental Health Journal, 35*(6), 544–554.

Clauss, D., & Baxter, S. (1997). *Post adoption survey of Russian and Eastern European children.* Belen, NM: Rainbow House International.

Cloitre, M. (2005). Beyond PTSD: Emotion regulation and interpersonal problems as predictors of functional impairment in survivors of childhood abuse. *Behavior Therapy, 36,* 119–124.

Cogen, P. (2008). *Parenting your internationally adopted child.* Boston MA: Harvard Common Press.

Cohen J. (2005). Treating traumatized children: Current status and future directions. *Journal of Trauma & Dissociation, 6,* 109–121.

Colvert, E., Rutter, M., Beckett, C., Castle, J., Groothues, C., & Hawkins, A. (2008). Emotional difficulties in early adolescence following severe early deprivation: Findings from the English and Romanian adoptees study. *Development and Psychopathology, 20*(2), 547–567.

Compton, R. (2016). *Adoption beyond borders. How international adoption benefits children.* New York: Oxford University Press.

Connor, T., & Rutter, M. (1999). Effects of qualities of early institutional care on cognitive attainment. *American Journal of Orthopsychiatry, 69*(4), 424–437.

Conradi, L., Taylor-Kletzka, N., & Oliver, T. (2010). A clinician's perspective on the trauma assessment pathway (TAP) model: A case study of one clinician's use of the TAP model. *Journal of Child & Adolescent Trauma, 3*(1), 40–57.

Conway, R., & Hopton, L. (2000). Application of a school-wide metacognitive training model: Effects on academic and planning performance. *Journal of Cognitive Education and Psychology, 1,* 140–153.

Cook, A., Blaustein, M., Spinazzola, J., & van der Kolk, B. (2003). Complex trauma in children and adolescents. National Child Traumatic Stress Network, Complex Trauma Taskforce. Retrieved from www.nctsnet.org/nctsn_assets/pdfs/edu_materials/ComplexTrauma_All.pdf

Cox, T. (1983). Cumulative deficit in culturally disadvantaged children. *British Journal of Educational Psychology, 53*(3), 317–326.

Cozoline, L. (2014). *The neuroscience of human relationships: Attachment and the developing social brain* (2nd ed.)., New York: W. W. Norton.

Cummins, J. (2003). Reading and the bilingual student: Fact and fiction. In G.G. Garcia (Ed.), *English learners: Reaching the highest level of English literacy* (pp. 2–33). Newark, DE: International Reading Association.

D'Andrea, W., Ford, J., Stolbach, B., Spinazzola, J., & van der Kolk, B. (2012). Understanding interpersonal trauma in children: Why we need a developmentally appropriate trauma diagnosis. *American Orthopsychiatry Association, 82*(2), 187–200.

Dalen, M. (2001). School performances among internationally adopted children in Norway. *Adoption Quarterly, 5*(2), 39–58.

Dalen, M., Vinnerljung, B., Lindblad, F., Hjern, A., & Rasmussen, F. (2010). School performance at age 16 among international adoptees: A Swedish national cohort study. *International Social Work Journal*, *53*(4), 510–527

Das, J.P. (2004). *The cognitive enhancement training program (COGENT)*. Edmonton: Developmental Disabilities Centre, University of Alberta.

Das, J.P., Hayward, D. Samantaray, S., & Panda, J. (2006). Cognitive enhancement training (COGENT) What is it? How does it work with a group of disadvantaged children? *Journal of Cognitive Education and Psychology*, *5*, 328–35.

De Bellis, M. Hooper, S., Spratt, E., & Woolley, D. (2009). Neuropsychological findings in childhood neglect and their relationships to pediatric PTSD. *Journal of the International Neuropsychological Society*, *15*, 868–878.

Dennis, M., Chan, Y., & Funk, R. (2006). Development and validation of the GAIN Short Screener (GAIN-SS) for psychopathology and crime/violence among adolescents and adults. *The American Journal on Addictions*, *15*(1), 80–91.

Desmarais, C., Roeber, B., Smith, M., & Pollak, S. (2012). Sentence comprehension in post-institutionalized school-age children. *Journal of Speech, Language, and Hearing Research*, *55*, 45–54.

DSM-5. (2013). Diagnostic and *s*tatistical *m*anual of *m*ental *d*isorders (5th ed.). Washington, DC: APA.

Dole, K. (2005). Education and internationally adopted children: Working collaboratively with schools. *Pediatric Clinic of North America*, *52*(5), 1445–1461.

Dorman C., Lehsten L., Woodin M., Cohen R., Schweitzer J., & Tona J. (2009). Using sensory tools for teens with behavioral and emotional problems. *Occupational Therapy Practice*, *14*(21),16–21.

Duncan, G., Claessens, A., & Huston, A. (2007). School readiness and later achievement. *Developmental Psychology*, *43*(6), 1428–1446.

Duszynski, R., Jonak, J., Garjaka, K., & Jankowska, A. (2015). The transition of adopted from abroad/post-institutionalized children to life in the United States. *School Psychology Forum*, *9*(1), 32–43

Eckerle J., Hill L., Iverson S., Hellerstedt W., Gunnar M., & Johnson D. (2014). Vision and hearing deficits and associations with parent-reported behavioral and developmental problems in international adoptees. *Maternal Child Health Journal*, *18*(3), 575–583.

Ehri, L., Dreyer, L., Flugman, B., & Gross, A. (2007). Reading rescue: An effective tutoring intervention model for language-minority students who are struggling readers in first grade. *American Educational Research Journal*, *44*(2), 414–448.

Eigsti, I., Weitzman, C., Schun, J., DeMarchena, A., & Casey, B. (2011). Language and cognitive outcomes in internationally adopted children. *Development and Psychopathology*, *23*, 629–646

Evan Donaldson Adoption Institute. (2010). Keeping the promise: The critical need for post-adoption services to enable children and families to succeed; *Policy & Practice Perspective*. Retrieved from https://affcny.org/wp-content/uploads/EBDKeepingThePromise.pdf.

Evans, A., & Coccoma, P. (2014). *Trauma-Informed Care: How neuroscience influences practice.* New York: Routledge.

Federici, R. (1998). *Help for hopeless child. A guide for families.* Alexandria, VA: Dr. Ronald S. Federici & Associates.

Feuerstein, R., Feuerstein, R. S., Falik, L., & Rand, Y. (2006). *The Feuerstein instrumental enrichment program.* Jerusalem, Israel: ICELP Press.

Fisher, S. (2014). *Neurofeedback in the treatment of developmental trauma.* New York: W. W. Norton.

Foli, K., Hebdon, M., Lim, E., & South, S. (2017). Transitions of adoptive parents: A longitudinal mixed methods analysis. *Archives of Psychiatric Nursing, 31*(5), 483–492.

Forbes, H. (2010). *Beyond consequences, logic and control* (2nd ed.),vol. 1 . Warren, NJ: Beyond Consequences Institute, LLC.

Freitag, C. (2007). The genetics of autistic disorders and its clinical relevance: A review of the literature. *Molecular Psychiatry, 12*(1), 2–22.

Friedman, M., Keane, T., & Resick, P. (2014). *Handbook of PTSD: Science and practice* (2nd ed.). New York: Guilford Press.

Gabowitz, D., Zucker, M., & Cook., A. (2008). Neuropsychological assessment in clinical evaluation of children and adolescents with complex trauma. *Journal of Child and Adolescent Trauma, 1*, 163–178.

Gauthier, K., & Genesee, F. (2011). Language development in internationally adopted children: A special case of early second language learning. *Child Development, 82*(3), 887–901.

Gaw, A. (2001). *Concise guide to cross-cultural psychiatry.* Washington, DC: American Psychiatric Publishing.

Genesee, F. (2016). Introduction. In F. Genesee & A. Delcenserie (Eds.), *Starting over – The language development in internationally adopted children,* 1–16. Amsterdam, the Netherlands: J. Benjamins Publishing.

Geren, J., Snedeker, J., & Ax, L. (2005). Starting over: A preliminary study of early lexical and syntactic development in internationally adopted pre-schoolers. *Seminars in Speech and Language, 26,* 44–53.

Gewirtz, A., Forgatch, M., & Wieling, E. (2008). Parenting practices as potential mechanisms for child adjustment following mass trauma. *Journal of Marital and Family Therapy, 34*(2), 177–192.

Gindis, B. (1998). Navigating uncharted waters: School psychologists working with internationally adopted post-institutionalized children. *NASP Communiqué,* Part I: 27(1), 6–9; Part II: 27(2), 20–23.

(2004a). Why a psycho-educational evaluation of a school age internationally adopted child is to be done as soon as possible? *Adoption Today, 6*(6), 56–59

(2004b). Language development in internationally adopted children. *China Connections, 10,* 34–37.

(2005). Cognitive, language, and educational issues of children adopted from overseas orphanages. *Journal of Cognitive Education and Psychology, 4*(3), 290–315.

(2006). Take charge: Home-based cognitive and language remediation for internationally adopted children. *Adoption Today, 8*(4), 12–18.

(2007). Test accommodations for internationally adopted children with disabilities. Retrieved from www.bgcenterschool.org/Newsletter/June_21_2007_Newsletter .htm).

(2008). "Institutional autism" in children adopted internationally: Myth or reality? *International Journal of Special Education, 23*(3), 124–129.

(2009). Children left behind: International adoptees in our schools. *Adoption Today, 2,* 42–45.

(2015). Socialization and peer interaction in internationally adopted children. *Adoption Today, 4*(4), 32–47.

(2019). *Child development mediated by trauma: The dark side of international adoption.* New York: Routledge.

Gindis, B. & Karpov, Y. (2000). Dynamic assessment of the level of internalization of elementary school children's problem-solving activity. In C. Lidz & J. Elliott (Eds.), *Dynamic assessment: Prevailing models and applications,* 133–154. Oxford, UK: Elsevier.

Glennen, S. (2005). New arrivals: Speech and language assessment for internationally adopted infants and toddlers within the first month home. *Seminars in Speech and Language, 26,* 10–21.

(2007a). Speech and language in children adopted internationally at older ages. *Perspectives on Communication Disorders in Culturally and Linguistically Diverse Populations, 14,* 17–20.

(2007b). Predicting language outcomes for internationally adopted children. *Journal of Speech, Language and Hearing Research, 50,* 529–548.

(2008). Speech and language "myth busters" for internationally adopted children. *The ASHA Leader, 13*(17), 10–13.

(2009). Speech and language guidelines for children adopted from abroad at older ages. *Topics in Language Disorders, 29*(1), 50–64

(2014). A longitudinal study of language and speech in children who were internationally adopted at different ages. *Language Speech & Hearing Services in Schools, 45,* 185–203.

(2015). Internationally adopted children in the early school years: Relative strengths and weaknesses in language abilities. *Language, Speech, and Hearing Services in Schools, 46,* 1–13.

(2016). Speech and language clinical issues in internationally adopted children. In F. Genesee & A. Delcenserie (Eds.), *Language development in internationally adopted children: Trends in language acquisition research,* 147–177. Amsterdam: John Benjamins Publishing.

Glennen, S., & Masters, M. G. (2002). Typical and atypical language development in infants and toddlers adopted from Eastern Europe. *American Journal of Speech-Language Pathology, 11,* 417–433.

Goldman, F., Lloyd, S., & Murphy, R. (2013). Child exposure to trauma: Comparative effectiveness of interventions addressing maltreatment. *Comparative Effectiveness Review* No. 89. (Prepared by the RTI-UNC Evidence-based Practice Center, Rockville, MD).

Goodman, S. (2013). Internationally adopted children & language-based school difficulties. *Bank Street College of Education.* Retrieved from http://educate .bankstreet.edu/independent-studies/119

Graham, S., Harris, K., & Troia, G. (2000). Self-regulated strategy development revisited: Teaching writing strategies to struggling writers. *Topics in Language Disorders, 20*(4), 1–14.

Green, R., & Ablon, S. (2006). *Treating explosive kids: The collaborative problem-solving approach.* New York: Guilford Publication.

Greenberg, K. H. (2000). *Cognitive enrichment advantage family-school partnership handbook.* Knoxville, TN: KCD Harris and Associates Press.

(2005). *Cognitive enrichment advantage teacher handbook.* Knoxville, TN: KCD Harris and Associates Press.

Gunnar M., van Dulmen M.; International Adoption Project Team. (2007). Behavior problems in post-institutionalized internationally adopted children. *Developmental Psychopathology, 19*(1), 129–148.

Gunnar, M. & Donzella, B. (2002). Social regulation of cortisol level in early human development. *Psycho-neuroendocrinology, 27*, 199–220.

Gunnar, M. & Quevedo, K. (2007). The neurobiology of stress and development. *Annual Review of Psychology, 58*, 145–173.

Hamblet, E. (2017) *From high school to college: Steps for success for students with disabilities.* Arlington, VA: Publication of the Council for Exceptional Children

Hamilton, L., Cheng, S., & Powell, B. (2007). Adoptive parents, adaptive parents: Evaluating the importance of biological ties for parental investment. *American Sociological Review, 72*(1), 95–116.

Harrison, P., & Oakland, T. (2015). *Adaptive behavior assessment system* (3rd ed.). Torrance, CA: Western Psychological Services

Harrison, R. (2015). *An evaluation on the Wilson Reading Program for students with learning disabilities: A longitudinal study.* Theses and Dissertations. Retrieved from https://rdw.rowan.edu/etd/325

Hartinger-Saunders, R., Semanchin-Jones, A., & Rittner, B. (2016). Improving access to trauma-informed adoption services: Applying a developmental trauma framework. *Journal of Child & Adolescent Trauma, 12*, 119–130.

Hawk, B., & McCall, R. (2011). Specific extreme behaviors of post-institutionalized Russian adoptees. *Developmental Psychology, 47*(3), 732–738

Haywood, H. C. (1987). The mental age deficit: Explanation and treatment. *Uppsala Journal of Medical Science, 44*, 191–203.

(2005). Transculturality and cognitive development: Some observations and some questions. *Journal of Cognitive Education and Psychology, 4*(3), 273–289.

(2010). Cognitive education: A transactional metacognitive perspective. *Journal of Cognitive Education and Psychology, 9*(1), 21–35

(2020). Cognitive Early Education. Oxford Research Encyclopedia of Education. Electronic edition. doi:10.1093/acrefore/9780190264093.013.971

Haywood, H., Brooks, P., & Burns, S. (1992). *Bright start: Cognitive curriculum for young children.* Watertown, MA: Charlesbridge Publishing.

Haywood, H. C., & Lidz, C. S. (2007). *Dynamic assessment in practice: Clinical and educational application.* Cambridge, UK: Cambridge University Press.

Heim, C., & Binder, E. (2012). Current research trends in early life stress and depression: Review of human studies on sensitive periods, gene–environment interactions, and epigenetics. *Experimental Neurology, 233*(1), 102–111.

Heim, C., & Nemeroff, C. B. (2002). Neurobiology of early life stress: Clinical studies. *Seminars in Clinical: Neuropsychiatry, 7*, 147–159.

Helder, E., Mulder, E., & Linder Gunnoe, M. (2016). A longitudinal investigation of children internationally adopted at school age. *Child Neuropsychology: Journal on Normal and Abnormal Development in Childhood and Adolescence, 22*(1), 39–64

Heller, L., & LaPierre, A. (2012). *Healing developmental trauma: How early trauma affects self-regulation, self-image, and the capacity for relationship.* Berkley, CA: North Atlantic Books.

Hellerstedt, W., Madsen, N., Gunnar, M., Grotevant, H., Lee, R., & Johnson, D. (2008). The International Adoption Project: Population-based surveillance of Minnesota parents who adopted children internationally. *Maternal and Child Health Journal, 12*(2), 162–171.

Hessels, M., & Hessels, S. (2013). Current views on cognitive education: A critical discussion and future perspectives. *Journal of Cognitive Education and Psychology, 12*, 108–124.

Hibbard, R., Barlow, J., & Macmillan, H. (2012). Psychological maltreatment. *Pediatrics, 130*(2), 372–378.

Hildyard, K., & Wolfe, D. (2002). Child neglect: Developmental issues and outcomes. *Child Abuse and Neglect, 26*, 679–695.

Hodgdon, H., Blaustein, M., Kinniburgh, K., Peterson, M. L., & Spinazzola, J. (2015). Application of the ARC model with adopted children: Supporting resiliency and family well-being. *Journal of Child and Adolescent Trauma, 1*, 11–21

Hodgdon, H., Kinniburgh, K., Gabowitz, D., Blaustein M., & Spinazzola, J. (2013). Development and implementation of trauma-informed programming in youth residential treatment centers using the ARC framework. *Journal of Family Violence, 28*(7), 679–692.

Hoksbergen, R., & Dijkum, C. (2001). Trauma experienced by children adopted from abroad. *Adoption & Fostering, 25*(2), 18–25.

Hoksbergen, R., Laak, J., Rijk, K., Dijkum, C., & Stoutjesdijk, F. (2005). Post-Institutional autistic syndrome in Romanian adoptees. *Journal of Autism and Developmental Disorders, 35*(50), 615–623.

Hostinar, C., Stellern, S., Schaefer, C., Carlson, S., & Gunnar, M. (2012). Associations between early life adversity and executive function in children adopted internationally from orphanages. *Proceedings of the National Academy of Sciences of the United States of America, 109*(2), 17208–17212.

Hough, S., & Kaczmarek, L. (2011). Language and reading outcomes in young children adopted from Eastern European orphanages. *Journal of Early Intervention, 33*, 51–57.

Hughes, D. (2011). *Attachment-focused parenting: Effective strategies to care for children*. New York: W. W. Norton & Co (Norton Professional Books)

Hulme, C., & Snowling, M. (2013). Learning to read: What we know and what we need to understand better. *Child Development Perspectives, 7,* 1–5.

IDEA. (2009). *Code of Federal Regulations, Title 34, Volume 2,* CITE: 34CFR300.304. Requirements for initial assessment of ELL students. Retrieved from www.law.cornell.edu/cfr/text/34/300.304, page 65–66.

International Society for Traumatic Stress Studies. (2020). Retrieved from https://istss.org/clinical-resources/assessing-trauma.

Jachuck, K., & Mohanty, A. K. (1974). Low socio-economic status and progressive retardation in cognitive skills: A test of cumulative deficit hypothesis. *Journal of Mental Retardation, 7*(1), 36–45

Jacobson, H. (2008). *Culture keeping: White mothers, international adoption, and negotiating of family difference.* Nashville, TN: Vanderbilt University Press.

Jensen, A. (1974). Cumulative deficit: A testable hypothesis? *Developmental Psychology, 10,* 996–1019

   (1977). Cumulative deficit in IQ of blacks in the rural South. Developmental Psychology, *13,* 184–191

Jewells, J. (2020). *The defiant children-Tips for parenting.* Retrieved at www.siue.edu/~jejewel/dr_jeremy_jewells_website_005._jeremy_jewells_homepage.html

Johnson, D. (2019). *The role of pre-placement medical review in contemporary adoptions: Setting expectations, assessing a child's needs, and supporting successful family formation.* Publication of National Council for Adoption. # 131. Retrieved from www.adoptioncouncil.org.

Johnston, R. (2017). Historical international adoption statistics, United States and world. Retrieved from www.johnstonsarchive.net/policy/adoptionstatsintl.html.

Jones, J., & Placek, P. (2017). *Adoption by the numbers. A comprehensive report of US adoption statistics.* Publication of National Council for Adoption (NCFA).

Judge, S. (2003). Developmental recovery and deficit in children adopted from Eastern European orphanages. *Child Psychiatry and Human Development, 34,* 49–62.

Juffer, F., & van IJzendoorn, M. (2005). Behavior problems and mental health referrals of international adoptees: A meta-analysis. *Journal of the American Medical Association, 293*(20), 2501–2515.

   (2012). Review of meta-analytical studies on the physical, emotional, and cognitive outcomes of intercountry adoptees In J. Gibbons & R. Smith (Eds.), Intercountry adoption: Policies, practices, and outcomes, 175–186. Southampton, UK: Ashgate.

Juffer, F., Palacios, J., Lemare, L., van IJzendoorn, M., & Verhulst, F. (2011). Development of adopted children with histories of early adversity. *Monographs of the Society for Research in Child Development, 76,* 31–61.

Julian, M. (2013). Age at adoption from institutional care as a window into the lasting effects of early experiences. *Clinical Child and Family Psychology Review, 16*(2), 101–145.

Julian, M., & McCall, R. (2016). Social skills in children adopted from socially-emotionally depriving institutions. *Adoption Quarterly, 19*(1), 44–62.

Kamin, L. (1978). A positive reinterpretation of apparent "cumulative deficit." *Developmental Psychology, 14*, 185–196.

Kaufman, S., & Sandilos, L. (2017). School transition and school readiness: An outcome of early childhood development, *Encyclopedia of Early Childhood Development*. Retrieved from www.child-encyclopedia.com/sites/default/files/textes-experts/en/814/school-transition-and-school-readiness-an-outcome-of-early-childhood-development.pdf

Kinniburgh, K., Blaustein, M., Spinazzola, J., & van der Kolk, B. (2005). Attachment, self-regulation & competency. *Psychiatric Annals, 35*(5), 424–430.

Kintsch, W., & Kinstch, E. (2005). Comprehension. In S. Paris & S. Stahl (Eds.), *Children's reading comprehension and assessment*, 71–92. Mahwah, NJ: Lawrence Erlbaum Associates.

Kirchberg, T. (2017). The secondary transition planning Process and effective outcomes for high school graduates with mild disabilities. Culminating projects in special education. 38. Retrieved from http://repository.stcloudstate.edu/sped_etds/38

Kisiel, C., Fehrenbach, T., Small, L., & Lyons, J. (2009). Assessment of complex trauma exposure, responses, and service needs among children and adolescents in child welfare. *Journal of Child & Adolescent Trauma, 2*, 143–160.

Kittle, K., & Reed, K. (2020). Improving long-term outcomes in adolescent adoption. *Adoption Advocate # 148*. Retrieved from https://adoptioncouncil.org/publications/adoption-advocate-no-148.

Kozulin, A. (1998). *Psychological tools: A sociocultural approach to education*. Cambridge, MA: Harvard University Press.

Krause-Grindlay, T. (2019). *Focus on adoption*. Online magazine. Retrieved from www.bcadoption.com/resources/articles/therapeutic-parenting-and-other-survival-skills)

Kumsta, R., Kreppner, J., Kennedy, M., Knights, N., Rutter, M., & Sonuga-Barke, E. (2015). Psychological consequences of early global deprivation: An overview of findings from the English & Romanian adoptees study. *European Psychology, 20*, 138–151.

Kuypers, L. (2011). *The zones of regulation: A curriculum designed to foster self-regulation and emotional control*. Santa Clara, CA: Social Thinking Publishing.

Landry, S., Smith, K., Swank, P., & Guttentag, C. (2008). A responsive parenting intervention: The optimal timing across early childhood for impacting maternal behaviors and child outcomes. *Developmental Psychology, 44*(5), 1335–1353.

Lange, B., Callinan, L., & Smith, M. (2019). Adverse childhood experiences and their relation to parenting stress and parenting practices. *Community Mental Health Journal, 55*, 651–662.

Lanius, U., Paulsen, S., & Corrigan, F. (2014). *Neurobiology and treatment of traumatic dissociation: Towards an embodied self.* New York: Springer Publishing Company.

Lawson, J., & Sibla, J. (2016). Caregiver perspectives of parenting children affected by trauma. *Psychology Research, 6*(7), 396–406.

Layne, C., Warren, J., Watson, P., & Shalev, A. (2007). Risk, vulnerability, resistance, and resilience: Toward an integrative conceptualization of post-traumatic adaptation. In M. Friedman, T. Keane, & P. Resick (Eds.), *Handbook of PTSD: Science and practice*, 497–520. New York: Guilford.

Leon, E., Steele, M., Palacios, J., Roman, M., & Moreno, C. (2018). Parenting adoptive children: Reflective functioning and parent-child interactions. A comparative, relational and predictive study. *Children and Youth Services Review, 95*, 352–360.

Lidz, C. (2000). The application of cognitive functions scale (ACFS): An example of curriculum-based dynamic assessment. In C. Lidz & J. Elliott (Eds.), *Dynamic assessment: Prevailing models and applications*, 407–439. Amsterdam: Elsevier.

(2007). *Early childhood assessment.* New York: Wiley.

Lidz, C., & Elliott, J. (Eds.). (2000). *Dynamic assessment: Prevailing models and applications.* Oxford, UK: Elsevier Science.

Lidz, C., & Gindis, B. (2000). *The SmartStart Program: Helping your internationally adopted child develop a foundation for learning.* Retrieved from www .bgcenter.com/smartstart.htm).

(2003). Dynamic assessment of the evolving cognitive functions in children. Chapter 5. In A. Kozulin, B. Gindis, & V. Ageev (Eds.), *Vygotsky's educational theory in cultural context*, 99–116. New York: Cambridge University Press

Light, W. (2015). (LRS-5) *Light's retention scale* (5th ed.). Novato, CA: Academic Therapy Publications.

Linck, J., Judith F., Kroll, J., & Sunderman, G. (2009). Losing access to the native language while immersed in a second language: Evidence for the role of inhibition in second-language learning. *Psychological Science, 20*(12), 1507–1515

Lindblad, F., Dalen, M., Rasmussen, F., Vinnerljung, B., & Hjern, A. (2009). School performance of international adoptees better than expected from cognitive test results. *European Child Adolescent Psychiatry, 18*(5), 301–318.

Lindblad, F., Ringback Weitoft, G., & Hjern, A. (2010). ADHD in international adoptees: a national cohort study. *European Child Adolescent Psychiatry, 19*, 37–44.

Loitre, M. (2005). Beyond PTSD: Emotion regulation and interpersonal problems as predictors of functional impairment in survivors of childhood abuse. *Behavior Therapy, 36*, 119–124.

Loman, M. (2012). *Is deprivation-related ADHD different from ADHD among children without histories of deprivation?* University of Minnesota Digital

Conservancy, Minnesota. Retrieved from https://conservancy.umn.edu/han dle/11299/138217.

Luber, M. (2009). Scripted protocols: Basics and special situations *of* EMDR. New York: Springer.

Luthar, S., Cicchetti, D., & Becker, B. (2000). The construct of resilience: A critical evaluation and guidelines for future work. *Child Development*, *71*, 543–562.

Mackner, L., Starr, R., & Black, M. (1997). The cumulative effect of neglect and failure to thrive on cognitive functioning. *Child Abuse & Neglect, 21*(7), 691–700.

Marinus H., & Juffer, M. (2011). Children in institutional care: Delayed development and resilience. *Monographs of the Society for Research in Child Development*, *76*(4), 8–30

Marlow, N., Rose, A., Rands, C., & Draper, E. (2005). Neuropsychological and educational problems at school age associated with neonatal encephalopathy. *Archives of Disease in Childhood, 90*(5), 380–387.

Marzbani, H., Marateb, H. R., & Mansourian, M. (2016). Neurofeedback: A comprehensive review on system design, methodology and clinical applications. *Basic and Clinical Neuroscience, 7*(2), 143–158.

Mason, P., & Narad, C. (2005). International adoption: A health and developmental prospective. *Seminars in Speech and Language, 26*, 1–9.

Mason, P., Stallings, J., & Worthman, C. (2000). The effect of institutionalization on growth and the stress response. *Pediatric Residency, 47*, 134–143

Mcacham, A. (2006). Language learning and the internationally adopted child. *Early Childhood Education Journal, 34*(1), 73–79.

McCarthy, H. (2005). Survey of Children Adopted from Eastern Europe. Retrieved from www.postadoptinfo.org/research/survey_results.php

(2017). *How to avoid the syndrome of parent burn out*. Warren, NJ: EMK Press. Retrieved from www.rainbowkids.com/adoption-stories/how-to-avoid-the-syndrome-of-parent-burn-out-2021

McConaughey, S. (2005). Direct observational assessment during test sessions and child clinical interviews. *School Psychology Review, 34*(4), 490–506.

McKenna, M. A., Hollingsworth, P. L., & Barnes, L. L. (2005). Developing latent mathematics abilities in economically disadvantaged students. *Roeper Review, 27*(4), 222–227.

Meese, R. (2005). A few new children: Post-institutionalized children of intercountry adoption. *Journal of Special Education, 39*(3), 157–167.

Meese, R. L. (2002). *Children of intercountry adoptions in school: A primer for parents and professionals*. Westport, CT: Bergin & Garvey.

Mercer, J. (2006). *Understanding attachment: Parenting, child care and emotional development*. Westport, CT: BookBuzz.

Merz, E., & McCall, R. (2010). Behavior problems in children adopted from psychosocially depriving institutions. *Journal of Abnormal Child Psychology, 38*(4), 459–470.

Mikolajczak, M., & Roskam, I. (2018). A theoretical and clinical framework for parental burnout: The balance between risks and resources. *Frontiers in Psychology*, *9*, 1–22.

Mikolajczak, M., Gross, J., & Roskam, I. (2019). Parental burnout: What is it, and why does it matter? *Clinical Psychological Science*, *7*(6), 1319–1329

Miller, L. (2005). *The handbook of international adoption medicine. A guide for physicians, parents, and provides.* New York: Oxford University Press.

Miller, L., Chan, W., Reece, R., Tirella, L., & Pertman, A. (2007). Child abuse fatalities among internationally adopted children. *Child Maltreatment*, *12*, 378–379.

Mottan, K., & Shanmugam, D. (2018). Role of parents in remedial pupil's academic achievement. *International Journal of Academic Research in Progressive Education and Development*, *7*(4), 166–178.

Mounts, B., & Bradley, L. (2019). Issues involving international adoption. *The Family Journal*, *28*(1), 33–39.

Multon, K., & Lapan, R. (1995). Developing scales to evaluate career and personal guidance curricula in a high school setting. *Journal of Career Development*, *21*, 293–305.

Murin, M., Willis, C., Minnis, H., Mandy, W., & Skuse, D. (2011). Discriminating reactive attachment disorder from autism spectrum disorders: Key symptoms and clinical characteristics. *International Society for Autism Research*. Retrieved from https://imfar.confex.com/imfar/2011/web program/Paper9121.html).

National Child Traumatic Stress Network. (2020). Retrieved from www.nctsn .org/treatments-and-practices/trauma-treatments/interventions).

National Council for Adoption. (2019). *The U.S. Department of Health and Human Services Adoption and Foster Care Analysis and Reporting System data for FY 2018*. Retrieved from www.adoptioncouncil.org/blog/2018/03/your-guide-to-the-2017-intercountry-adoption-stats).

National Survey of Adoptive Parents. (2009). Retrieved from https://aspe.hhs .gov/national-survey-adoptive-parents-nsap.

Nemeroff, C. B. (2004). Neurobiological consequences of childhood trauma. *Journal of Clinical Psychiatry*, *65*(1), 18–28.

Neubert, D., & Leconte, P. (2013). Age-appropriate transition assessment: The position of the division on career development and transition. *Career Development for Exceptional Individuals*, *20*(1), 69–79

Oakhill, J., & Cain, K. (2016). Supporting reading comprehension development: From research to practice. *Perspectives on Language and Literacy*, *42*(2), 124–139.

Odenstad, A., Hjern, A., Lindblad, F., Rasmussen, F., Vinnerljung, B., & Dalen, M. (2008). Does age at adoption and geographic origin matter? A national cohort study of cognitive test performance in adult inter-country adoptees. *Psychological Medicine*, *38*(12), 1803–1814.

Ogden, P., Kekuni, M., & Pain, C. (2006). *Trauma and the body: A sensorimotor approach to psychotherapy.* New York: W. W. Norton and Co..

Palacios, J., Moreno, C., & Roman, M. (2013). Social competence in internationally adopted and institutionalized children. *Early Childhood Research Quarterly, 28*(2), 357–365

Pearson, C. (2008). First language attrition in internationally adopted children. *Family Focus, FRUA Journal, 14*(3), 1–14.

Perry, B.(2006). The neuro-sequential model of Therapeutics: Applying principles of neuroscience to clinical work with traumatized and maltreated children. In Nancy Boyd-Webb (Ed.), *Working with traumatized youth in child welfare* , 27–52. New York: The Guilford Press.

Petersen, S. (2012). Therapeutic parenting information skills and support for parents of children with additional emotional and behavioral needs. *Australian Journal of Adoption, 6*(1), 1–17.

Pinderhughes, E., Matthews, J., Deoudes, G., & Pertman, A. (2013*). A changing world: Shaping best practices through understanding of the new realities of intercountry adoption.* New York: Publication of the Donaldson Adoption Institute.

Pollak, S., Nelson, C., Schlaak, M., Roeber, B., Wewerka, S., Wiik, K., Frenn, K., Loman, M., & Gunnar, M. (2010). Neurodevelopmental effects of early deprivation in post-institutionalized children. *Child Development, 81,* 224–236.

Pomerleau, A., Malcuit, G., Chicoine, J., Séquin, R., Belhumeur, C., & Germain, P. (2005). Health status, cognitive and motor development of young children adopted from China, East Asia, and Russia across the first 6 months after adoption. *International Journal of Behavioral Development, 29,* 445–457.

Price, P. (2000). FRUA's health and development survey. *The Family Focus, 6*(3), 1–3.

Purvis, K. B., & Cross, D. R. (2007a). Facilitating behavioral change in adopted children suffering from sensory processing disorder. In T. Atwood, L. Allen, V. Ravenel & N. Callahan (Eds.), *Adoption factbook IV,* 375–379. Washington, DC: National Council for Adoption.

Purvis, K. B., Cross, D. R., & Pennings, J. (2009). Trust-based relational intervention: Interactive principles for adopted children with special social-emotional needs. *Journal of Humanistic Counseling, Education, and Development, 48,* 3–48.

Purvis, K. B., Cross, D. R., & Sunshine, W. L. (2007b). *The connected child: Bring hope and healing to your adoptive family.* New York: McGraw-Hill.

Purvis, K. B., Gross, D., Dansereau, D., & Parris, S. (2013). Trust-based relational intervention (TBRI): A systemic approach to complex developmental trauma. *Child and Youth Service, 34*(4), 360–386.

Putnam, F. (2006). The impact of trauma on child development. *Juvenile and Family Court Journal, 57*(1), 1–11.

Quenk, N. (2009). *Essentials of Myers-Briggs type indicator assessment* (2nd ed.). Hoboken, NJ: John Wiley & Sons

Quiroz, P. (2012). Cultural tourism in transnational adoption: "Staged Authenticity" and its implications for adopted children. *Journal of Family Issues, 33*(4), 527–555

Rittle-Johnson, E., Fyfe, E., McLean, L., & McEldoon, K., (2013). Emerging understanding of patterning in 4-year-olds. *Journal of Cognition and Development, 14*(3), 375–395.

Robinson, G. (1998). *Old children adoption.* Chestnut Ridge, NY: Crossroad Classic.

Roskam, I., Stievenart, M., Tessier, R., Muntean, A., Escobar, M., Santelices, M., Juffer, F., van IJzendoorn, M., & Pierrehumbert, B. (2013). Another way of thinking about ADHD: The predictive role of early attachment deprivation in adolescents' level of symptoms. *Social Psychiatry and Psychiatric Epidemiology, 49*(1), 1–19.

Rothschild, B. (2000). *The body remembers. The psychophysiology of trauma and trauma treatment.* New York: W.W. Norton and Co..

Rutter, M., Andersen-Wood, L., Beckett, C., Bredenkamp, D., Castle, J., & Groothues, C. (1999). Quasi-autistic patterns following severe early global privation. *Journal of Child Psychology and Psychiatry, 40*, 537–549.

Rutter, M., Kreppner, J., & Croft, C. (2007). Early adolescent outcomes of institutionally deprived and non-deprived adoptees. *Journal of Child Psychology and Psychiatry, 48*(12), 1200–1207

Rutter, M., Kreppner, J., & O'Connor, T. (2001). Specificity and heterogeneity in children's responses to profound institutional privation. *British Journal of Psychiatry, 179*, 97–103.

Rutter, M., Kumsta, R., Kreppner, J., Kennedy, M., Knights, N., & Sonuga-Barke E. (2015). Psychological consequences of early global deprivation: An overview of findings from the English & Romanian adoptees study. *European Psychology, 20*, 138–151.

Ryan, A. (2000). Peer groups as a context for the socialization of adolescents' motivation, engagement, and achievement in school. *Educational Psychologist, 35*(2), 101–111

Saco-Pollitt, C., Pollitt, E., & Greenfield, D. (1985). The cumulative deficit hypothesis in the light of cross-cultural evidence. *International Journal of Behavioral Development, 8*(1), 75–97.

Sattler, J. (1992). Assessment of children. Revised and updated 3rd edition. J. Sattler, Publisher, San Diego.

Sayeski, K., Earle, G., Davis, R., & Calamari, J. (2019). Orton Gillingham: Who, what, and how. *Teaching Exceptional Children, 51*(3), 240–249

Schmid, M. (2002). *First language attrition, use and maintenance: The case of German Jews in anglophone countries.* Amsterdam/Philadelphia: John Benjamins Publishing Co.

(2007). The role of L1 use for L1 attrition. In B. Köpke, M. S. Schmid, M. Keijzer & S. Dostert (Eds.), *Language attrition: Theoretical perspectives,* 135–153. Amsterdam/Philadelphia: John Benjamins.

(2012). First language attrition: State of the discipline and future directions. *Linguistic Approaches to Bilingualism, 3*(1), 97–116

Schmid, M., & Dusseldorp, E. (2010). Quantitative analyses in a multivariate study of language attrition: The impact of extralinguistic factors. *Second Language Research, 26*(1), 125–160.

Schmid, M., Köpke, B., & de Bot, K. (2012). Language attrition as a complex, non-linear development. *International Journal of Bilingualism, 17*(6), 675–682.

Schrager, A. (2020). The real reason international adoptions are failing. *Quartz Media*. Retrieved from https://qz.com/125451/the-real-reason-international-adoptions-are-failing/

Scott, K., Roberts, J., & Glennen, S. (2011). How well do children who are internationally adopted acquire language? A meta-analysis. *Journal of Speech, Language, & Hearing Research, 54*, 1–17

Searight, H. R., & Searight, B. K. (2009). Working with foreign language interpreters: Recommendations for psychological practice. *Professional Psychology: Research and Practice, 40*(5), 444–451.

Seol, K. O., Yoo, H. C., Lee, R. M., Park, J. E., & Kyeong, Y. (2016). Racial and ethnic socialization as moderators of racial discrimination and school adjustment of adopted and nonadopted Korean American adolescents. *Journal of Counseling Psychology, 63*(3), 294–306

Shannon, S., van Dyke, D., Hongjun, S., Vigil, G., & Walton, S. (2004). Cultural and socio-emotional issues of internationally adopted children. *International Pediatrics, 19*(4), 208–216

Shapiro, F., & Laliotis, D. (2015). EMDR therapy for trauma-related disorders. In U. Schnyder & M. Cloitre (Eds.), *Evidence based treatments for trauma-related psychological disorders*. New York: Springer.

Shapiro, L. (2004). *101 ways to teach children social skills: A ready-to-use reproducible activity book*. Retrieved from www.amazon.com/Teach-Children-Social-Skills-Ready/dp/1566887259).

Shaywitz, S. E. (2003). *Overcoming dyslexia: A new and complete science-based program for reading problems at any level*. New York: Knopf.

Slavin, R., Lake, C., Davis, S., & Madden, N. (2011). *Effective programs for struggling readers: A best-evidence synthesis*, 1–26. Baltimore, MD: Johns Hopkins University, Center for Research and Reform in Education.

Snowling, M., & Hulme, C. (2012). Interventions for children's language and literacy difficulties. *International Journal of Language & Communication Disorders, 47*, 27–34.

Sonuga-Barke, E., Schlotz, W., & Kreppner, J. (2010). Differentiation developmental trajectories for conduct, emotion and peer problems following early deprivation. *Monographs of the Society for Research in Child Development, 75*, 102–124.

Sonuga-Barke, S., Edmund, J., & Kreppner, J. (2012). The development and care of institutionally reared children. *Child Development Perspectives, 6*(2), 174–180.

Standards for Educational and Psychological Testing. (2014). *AERA (American Educational Research Association), APA (American Psychological Association) and NCME (National Council on Measurement in Education) (2014)*. Washington, DC: Published by APA.

Stern, M., & Gold, T. (2007). *Structural arithmetic I & ll*. Stern Math, LLC. Available at http://sternmath.com/.

Stevens, J., van Rooij, S., & Jovanovic, T. (2016). Developmental contributors to trauma response: The importance of sensitive periods, early environment, and sex differences. In *Journal of Behavioral Neurobiology of PTSD*, 1–22. Berlin, Heidelberg: Springer.

Tan, T., & Robinson, E. (2018). Institutionalized Chinese children with congenital medical conditions: Placement delay, developmental issues at arrival and current wellbeing. *Child Youth Services Review, 88*, 380–386.

Tarullo, A., & Gunnar, M. (2005). Institutional rearing and deficits in social relatedness: Possible mechanisms and processes. *Cognition, Brain, Behavior, 9*(3), 329–342

Taylor, J. (2001). *From defiance to cooperation: Real solutions for transforming the angry, defiant, discouraged child*. New York: Three Rivers Press.

The AFCARS Report #27. (2020). U.S. Department of Health and Human Services, Administration on Children, Youth and Families, Children's Bureau. Retrieved from www.acf.hhs.gov/sites/default/files/cb/afcarsreport27.pdf

The Free Dictionary by Farlex. (2020). Retrieved from https://legal-dictionary .thefreedictionary.com/adoption.

Therapeutic Parenting Journal. (2015). Issue #3, published by Attachment & Trauma Network, Inc. Retrieved from 2015AprilATNTherapeuticParentingJournal.pdf (attachmenttraumanetwork.org)

Thomas, K. (2016). Adoption, foreign-born status, and children's progress in school. *Journal of Marriage and Family, 78*(1), 75–90

Thompson, M., & O'Neill, G. (2001). *Best of friends, worst of enemies: Understanding the social lives of children*. New York: Random House.

Tieman, W., van der Ende, J., & Verhulst, F. C. (2005). Psychiatric disorders in young adult intercountry adoptees: An epidemiological study. *American Journal of Psychiatry, 162*(3), 592–598.

Tirella, L., Chan, W., & Miller, L. (2009). Educational outcomes of children adopted from Eastern Europe, Now Ages 8–12. *Journal of Research in Childhood Education, 20*(4), 245–254. https://www.acf.hhs.gov/cb/ resource/trends-in-foster-care-and-adoption

Turstra, L., Cicia, A., & Seaton, C. (2003). Interactive behaviors in adolescent conversation dyads. *Language, Speech, and Hearing Services in School, 34*, 117–127.

Tzuriel, D., Isman, E. B., Klung, T., & Haywood, H. C. (2017). Effects of teaching classification on classification, verbal conceptualization, and analogical reasoning in children with developmental language disorders. *Journal of Cognitive Education and Psychology, 16*(1), 107–124.

US Department of Education. (2017). Office of Planning, Evaluation and Policy Development, Resource Guide: Building a Bright Future for All, Washington, DC. Retrieved from www2.ed.gov/about/overview/focus/ early-learning-teacher-and-parent-resource-guide.pdf

US Department of State. (2019). Bureau of Consular Affairs report. Retrieved from https://travel.state.gov/content/travel/en/legal/visa-lawo/visa-statistics/ immigrant-visa-statistics/monthly-immigrant-visa-issuances.html

US Department of State. (March 2020). Annual Report on Intercountry Adoptions, FY 2019 and previous years. Washington, DC: Author.

Updated Transition Guide. (2017). Published by the Office of Special Education and Rehabilitation Services United States Department of Education. Retrieved from www2.ed.gov/about/offices/list/osers/transition/products/postsecondary-transition-guide-may-2017.pdf

US Citizenship and Immigration Services Glossary. (2020). USCIS.gov an online dictionary. Retrieved from www.uscis.gov/tools/glossary/orphan.

US Department of Education. (2020). Developing Programs for English Language Learners: Legal Background. Retrieved from www2.ed.gov/about/offices/list/ocr/ell/legal.html.

(2018). Annual report on intercountry adoption. Retrieved from www.passportsusa.com/family/adoption/stats/stats_451.html).

van der Kolk, B. (2003). The neurobiology of childhood trauma and abuse. *Child Adolescent Psychiatric Clinic of North America, 12*, 293–317.

(2005). Developmental trauma disorder: Toward a rational diagnosis for children with complex trauma histories. *Psychiatric Annals, 35*(5), 401–408

(2015). *The body keeps the score – Brain, mind, and body in the healing of trauma.* New York: Viking Press.

van der Vegt, E., van der Ende, J., Ferdinand, R., Verhulst, F., & Tiemeier, H. (2009). Early childhood adversities and trajectories of psychiatric problems in adoptees: Evidence for long lasting effects. *Journal of Abnormal Child Psychology, 37*, 239-249.

van IJzendoorn, M. H., Juffer, F., & Poelhuis, C. W. K. (2005). Adoption and cognitive development: A meta-analytic comparison of adopted and non-adopted children's IQ and school performance. *Psychological Bulletin, 131*(2), 301–316.

van IJzendoorn, M., & Juffer, F. (2006). Adoption as intervention: Meta-analytic evidence for massive catch-up and plasticity in physical, socio-emotional and cognitive development. *Journal of Child Psychology and Psychiatry, 47*, 1128–1245.

van IJzendoorn, M., Juffer, F., & Klein, P. (2005). Adoption and cognitive development: A meta-analytic comparison of adopted and nonadopted children's IQ and school performance. *Psychological Bulletin, 131*(2), 301–316.

van Londen, W., Juffer, F., & van IJzendoorn, M. (2007). Attachment, cognitive, and motor development in adopted children: Short-term outcomes after international adoption. *Journal of Pediatric Psychology, 32*(10), 1249–1258.

Vygotsky, L.S. The collected works of L. S. Vygotsky: Problems of general psychology, including the volume thinking and speech, Volume 1 (1987); Volume 2. The Collected Works of L.S. Vygotsky: Volume 2: Fundamentals of defectology, Volume 2 (1993); Volume 5. The collected works of L.S. Vygotsky: Child psychology, Volume 5. (1998). New York & London: Plenum Press.

Walker, A., Kortering, L., Fowler, C., & Rowe, D. (2010). *Age-appropriate transition assessment guide* (2nd ed.). Charlotte, NC: National Secondary

Transition Technical Assistance Center. Retrieved from www.nsttac.org/content/age-appropriate-transition-assessment-toolkit

Wanzek, J., & Vaughn, S. (2007). Research-based implications from extensive early reading interventions. *School Psychology Review, 36,* 541–561.

Warner, E., Koomar, J., & Lary, B. (2013). Can the body change the score? Application of sensory modulation principles in the treatment of traumatized adolescents in residential settings. *Journal of Family Violence, 28,* 729–738.

Waters, F. S. (2016). *Healing the fractured child: Diagnosis and treatment of youth with dissociation.* New York: Springer Publishing Company.

Wehmeyer, M., & Fied, S. (2007). *Self-determination: Instructional and assessment strategies.* Thousand Oaks, CA: Corwin Press.

Welsh, J., & Viana, A. (2012). Developmental outcomes of internationally adopted children. *Adoption Quarterly, 15*(4), 241–264.

Welsh, J., Andres G., Viana A., Petrill, S, & Mathias, M. (2007). Interventions for internationally adopted children and families: A review of the literature. *Child and Adolescent Social Work Journal, 24,* 285–311.

Werum, R., Davis, T., Simon Cheng, S., & Browne, I. (2017). Adoption context, parental investment, and children's educational outcomes. *Journal of Family Issues, 39*(3), 720–746

Wesselmann, D., Schweitzer, C., & Armstrong, S. (2014). *Integrative parenting: Strategies for raising children affected by trauma.* New York: W. W. Norton & Company.

Wevodau, A. (2016). *Review of trauma screening tools for children and adolescents.* Retrieved from www.nysap.us/Review%20of%20Trauma%20Screening%20Tools%20for%20Children%20&%20Adolescents.pdf)

White, R. (2017). Adoption UK's schools & exclusions report. Adoption UK Retrieved from www.adoptionuk.org/faqs/adoption-uks-schools-exclusions-report

Whitten, K. L., & Weaver, S. R. (2010). Adoptive family relationships and healthy adolescent development: A risk and resilience analysis. *Adoption Quarterly, 13*(3/4), 209–226.

Willingham, D. (2017). *The reading mind: A cognitive approach to understanding how the mind reads.* San Francisco, CA: Jossey-Bass.

Winsler, A., & Carlton, M. (1999). School readiness: The need for a paradigm shift. *School Psychology Review, 28*(3), 338–352.

Wolfgang, J. (2011). International adoption in the U. S: Traumatic stress and normal developmental responses. *The Counseling Psychologist, 31,* 711–744.

World Health Organization. (2013). Guidelines for the management of conditions that are specially related to stress. Glossary page 1. Geneva. Retrieved from www.who.int/mental_health/emergencies/stress_guidelines/en/

Zamostny, K., O'Leary Wiley, M., O'Brien, K., Lee, R., & Baden, A. (2003). Breaking the silence: Advancing knowledge about adoption for counseling psychologists. *The Counseling Psychologist, 31*(6), 647–650.

Zill, N. (2015) The paradox of adoption. Publication of the Institute for Family Studies. Retrieved from https://ifstudies.org/blog/the-paradox-of-adoption.

(2016). How adopted children fare in middle school. Publication of the Institute of Family Studies. Retrieved from https://ifstudies.org/blog/how-adopted-children-fare-in-middle-school.

(2017). Analysis of data from the Early Childhood Longitudinal Study of the Kindergarten Class of 2010–2011. National Center for Education Statistics, U.S. Department of Education. Retrieved from https://ifstudies.org/blog/the-changing-face-of-adoption-in-the-united-states

(2020). *An Update on the Changing Face of Adoption*. Retrieved from https://ifstudies.org/blog/an-update-on-the-changing-face-of-adoption

Zill, N., & Bradford, W. (2018). The adoptive difference: New evidence on how adopted children perform in school. Publication of the Institute for Family Studies. Retrieved from https://ifstudies.org/blog/the-adoptive-difference-new-evidence-on-how-adopted-children-perform-in-school.

Index

Milton Keynes UK
Ingram Content Group UK Ltd.
UKHW022232201023
431061UK00014B/60